12 ROUNDS IN LO'S GYM

D0107235

12 ROUNDS IN LO'S GYM

Boxing and Manhood in Appalachia

Todd D. Snyder

West Virginia University Press
Morgantown 2018

Copyright 2018 West Virginia University Press

First edition published 2018 by West Virginia
University Press
Printed in the United States of America

ISBN:
PB: 978-1-946684-12-7
EPUB: 978-1-946684-13-4
PDF: 978-1-946684-14-1

Library of Congress Cataloging-in-Publication
Data is available from the Library of Congress

Book and cover design by Than Saffel.
Cover image by Stephanie Snyder.

To Stephanie Nicole
and Huntington Jay
for filling my life with joy and purpose,
and in memory of
Naton D. Leslie (1947–2013),
an Ohio Steel Valley fighter

CONTENTS

————

Part III

Split Decisions:
Stories from the Championship Rounds

Prelude

MOUNTAIN VIOLENCE

Shot fighters are always the last to know they are *damaged goods*. These are the guys who keep at it well past their prime, sluggers and maulers who just can't seem to recognize what is obvious to the rest of us—*the show's over, it's time to call it quits*. Ask any competent boxing trainer and he'll lay it out for you. *Shot fighters* require somebody to come along and prove it. The *shot fighter* always thinks he has one more in him. He's the last to know it's his turn to taste the canvas.

This book is an old Appalachian yarn, a collection of tall tales, set in the final round of an aging West Virginia pugilist's career. This is the story of a *shot fighter*.

***

In 1742, explorer John Peter Salling made his way across the Allegheny Mountains, discovering an outcropping of coal along a tributary of the Kanawha River.[1] He and his cohorts named the tributary Coal River. Sally was an out-of-towner, born in Germany, but his was the discovery that set things into motion for all of us. Sally was in Boone County before Boone County was Boone County. This was more than a century before West Virginia came to be known as such.

I

"There is coal in those mountains."

"The kid is gonna be a champion," I imagine Sally predicting.

***

In the early days it was a pick-and-shovel operation, dangerous as hell. Most of the workers were local farmers—some were African slaves. They'd shovel and sack and lug coal out of the mountains. This was before the continuous miner, the dragline, the longwall.[2] Before those fancy gadgets came along, it was all picks and shovels and sacks of coal; the farmers and African slaves were collateral damage.

It was a long road to the top. There weren't enough good ol' West Virginia boys to put to work back then. Because most coal mines were located far from established towns, immigrants from Wales, England, Germany, and Scotland were shipped over to do the job. Coal camps were erected that later became townships. Company-owned houses, stores, schools, and churches were built for the workers and their families. Workers were paid in company scrip that could be spent only at the company-owned stores. Coal was the economy, ideology, and religion of the people. The railroad tycoons, the captains of industrialization, came along at just the right time.

Ask any competent boxing trainer and he'll lay it out for you—timing is everything.

***

John Cowen was born near Millersburg, Ohio, in 1844.[3] Cowen graduated from Princeton College in 1866 and moved to Baltimore, Maryland, in 1872, a newly appointed counsel member of the Baltimore and Ohio Railroad.[4] Cowen must have been a social climber, a real overachiever. By 1896, Cowen was president of the whole B&O shebang.[5]

It was a good time to be a railroad man. By the mid-1800s, extractive industry corporations were established under Virginia state laws for the purpose of encouraging financial investments from foreign countries. Most of the mining operations were funded by out-of-state capital, run by absentee owners. Before the days of labor unions, workers' rights, emissions regulations, and environmental protection agencies, it was a meteoric rise to fame for the extractive industry giant that came to be known as King Coal.

John Cowen laid the tracks that gave King Coal his shot at the title. Around my way, they name towns after guys like that.[6]

***

Cowen, West Virginia, never had much of a chance at becoming anything other than a *crossroads opponent*. Located slightly east of the geographic center of the state of West Virginia, Cowen is tucked away from the rest of the world, hidden deep within the Appalachian Mountains. Born August 2, 1899, just six years before the formation of the West Virginia Department of Mines, Cowen, like most fighters, was hardened by the socioeconomic limitations of its surroundings.[7] When King Coal was winning, life in our little West Virginia mining town wasn't so bad, they say.

By the time I came along in December 1981, King Coal's best years were already behind him. The once-mighty champion had become a shell of himself. It's never the one-punch knockout that causes the hematoma. It is the accumulation of damage that takes its toll on a fighter.

Our fathers were born into the final years of King Coal's long title reign; they were just old enough to have firsthand memories of the good old days. My generation was the first to see it coming, the first to ship off to college in droves. We were teenagers, about to set off into the real world, when windmills, solar panels, and hydraulic fracking technologies came along. We watched our fathers get laid off or transferred, get sick, or be killed.

"This ol' boy is destined for a fall," we figured.

***

Never ask a *shot fighter* when he's going to hang up the gloves. He'll never give you a straight answer. The *shot fighter* would rather die in the ring than hang 'em up. He'd rather die than have to imagine himself differently. Even when he's up against the ropes, taking one hell of a beating, the *shot fighter* doesn't know how to be anything other than a fighter.

I spin this old Appalachian yarn, this collection of tall tales, moments before the white towel finds its way to the canvas, bringing a halt to the slugfest. The bell is about to sound.

We are the sons of hard men. Our fathers and grandfathers proved it to us each time they arrived home covered in blackness. Theirs was a world designed to promote and reward a particular brand of hypermasculine identity. They were *goddamned* tough because that's what folks around town had to be. But ask any competent boxing trainer and he'll lay it out for you—*tough* can get you hurt.

We are a generation in transition, I suppose, caught in the middle—unsure if we are allowed to be anything other than miners and fighters. Ours are stories from the final round. And the ref is about to call it.

> *The show's over—it's time to call it quits.*
> *It's time to imagine life after fighting . . .*
>
> —T. D. Snyder

Then the King will say to those on his right, "Come, you who are blessed by my Father; take your inheritance, the kingdom prepared for you since the creation of the world. For I was hungry and you gave me something to eat, I was thirsty and you gave me something to drink, I was a stranger and you invited me in, / I needed clothes and you clothed me, I was sick and you looked after me, I was in prison and you came to visit me." Then the righteous will answer him, "Lord, when did we see you hungry and feed you, or thirsty and give you something to drink? / When did we see you a stranger and invite you in, or needing clothes and clothe you? / When did we see you sick or in prison and go to visit you?" The King will reply, "Truly I tell you, whatever you did for one of the least of these brothers and sisters of mine, you did for me."

—Matthew 25:34–40

There is a Taoist story of an old farmer. One day his horse ran away. Upon hearing the news, his neighbors came to visit. "Such bad luck," they said. "Maybe," the farmer replied. The next morning the horse returned, bringing with it three wild horses. "How wonderful," the neighbors exclaimed. "Maybe," replied the old farmer. The following day, his son tried to ride one of the untamed horses, was thrown, and broke his leg. The neighbors again came to offer their sympathy. "Such bad luck," they said. "Maybe," answered the old farmer. The day after, military officials came to the village to draft young men into the army. Seeing that the son's leg was broken, they passed him by. The neighbors congratulated the farmer on how well things had turned out. "How wonderful," they said. "Maybe" replied the farmer.

—Taoist proverb

PART I

CORNER MEN

The Eden Story
of Lo's Gym Boxing Club

Chapter 1

—

FIGHTING NOAH MILTON

—

I can't remember if his name was Noah Milton or if his name was Noah and he was from Milton, West Virginia. Either way, he was the first person to kick my ass. Noah was bigger and more intimidating than me. He had thick veiny biceps and a squared jawline. There was something redneck about him. He sported a tobacco-stained shit ring around his mouth, just like the vo-tech boys at my high school. He looked like the kind of kid whose papaw gives him a dip of snuff every now and then. Noah probably had a snuff-dipping papaw who made him chop firewood and carry around buckets of coal. That's where the shit ring and biceps came from, I figured. Noah Milton looked the part and I sure as hell didn't. I was Don Knotts in boxing gloves, a young Barney Fife in satin blue trunks, all knees and elbows. It wasn't much of a fight.

When the opening bell rang, I shot out of the corner like the righteous stone that TKO'd Goliath. But this righteous stone ran into a sneaky right uppercut and went down with a thud. It was the first punch of the fight. The next thing I remember is my ass hitting the canvas with tailbone-jarring force.

When I was 17 years old, I wanted nothing more than to be the kind of fighter my father was in the ring, to be the kind of man he was outside of it. Seconds into my boxing career, I came to the realization that I'd likely fall short of becoming either.

But, like a coward, I got back up. I was on my feet before the referee could reach the count of three. He administered the mandatory eight-count and sent me back into a sea of punches.

My only regret is that I didn't throw back. I should have had the balls to fight back, but I didn't. That part of the story is hard to swallow, even now. I'd thrown a hard left-right combination on my way to getting tagged by that sneaky right uppercut, but neither punch landed and by the time I made it back to my feet, I was all out of balls and righteousness.

The second time around was more of a gradual collapse, the kind of slow but violent death one witnesses in a condemned building imploded from within. My knees hit the canvas first. The gloves broke my fall. I was embarrassed and ashamed, but I wasn't exactly hurt or stunned. Noah Milton hadn't knocked me down this time, not really. He'd convinced me that standing was a bad idea. He'd convinced me that I wasn't a fighter, at least not the kind of fighter who laces up the gloves.

I made it back to my feet by the count of five. That didn't matter. The ref called it because he knew that I wasn't going to fight back. Some referees are sadists; they'll make you take your medicine. This guy had a heart. Objection echoed off the dingy brick walls of Simon's Gym as I drowned in Noah's flood. The rowdy Morgantown crowd was poor, drunk, and angry. They wanted to see Don Knotts take a few more punches. After that night, I never felt the same about trying to impress my father.

Back in the dingy locker room I sat on the hard wooden bench, my face buried in a dirty gym towel, in the same posture flight emergency cards ask you to adopt when the plane is crashing. Hunkered down on one knee, unlacing and removing my boxing shoes as quickly as possible, my father was a NASCAR pit-crew worker trying to change a tire. I don't remember either of us saying a word.

When Noah Milton and his trainer walked through the locker room door, I kept my head down and tried my best not to look up. My father offered some sort of congratulatory statement to Noah and his trainer and they said something back to him, but I don't recall any of it.

"Kid, you're a real fighter."

Noah's trainer placed his hand on my shoulder.

"You know how I can tell that you are a real fighter?"

I don't recall answering or nodding or even acknowledging his sentiment.

"You got up! That's what real fighters do. When they get knocked down, they get up."

We shook hands.

Noah's trainer had thick sandpaper hands like my father. He had a shit ring around his mouth too. Everyone in Milton, West Virginia, must chew Skoal.

"That's a fighter's instinct. Fighters get back up. That's the truth."

We shook hands again, for some reason.

Noah and his trainer disappeared behind the partition of lockers and I'd never see either of them ever again, although both have occupied my imagination for some time.

Boxing commentator Larry Merchant once referred to heavyweight champion Joe Frazier as a truth machine. When you fought Smokin' Joe Frazier, the truth came out. If you weren't in shape or couldn't take a punch, Joe would expose it. My father was fond of Merchant's analogy. He would often extend that analogy to the boxing ring.

"When you crawl through the ropes, you can't hide from the truth. If you are brave, the world will see it. If you are a coward, that'll come out too," he'd say.

That night in Simon's Gym, the truth was there for both of us to see. My father and I were yin and yang, opposite and contrary forces both interdependent and interconnected to one another.

***

In the second chapter of Alex Haley's *The Autobiography of Malcolm X*, we meet a 13-year-old version of the civil rights legend, a young bantamweight making his ring debut at Prudden Auditorium in Lansing, Michigan. Malcolm is matched up with a white boy named Bill Peterson. It isn't much of a fight.

"He knocked me down fifty times if he did once," Malcolm recalls.[8]

The 13-year-old version of Malcolm X is trying to impress his older brother Philbert, an up-and-coming amateur pugilist. He doesn't. The white boy gives Malcolm a pretty good beating.

After the loss, the 13-year-old version of Malcolm X goes into hiding. He can't show his face around his Detroit neighborhood after getting whooped by a white boy.

But the humiliation weighs on Malcolm's pride; it lures him back into the gym. Malcolm skips rope, beats the heavy bag, and signs up to fight Bill Peterson again, this time in Alma, Michigan. The rematch doesn't go much better.

"It was probably the shortest fight in history," Malcolm jokes.[9]

Second time around, the white boy renders Malcolm unconscious.

It was the first punch of the fight.

"We are what we pretend to be, so we must be careful about what we pretend to be," Kurt Vonnegut famously warns in his novel *Mother Night*.[10]

This is a lesson for guys like Malcolm and me and any romantic fool who climbs through the ropes of a boxing ring. Be careful what you pretend to be because getting your ass kicked isn't much fun. I'm paraphrasing.

By the time Malcolm X sat down with Alex Haley to tell his life's story, he viewed it all from a much different vantage point, however.

"In these later years since I became a Muslim, I've thought back to that fight and reflected that it was Allah's work to stop me," Malcolm states.[11]

That's a splendid way to look at it, I suppose. Maybe it was Allah, or Jesus, or God, or Fate who brought Noah Milton into my life. Maybe one of the millions upon millions of minute purposes of Noah's being was to land that sneaky right uppercut on my chin, redirecting my path, so to speak. If you've read the Old Testament, you know that God employed the original Noah to steer folks in all kinds of specific directions.

After that night in Simon's Gym, I gave up on the idea of becoming my father and decided to become everything he wasn't; I shipped off to college the following September. I was the first in my family to ship off to college. Shipping off to college turned out to be a much wiser life choice.

So maybe Malcolm knows what he's talking about; maybe God uppercuts a chosen few of us in the right direction every now and then. After all, Malcolm Little took those ass whoopings from Bill Peterson and went on to become Malcolm X. I took my ass whooping from Noah Milton and went on to become Dr. Snyder. In the end, both Malcolm and I found our way. Divine intervention?

I once told my wife, Stephanie, that if I were to write a book about my life, I'd open with Noah Milton whooping my ass in Simon's Gym—that's how important the experience was to me. If she had accused me of plagiarizing the idea from Alex Haley, I wouldn't have argued the point. But this isn't a memoir. This isn't the story of my life. I'm much too young for that sort of thing. This is the story of an odd little chapter in my existence.

I write these words on a balmy summer afternoon in upstate New York, playing Faust to memories of that old self I once sheepishly occupied. Today, I am a 35-year-old husband and father, a published author, an associate professor of rhetoric and composition at Siena College in Albany, New York, a man so far removed from the social circumstances of the scrawny kid who entered the ring against Noah Milton that writing about him almost feels as if I am writing about someone else. Memories of those failed attempts at proving my working-class Appalachian masculinity don't quite sting like they used to. Why should they? At 35, I've been fortunate enough to see most of my humble little career dreams come to fruition. My ivory tower status affords me the privilege of looking back on my clash with Noah Milton as nothing more than the first paragraph of an odd little chapter in my existence.

But this isn't the story of my journey as a first-generation college student—that book has already been written; it's blue and has a picture of a hillbilly on the cover.[12] This book is about the thorny, often-contradictory, messages that we, as Appalachian men, receive about manhood. It is about the working-class Appalachian man I was so desperately attempting to emulate when I caught that beating from Noah Milton back in September 1999—my father. More specifically, this book is about the man he became after that night in Morgantown, West Virginia.

I begin with mythos.

***

My father was Beowulf. He'd spin war stories about the man he used to be. Until Lo's Gym came along, the stories were all I had to go by. His versions of the past were fantastic and unreliable, but I wanted to hear them anyway because they were that damn good. My father lived in those stories.

"I played my entire senior year of football with three broke ribs."

"I picked up the fumble and ran it back 60 yards for the game-winning touchdown."

"I hit that son-of-a-bitch with a right uppercut and knocked him colder than a wedge."

My father would tell the same stories over and over, but I didn't care. I would indulge him every single time. When he would spin those war stories to my trailer park buddies, I'd feel like the son of a great man, the next in line for the throne.

"Your dad's muscles are bigger than He-Man's muscles."

"I bet your dad could whip the Terminator."

"How come your dad don't box no more?" the trailer park kids would ask.

The trailer park kids wanted to believe my father's war stories just as much as he did. My father was younger, bigger, and stronger than their dads, if they had dads, and nobody ever called bullshit, so we treated those stories like the gospel. I never had the chance to see my father street fight, or see him play football, or box, but I've heard so many war stories I somehow feel as if I did. All of us kids felt that way, I think. Mike "Lo" Snyder was the toughest guy in Willoughby Trailer Park. He was John Henry, if John Henry played football and boxed and mined coal rather than battling steam engines. He was Beowulf before Beowulf's bout with the dragon.

You can spin a Beowulf story in a town like Cowen, West Virginia. My hometown is a half-enclosed bus house with "Stop 1–66"[13] splattered along the side in graffiti. It is a dilapidated hardware store, long gone out of business. It is Big Ditch Lake. It is a few shirtless townies who set on the curb and drink Mountain Dew and smoke cigarettes. Cowen, West Virginia, is train tracks, a few log trucks barreling down the mountain. It is a puff of black smoke. The windows in our trailers shake when they blast dynamite down at the mines. The churches pass velvet-lined collection plates and they baptize us in Williams River. Cowen, West Virginia, is a gorgeous backdrop of trees and mountains and hollers and back roads and none of us know about much else. There is only one stoplight in the entire county and that stoplight isn't even necessary. Nothing much happens and when something happens that looks like something, everyone talks about it. You can be a big fish in a small pond in a town like Cowen, West Virginia. You can be the prettiest girl in school or the richest kid in town or the toughest guy on the block. That's what my father was—a big fish in a small trailer park. He was a myth and my father. He couldn't have happened anywhere else.

Everyone in Cowen refers to my father as "Lo" (pronounced "Low"). The mythology behind that nickname is sketchy. I've had a few people tell me the nickname originated during my father's days on the football field. He was a standout running back at Webster County High School; he ran for over 1,000 all-purpose yards in both his junior and senior seasons. In a town like Cowen, West Virginia, that sort of thing matters. "Lo" was number 22 coming out of the backfield. Number 22 was his identity. Back when I played Little League sports, there was never a question as to what number I would wear. Lo's boy was number 22. My coaches would always make sure of it.

"Your daddy hit those holes so low to the ground . . . Coach Gothard started calling him Mike 'Lo' Snyder," they'd say.

But "Lo" didn't make it to Monday Night Football. This isn't that type of book. When my father was offered a partial scholarship to play college football at a small Division III school, he turned down the offer for a job at the Smooth Coal Company.[14] In this regard, he was no different than most high school heroes from around my way; they tend to trade in their football cleats for mining boots.

"This will be the biggest regret of your life," the college recruiter told him.

It was.

Others claim the nickname had something to do with my father's boxing stance. A few months after accepting his post at Smooth Coal Company, my father took up amateur boxing. And why not? He'd long fancied himself a street fighter, grew up listening to the sweet science on the radio, hated his job at the coal mines, and didn't have anything better to do with his free time. My father took to the sport quickly.

"Back when your daddy fought, he was a bulldog, low to the ground— mean and nasty," they'd say.

"We called him Smokin' Lo," they'd add.

But my father's amateur boxing career didn't last much longer than mine. In a span of about 15 months, my father tallied a record of five wins and no losses, with all five wins coming by way of first-round knockout. Coal mining kept my father from fully dedicating himself to the sport; the untimely death of his best friend, Rick Cogar, due to a logging accident, caused him to temporarily lose focus; and by December 1981, he'd become a father.

"Smokin' Lo" named his only begotten son Todd Daniel Snyder so that his son's initials would read T. D. Snyder, short for "Touchdown." He imagined some Howard Cosell type calling his son's name out to the masses.

"Annooother TD for T. D. Snyder."

"Touchdown Snyder does it again, folks."

"Todd 'Touch Down' Snyder runs it back for a 50-yard TD."

"Touch Down" Snyder never made it to the end zone. As a youngster, I was the kind of kid who smiled when I talked, sometimes fumbled my words when trying to make an important point. I was overly apologetic, and had a bad habit of looking down when I spoke. I was the kind of kid who lived in my own imagination, a coal miner's son who not so secretly dreamed of one day becoming a writer.

"You'd better be the next Stephen King, otherwise your family will starve," my sixth grade teacher warned.

"Where are you going to get a job like that around here?" she added.

"Touch Down" Snyder didn't argue the point, or any point. I was the kind of kid who said, "I'm sorry," when it wasn't necessary; the kind of kid who walked to the back of the line. "Smokin' Lo" didn't get a Dick Butkus. He didn't get a Mike Tyson either. Knowing this bothered his son much more than it did him.

But then again, maybe the nickname had something to do with my father's physical stature. He was short and stocky, about five-feet ten-inches tall, and around 220 pounds. He looked like the kind of guy you'd call "Lo." He had sandpaper hands, tattooed arms, and a raspy voice. My father looked like how Mr. Clean might look if Mr. Clean played football and boxed and mined coal rather than selling products for Procter and Gamble. His skin was the hue of a two-day-old sunburn, his eyes were the color of regret; the demoralized frown my father wore on his coal-covered face when he returned home from work each evening told the story. From a physical standpoint, the moniker "Lo" suited him well.

My father's bulldog physicality aided his small-town mythos. His muscular arms were storytellers; his tattoos a cliché that made perfect sense only to him. The large gothic-style cross inked just above his right bicep didn't have anything to do with Christianity. My father wasn't a religious man, not in the traditional sense. He knew a little bit about the Bible. He believed in God. He liked the part about "remembering the least." He liked Jesus and his take on things, but, to be completely honest, didn't care much for church or church people. He didn't care much for people who came from privilege either. This was his most obvious character flaw. Matthew 25:34–40 was his personal mantra, although we wouldn't have called it a mantra. It's the part where God aligns himself with the poor, the part where he judges us by our treatment of those from the lower rungs of society. "Lo" was a Sermon on the Mount kind of guy.

And like the man they served, my father's storytelling arms were a contradiction. The interlocking black-and-white ebb and flow of the sun-drenched yin-yang tattooed on his left arm had nothing to do with Taoism or Confucianism; he'd never heard of either concept. The yin-yang, for my father, symbolized a "what-goes-around-comes-around" world view that heavily influenced the way he dealt with others. If you are good to people, some of it might come back to you. If you are bad to people, you'll get yours. That's how "Lo" saw it.

My father viewed the world as flawed and unfair. He was raised in a small West Virginia town shaped and modeled by the outside interests of extractive industry officials. Although located in the vicinity of pioneering settlers, the town of Cowen never truly existed until railroad tracks were laid in 1898.[15] In its infancy, it was the kind of place where workers were housed in company homes and paid in company scrip that could be spent only at the company store. My father sprang from a long line of West Virginia coal miners. He grew up recognizing the sociopolitical landscape of his hometown community as one designed to take advantage of those who couldn't fight for themselves.

"If you think the world is out to fuck you over, you're right . . . it is," he'd say.

"Life ain't a fair fight," he'd add.

For my father, the cross and yin-yang, when paired together, were symbolic of such a world view. As soon as I was legally old enough to do so, I jumped in Cowboy Jack's chair and got both tattoos on my arms. If I couldn't be my father on the football field or the boxing ring, I'd have to settle for taking part in my father's symbolism. That's how Touch Down Snyder spent much of his teenage years, pushing the Sisyphean boulder that was his father's mythology. The limits of my father's greatness were the limits of my imagination.

Or maybe the nickname had something to do with my father's middle name, Lowell. He was, after all, Lowell Snyder's boy—"Lo." For years, he and my grandfather worked side by side at the Smooth Coal Company. Most young men from Cowen, West Virginia, dream of becoming something better than their fathers, but their fathers are what they eventually become. That's how cyclical poverty works. Follow in the coal dust footsteps made by your Pa's mining boots and you're bound to catch a nickname.

***

"Human beings, truth be told, are inept narrators of their own lives," my old graduate school professor Dinty W. Moore writes.[16] "We often don't see what is right in front of us; frequently what we think we have seen isn't there. In almost every case we see a decidedly distorted view, as if peering through a rippled window," he adds.[17]

My father was an inept narrator of his own life. He was the kind of fellow who was always much happier in retrospect, never quite enjoying the moment itself. By the time he turned 35 years old, my father resigned himself to the fact that he'd accomplished all that he was ever going to accomplish. He was a wandering Moses lost in the desert, those touchdowns and TKOs hadn't gotten him anywhere but right back to the place where folks had always told him he'd end up.

Every now and then my father would work up the courage to become the person he used to be, but the reunions were always short-lived. Back in 1979, my father founded our town's first-ever Little League football team, the Cowen Raiders. He'd rush from the coal mines to the football field every evening, mentoring the little coal miners-to-be in his dust-covered Smooth uniform. My father coached the Cowen Raiders for a few seasons and did well. This success earned him a gig as the head football coach at Glade Elementary Junior High School. My father coached the Glade Bulldogs for a few years, but that didn't last either; my father wasn't a college boy and state law required that hiring preferences be given to college boys. It hurt my father, having to give up that coaching gig. He had far too much working-class pride to play assistant coach to some pencil-neck college boy. So, Moses wandered on, telling stories of past victories to us trailer park kids, peering into the rippled windows of his past, living off the successes of his youth. And why not? Our family didn't have much to cheer about back in the Willoughby Trailer Park days.

But the "Good Book" warns of the ills of looking back. You can get turned into a pillar of salt doing that kind of thing. Looking back is no way to live. I'm paraphrasing again. So maybe Noah Milton's divine uppercut was intended for both my father and me? Our lives started moving forward after that night. We became unstuck from the past upon impact.

It was a rubber gym mat wrapped in a thick green canvas. It was nylon ropes and duct tape. It was crudely welded steel posts and hooks and levies. It wasn't pretty.

One week after my epic loss to Noah Milton, my father began constructing a makeshift boxing ring in the spare room in the back of Classic Curl Beauty Shop. The materials used to construct the makeshift boxing ring were generously donated by some of my father's business associates who have yet to be informed of their generosity. My father held a PhD in Robin Hood ethics from the School of Hard Knocks.

The story of how my father's makeshift boxing ring found its temporary home in the back of a women's hair salon, however, begins not with Noah Milton but with a pretty young brown-eyed McCoy girl from Point Mountain, West Virginia. What's an old Appalachian yarn without a McCoy girl?

After high school, Cheryl Jean McCoy entered a 12-month program at the Clarksburg Beauty Academy. Upon completing the program, she returned to Webster County and started cutting hair. Cheryl Jean McCoy was the product of a rather humble upbringing; she grew up on a small farm with eight siblings and two sick parents. By the time Cheryl Jean McCoy was 18 years old, she fully understood both the social and economic limitations placed on Appalachian women. Cheryl Jean McCoy didn't want to be a housewife or a secretary or a cleaning lady; she wanted to be a hairdresser. Cheryl Jean McCoy's career ambitions were in opposition to all that she'd been taught about small-town Appalachian pragmatism.

"Sherrie, you need to get you a secretary job with Dr. Mace or go down to the courthouse and see if they have any secretary work."

"I don't know about all this hairdresser business. Not here, not in Webster County. You'll end up in the poorhouse," they said.

Cheryl Jean McCoy didn't listen. Against her parents' wishes, she enrolled in the 12-month program in Clarksburg, thus becoming the first of her brothers and sisters to obtain any measure of postsecondary education.

It wasn't long after Cheryl Jean McCoy returned to Cowen that many of Webster County's most eligible bachelors began lining up to get their hair cut by the pretty young brown-eyed McCoy girl from Point Mountain. Mike "Lo" Snyder, number 22 coming out of the backfield, was one of those guys. He strolled into Classic Curl Beauty Shop, got a haircut he didn't need, asked Cheryl Jean McCoy out on a date, and the two were an item from that point forward. That first date was at a boxing match hosted at the old Webster Springs High School. If my mother didn't read the signs, she wasn't paying attention. If you marry a fighter, you'd better be a fighter yourself. Her beauty shop would be transformed into a boxing gym in due time.

The spare room at the back of Classic Curl Beauty Shop was not an ideal space; it was just large enough to house our 16-by-16-foot makeshift boxing ring, a sand-filled heavy bag, and a half-deflated speed bag. It was an odd spatial juxtaposition. The front room was all curlers, wigs, and *Better Homes and Gardens* scattered about. The back room was our own miniature Gleason's Gym. By day, my mother's shop was full of elderly Appalachian women with curlers in their hair—the wives of coal miners, loggers, and army veterans. By night, the back of her shop was abuzz with the ricochet of a speed bag, the thump of fists pounding a sand-filled heavy bag, and the ding of the ring timer that signaled the start and end of every round, sounds and rhythms put into motion that night in Simon's Gym.

***

Like the 13-year-old version of Malcolm X, it was pride that inadvertently lured my father back into the sport of boxing after a 17-year absence; he felt primarily responsible for my ass whooping at the hands of Noah Milton. That makeshift boxing ring was built with stubborn regret.

"The ring will make all the difference."

"You can't learn to box without a boxing ring," he preached during the construction process.

That much was true. There wasn't another boxing gym located within two hours of our small Appalachian town; the club where my father had boxed as a young man lasted no more than three years. We'd been training like cavemen leading up to the Noah Milton fight, hitting the mitts out in the backyard and sparring in the driveway. Neither of us really knew what we were doing.

A few months prior to the Noah Milton bout, I'd coaxed my father into teaching me how to box. We were on the way home from the Beckley Toughman Contest when I first made the proposition. I'd seen hundreds of televised professional bouts over the years, but this was my first time watching a fight in person. That night a LeRoy Neiman painting came to life and I fell in love. I was lost in the pageantry and spectacle of it all.

For those from outside West Virginia, Toughman competitions are two-day semiprofessional boxing tournaments that, more often than not, feature out-of-shape coal miners, beer-bellied lumberjacks, possibly drunken college students, and a few roughnecks who actually know how to box. The working-class brand of masculinity that dominates the cultural landscape of my home state provides the perfect backdrop for this sort of public display. But I digress.

My father taught me a thing or two about boxing that summer. It wasn't long before he convinced himself that boxing was in my blood; we started gym hopping our way around the state of West Virginia in the fall.

Simon's Gym was located in Morgantown, West Virginia, just a few blocks outside of the campus of West Virginia University. It was the first boxing gym I ever visited. Hidden in the basement of what appeared to be an out-of-business furniture store, Simon's Gym wasn't easy to find if you were from out of town. Although a little off the beaten path, the gym was located in prime real estate for a West Virginia boxing club; it was host to a strange mix of working-class tough guys, WVU students, and sometimes, WVU football players. Once a month, Steve Simon, the owner and head trainer, organized an amateur boxing showcase, usually consisting of 10–12 fights. This primal display of Appalachian manliness consistently lured paying customers down into the basement of Simon's Gym for a boxing peep show. Working-class poverty kept Steve supplied with tough fighters, the 30,000 college students down the street kept him in business. Steve's amateur boxing peep shows made Simon's Gym the place to be in Morgantown on Saturday nights, at least for a certain crowd.

Steve wasn't from West Virginia; his accent was a dead giveaway. If I remember correctly, he'd spent time down in Charlotte, North Carolina, migrated north to Pittsburgh, Pennsylvania, and then traveled down 1–79 to Morgantown. During his time down in the Carolinas, he somehow hooked up with former heavyweight champion James "Bonecrusher" Smith and the two were in the process of starting a promotional company that, at this point, wasn't completely off the ground yet. My cousin John, a sophomore at West Virginia University, had been to a few of Steve's boxing peep shows, had a few buddies who trained at Simon's Gym from time to time, and, after we asked him to do so, helped us score Steve's phone number. As far as we knew, Simon's Gym was the only boxing gym still going in the state of West Virginia; all of my father's boxing associates from back in the day were long gone, likely in nursing homes or graveyards.

Simon's Gym was the beginning of our boxing journey, but you already know how that turned out. I ran into a sneaky right uppercut, gave up coal country pugilism, and shipped off to college the following September. My father ended up with a makeshift boxing ring in the back of a beauty shop. In the end, we both found our way. Lucky punch?

At first, my father asked me to keep the makeshift boxing ring a secret. He didn't want townies or streetwalkers trying to break in and steal our equipment. Nor did he want a long line of local tough guys dropping by to interrupt our workouts. So, for a while, Lo's Gym was just my father and I. We'd spend evenings after work and school boxing in the back of Classic Curl Beauty Shop. I enjoyed this time with my father very much; I enjoyed learning about the fight game and listening to his old fight stories. I was content just spending this time with him, content with just working out and bonding with my father. But the makeshift boxing ring was a secret my father couldn't keep. As my skills improved and I started to look a little more like the son he'd dreamed up 17 years earlier, my father couldn't resist the urge to invite a few local boys down to Classic Curl to spar his son. He wanted to see me Noah Milton a few kids who'd never been in a boxing ring before. And I did.

It was something akin to a shrewd scam. The three of us would work out for a while; my father, the pugilistic grifter, would teach the guy a few things, puff him up a bit, and about a half an hour into the workout he would say something like, "You boys should get in there and spar." And, for some reason, they never caught wind of what was going on. They would happily strap on the headgear and bounce into the ring ready to impress my father. I'd beat these kids senseless and my father was addicted to watching it. By spring of 2000, Pandora was completely out of the box. The gossip traveled faster than our town's dial-up internet service. Everyone was talking about my father's makeshift boxing gym.

Classic Curl Beauty Shop wasn't much, but it was located right in the middle of Cowen, along Main Street, just down the road from Foodland, across the street from the only gas station in town. In a spot like that, you'd get the townies and streetwalkers. You'd get the alternative school kids and the unemployables. You'd get the fighters. Advertising wasn't necessary. The conditions were ideal, I suppose. With the dawning of the twenty-first century, King Coal's deteriorating condition quickly began to reveal itself to folks around my way. The inevitable downward spiral came in the form of a series of socioeconomic flash knockdowns. Some West Virginia coal mines were bought by out-of-state bigwigs and consolidated; others simply laid folks off or shut down, a metaphoric castration long in the works. Hard times were around the corner. Cowen was in for a fight.

As a young boy, I'd fallen in love with the sport of boxing because the act of fighting so clearly personified my father's ambition. He was a *real man*, like the sluggers and maulers on television. My father's childhood dream was to climb through the ropes at Madison Square Garden, to beat the hell out of some poor fellow on national television and score a symbolic victory for the town of Cowen—for all of Appalachia perhaps.

"If the right person would'a came along and paid some attention to me, I could'a made something out of this boxing shit," my father would often lament.

Back in the spring of 2000, my father couldn't have possibly known that his makeshift boxing ring would serve as a pathway to vicariously realizing this small-town masculine fantasy. He couldn't have possibly cooked up a scenario where a boy from Cowen, West Virginia, one of his pupils, would get the opportunity to fight on an HBO Pay-Per-View event at Boardwalk Hall in Atlantic City. But then again, maybe I am underestimating Beowulf's hubris. In retrospect, a sneaky right uppercut feels like the appropriate place to begin. In hindsight, it almost feels as if Lo's Gym Boxing Club started itself.

Chapter 2

———

TOUGH MEN

———

Art Dore understood that everyone thinks they can box until they give it a try. He understood how most working-class men are conditioned to think about manhood. The business plan was simple but ingenious. The Toughman story begins in Bay City, Michigan, back in 1979.[18] Dore, a former boxer and then promoter, rented cheap venues in remote sections of the state, and hung up colorful flyers that dared local tough guys to slug it out in front of their friends and families for small-town bragging rights. The locals took to it quickly. After two nights of boxing, some fella would walk away with a nylon jacket that said he was the toughest guy around. Fighters with professional experience, or more than five amateur fights, were barred from competition. Dore wanted the Everyday Joes.

In those early days, The Toughman Contest "was billed clean, down-to-earth, back to basics fighting. No professionals, and no ringers, just big, tough guys that would get knocked down, and keep coming back for more until there would be only one left . . . the *Toughest Man in Town*,"[19] the official website tells me.

Business was good. Dore's Toughman events quickly spread throughout his home state of Michigan and eventually expanded to Ohio and then West Virginia, where Dore hooked up with local fight promoter Jerry Thomas, the brother of Tommy Franco Thomas, one of the most celebrated and accomplished professional fighters in the history of West Virginia boxing. Over a nine-year career as a professional boxer, Tommy

Thomas compiled a record of 34–8 (with 21 knockouts).[20] Along the way, Tommy faced an impressive array of professional fighters, a list that includes heavyweight greats Leon Spinks, Michael Dokes, and Jimmy Young. By the time I first met Tommy, he'd been retired from the ring for over ten years and was working as a police officer in Clarksburg, West Virginia. Although Tommy was older, a little out of shape, and had an overall pleasant demeanor, the look in his eyes and the size of his massive hands reminded you that he probably wasn't someone you wanted to mess with. His younger brother Jerry, on the other hand, looked the part of the well-dressed Sicilian businessman; he was a Frank Sinatra–era, old-school-class kind of guy. Jerry always sported nice clothes, a well-groomed mustache, and, for the most part, the kind of vocabulary and diction one doesn't come across often in working-class Appalachia.

When Tommy retired from the ring, he and Jerry opened a boxing club in their hometown of Clarksburg—The Tommy Thomas Boxing Club. Tommy was the trainer, working with both amateurs and professionals, while his younger brother, Jerry, was the manager and promoter. After my epic loss to Noah Milton, Steve Simon introduced my father to the boxing Thomas brothers of Clarksburg. Soon thereafter, my father started driving me up to Clarksburg for bimonthly sparring field trips. On one occasion, I whipped an Italian kid named Mitch something-or-other—almost put him through the ropes, perhaps my finest moment in a boxing ring.

"You knocked the cock off him," my father proudly declared afterward.

As a businessman, Jerry Thomas quickly made a name for himself promoting Toughman Contests throughout the state of West Virginia. "Toughman Season," as Jerry called it, ran from November to April of each year and eventually grew to encompass 12 different West Virginia towns: Huntington, Morgantown, Beckley, Lewisburg, Wheeling, Parkersburg, Short Gap, Martinsburg, Elkins, Glenville, Logan, and Clarksburg. And, like his comrade Art Dore, Jerry Thomas had a sure-shot business plan; he brought boxing back to West Virginia by giving all of those washed-up could-have-beens and would-have-beens a chance to prove their manhood. He couldn't have picked a better location.

I watched Jerry Thomas do his Michael Buffer routine for the first time at the Beckley Toughman Contest back in April 1999; in those days, Jerry doubled as both promoter and ring announcer. The Beckley National Guard Armory was Madison Square Garden, for all I knew. The yellow-and-black professional-style boxing ring was decorated with barbed-wire graphics. The DJ. The loudspeakers. The music. The big-busted ring girls. The smoke machines. The drunken cheers from the crowd. The drunken fights in the crowd. It was a cathedral of Appalachian masculinity. Shaking hands with Jerry Thomas back in 1999 felt like shaking hands with Don King or Michael Buffer (I'd actually shake hands with both King and Buffer years later when I moved to New York). I implored my father to teach me how to box all the way home.

Thanks to the Smooth Coal Company, my father missed out on all the Toughman fun. Jerry Thomas promoted his first West Virginia Toughman Contest in 1980, just a few months before I was born. My father was, at the time, working 70 hours a week down at Smooth, a 21-year-old father-to-be, with goals of getting his family out of Willoughby Trailer Park. By the time my sister, Katie, was born, my father had long abandoned his pugilistic dreams. He'd hung 'em up, as the old timers say. My father didn't attend his first Toughman Contest until the late 1980s. But there would always be guys coming around the trailer park, wanting my father to show them a thing or two on the mitts or the heavy bag. Tough Men. They'd always go off to Beckley and get thumped by guys who could actually box.

Jerry's traveling Toughman circus gradually came to be seen as something of a rite of passage for roughnecks from around my way. When you turn 18 years old, you get to chew snuff, buy lottery tickets, and sign up for your first Toughman Contest. The allure tugs at our overhauls. And why not? Sam Scaff won the Huntington Toughman Contest in 1981, turned professional, and got a shot at Mike Tyson. That didn't go too well for Scaff. Billy Fox won back-to-back Toughman Contests in 1990 and 1991, turned professional, and went on to become a successful professional boxer. Even Tommy Small, of Beckley, West Virginia, got his start in the Toughman circuit. Tommy won the vacant World Boxing Federation title against Harry Arroyo back in 1991, and by the time I met him, had squared off with some of boxing's most celebrated legends—Hector "Macho" Camacho, Julio Cesar Chavez, and Meldrick Taylor, just to name a few. Jerry Thomas's Toughman circus produced its fair share of Appalachian Cinderella men.

But the working-class man-boys from my town always had their carriages turned back into pumpkins. Nobody from Webster County ever won the whole damn thing. And that's how it was for almost 20 years.

That's how it was until Curtis "The Ice Man" Wright walked off the streets of Cowen and into the back of Classic Curl Beauty Shop.

***

Everyone used to call him "Ice Man." Hell if I know how he got the nickname. It probably had something to do with Val Kilmer's character in *Top Gun*. That's my guess. All the boys in my town loved that movie, for some reason. I'm pretty sure the nickname didn't have a thing to do with the play by Eugene O'Neill.

Curtis Wright looked like Hercules might look if Hercules were more than a myth. Without doing a sit-up, he wore rippled six-pack abs like a shield of honor. His rock-hard biceps forced his t-shirts to cling helplessly to his arms. His lateral muscles gave him the appearance of a turtle about to sink back into his shell. He was only five feet ten inches and 195 pounds but he was pure muscle. With his blond and closely cropped, military-cut hairstyle, Curtis looked like G.I. Joe might look if action figures could fight at cruiserweight. I'd put money on the fact that Curtis was always the best athlete in his class, the first kid picked on the playground. In high school, he'd been a multisport athlete, an all-star running back, just like my father. Curtis's life, in some ways, was a life my father had already lived.

Curtis was the good, hard-working, Appalachian high school sports star who graduates and picks up his dinner bucket and gets in line at the coal mine or the local sawmill. He was the good Appalachian boy who marries his high school sweetheart, has a few kids, buys a house, and settles down into a nice rut. After high school, Curtis traded in newspaper headlines and sports trophies for a wedding ring, a dinner bucket, a mortgage, and baby bottles. Like an earlier version of my father, he must have felt too young to be so complete. His life had become a short story, but he'd dreamed of becoming a novel.

As word of the makeshift boxing ring spread around our small town, pugilistic walk-ins became a frequent occurrence during our training sessions at Classic Curl Beauty Shop. Initially, my father wasn't concerned with training any of them. If they were too big or too old to feed to his son, he didn't want anything to do with it. Curtis "The Ice Man" Wright changed everything. Curtis Wright arrived on the scene in November 1999, a few months after my loss to Noah Milton. Uninvited and unannounced, Curtis shouted, "I heard you had a boxing ring down here," just loud enough so that we could hear him over the blasting music; we'd apparently forgotten to lock the back door.

Driving through town on his way home from his job at Columbia Forest Products in Nicholas County, Curtis spotted my father's silver pickup truck parked in front of my mother's shop after hours. He couldn't help himself. Curtis made a U-turn at the only gas station in town and came back to give it a second look. He'd heard that my father had been harboring a boxing ring in the spare room and couldn't resist the urge to see if there was some truth to the rumor.

"Damn, I wish I'd have known you boys had all of this set up down here," Curtis shouted over the music once he had our attention.

The Curtis Wright who walked through the door that day was in his mid-twenties, was still in pretty good shape, but was visibly jaded from his time at Columbia. The look in Curtis's eyes was a polite desperation, a look or prerequisite that I would eventually learn to spot in fighters. I don't remember much of what was said that first day, but I do remember the look on Curtis's face as he took in the sway of the heavy bag, the back and forth of a recently struck speed bag, the ropes, the green canvas, the black-and-white fight posters lining the wall. Curtis had that same look that adorns the face of the Hollywood cuckold who bursts into an unfaithful wife's bedroom. His suspicions had been confirmed—there was a boxing ring hiding in the back of a beauty shop in his town and he wanted in on it. Curtis didn't need to say another word; he walked into our makeshift boxing gym wearing his intentions.

When my father and I pulled into the parking lot of Classic Curl the following evening, Curtis Wright was standing in front of the shop waiting for us. His hands were already wrapped. At this point, we really didn't know Curtis that well. My father and I used to watch Curtis play football on Friday nights, but I don't recall either of us ever speaking with him during his high school glory days. After high school, Curtis married my cousin Angel, from my mother's side of the family, so we would occasionally see him at family get-togethers. We knew that Curtis was a good athlete, that he was married to my cousin Angel, that he'd fought in a few Toughman Contests, but that was about it. Maybe it was my uncle Randy, Angel's father, who gave our secret away. It could have been one of the local kids who we grifted in the back of my mother's beauty shop. Regardless of the source, Curtis Wright found his way into our hidden boxing gym and my father and I knew getting rid of him would not be easy.

Curtis had signed up for the Toughman Contest in Lewisburg that was only a week away, and like most boxing virgins, believed a few days in a boxing ring and a few rounds on a heavy bag would make some measure of difference. Curtis always had a "yes sir, no sir" disposition with my father, and, like all coaches, my father was the kind of guy who ate that stuff up. I gritted my metaphorical teeth when my father invited him to come back down to our makeshift ring and train with us for the rest of the week.

Curtis Wright's first day of training got off to a precarious start. My father was working Curtis on the mitts and I was hitting the heavy bag when the three of us were interrupted by an uninvited voice. We hadn't been training for a full 30 minutes when it happened again.

"I heard you guys were boxing down here."

Déjà vu?

We'd forgotten to lock the back door.

This time it was Mitch Cooner,[21] a local tough guy just a few years older than me, one of those corn-fed, Noah Milton, chaw-of-tobacco kind of guys you meet from time to time when you grow up in rural Appalachia. Unlike my father and Curtis, Mitch wasn't a local sports star, or a prom king, or voted most likely to make it to Monday Night Football. Mitch, as I remember him, was a hillbilly caricature of the Jethro Bodine variety.

"I'm f[eye]tin' in that boxing tournament in Lewisburg this weekend . . . you boys mind if I train with ya?" he shouted over the music.

I figured Curtis and Mitch would end up scrapping before the end of the night; they were two uninvited dinner guests vying for the same place at the table.

Curtis and Mitch trained with us on Tuesday, Wednesday, and Thursday of that week. From what I can remember, my father didn't really offer Curtis or Mitch any tactical advice or give them any specific encouragement. The mood was a little tense, seeing that both guys were training for the same tournament, but, for the most part, everyone got along. It was the first time our little makeshift gym was occupied by more than two fighters at a time, the first time that outsiders had been welcomed to use our equipment and to use my father.

Neither Curtis nor Mitch really knew what they were doing. They were both older and larger than me, but were boxing adolescents nonetheless. They held their hands the wrong way, threw punches like drunken brawlers, and didn't know much about boxing history apart from Rocky Balboa movies. I didn't like having them in the gym, didn't like the way my father encouraged them despite their lack of technique. He was humoring them the same way he had humored me on the way home from the Noah Milton fight.

After the Thursday evening training session, my father wished Curtis and Mitch good luck and we headed back to the house.

"Why didn't you let them spar? I wanted to see Curtis kick his ass," I smirked on the way home.

My father didn't know it at the time, but Mitch Cooner and I were not the best of friends. Mitch, a junior when I was a high school freshman, was one of the local boys who used to give me hell for listening to rap music. He'd called me a nigger lover or told someone that I was a nigger lover or told someone that he wanted to kick my ass because I was a nigger lover or something like that. If Mitch was going to come into my gym and use my father, I was at least hoping to see Curtis "The Ice Man" Wright give him the ass kicking that I couldn't.

"Son, Mitch might have knocked Curtis out if I'd let them spar. He hits like a mule," my father answered without taking his eyes off the road.

His saying that hurt my feelings. I didn't like his choosing Mitch over Curtis or his choosing both of them over me. I didn't say a word the rest of the way home.

When my father made it home from the coal mines the following evening, he poked his head into my bedroom and said, "Get dressed, I want to go to Lewisburg and watch those fights."

My father always had a funny way of doing that sort of thing, dressing up a calculated choice so that it looked like a spontaneous gesture.

"You know your father is going to want to go to those fights when he gets home," my mother said at the dinner table an hour or so earlier.

That night in Lewisburg was thick with irony. In a tournament full of over 20 light heavyweight combatants from around the state, Curtis Wright and Mitch Cooner were matched up to fight each other in the opening round of competition.

At first, Curtis and Mitch were sportsmanlike.

"No hard feelings," Curtis said to Mitch, shaking his hand before the fight.

It was a loaded comment, one of those gentlemanly sentiments a Hollywood gunslinger spouts before a duel.

"You'll probably kick my ass," Mitch said mid-handshake.

Mitch was visibly shaken—he'd been matched up against a Webster County sports legend, and he knew that he'd never hear the end of it when he returned to Cowen. I loved seeing Mitch look that way; I got a real kick out of it.

I loved watching Curtis beat the redneck out of Mitch in the first round as well; Curtis drove Mitch into the corner of the boxing ring and whaled away on him for the entire two minutes. Finally, I was getting to see the show my father had denied me of just one day earlier. I couldn't have enjoyed the first round more.

Curtis may have been enjoying all of this a little bit too much as well. In the second round Curtis became overly cocky and reckless; he looked like Babe Ruth at a company softball game—swinging for the fences with every punch. Toward the end of the round, Curtis missed a looping overhand right, walked into a thunderous redneck uppercut, and went down with a thud.

Stumbling out of the ring, with his head hung low was my father's premonition. It was the first but not the last time my father would do that sort of thing to me.

Mitch Cooner lost his fight the following night. He quit on the stool. As far as I know, he never fought again. Curtis Wright would go on to become Lo's Gym's first and perhaps greatest champion. And, as far as my father is concerned, it was because of that night in Lewisburg.

"You know how I can tell that you are a real fighter, Curtis?"

"No, sir."

"You got up! That's what real fighters do."

"Yes, sir."

"When they get knocked down, they get up," my father said.

***

When Curtis Wright's pickup truck pulled into our driveway in August 2000, my father was grilling hamburgers out on the front porch, as my mother, sister, and I prepared the picnic table. Nine months had passed since his loss to Mitch Cooner, but Curtis hadn't missed out on much; our little makeshift boxing gym was stuck in neutral. Private workouts with my father, and a few grifting/sparring sessions, had turned me into a more seasoned amateur boxer, but I had yet to get back on the horse, so to speak. I had cold feet.

"We'll sign you up for your next fight when *you* know you're ready," my father said.

"If you gotta ask me if you're ready, you ain't," he'd add.

When Curtis Wright arrived at our summer cookout, my freshman year of college was only a few weeks away, and my boxing career, it seemed, was all but over. I was a wandering Moses lost in the desert.

The college arguments were tense that summer. On more than one occasion, I tried to use boxing as a way to avoid my having to ship off to college.

"You can box when you come home in the summers."

"But . . ."

"College is more important than boxing," my mother would say.

When my father was out of earshot, she would break it down for me.

"Do you have any idea how bad your father regrets not going to college? Do you have any idea how bad it hurts him to hear you say that?"

"Mom, I'm just saying . . ."

"We are going to see to it that you have all the opportunities we didn't have . . . we don't want you coming home to your wife covered in coal dust every evening."

"But . . . I'm almost ready for my next fight."

"Your father was working himself to death to see you become the first man in this family to attend college and you're going to at least give college a try."

And that was the end of the conversation. My mother had no way of knowing that I'd one day become a rhetoric professor, but she did have the foresight to recognize my boxing argument as empty rhetoric.

Curtis Wright climbed out of his truck, still in his Columbia Forest Products work clothes, and sat down on the cinderblock wall that lined our driveway. He couldn't have picked a better time to proposition my father.

Fifteen minutes into the conversation, Curtis finally got to it.

"Lo, I'd like to ask you to train me for the Toughman—the one in Lewisburg," he finally said.

"I'll do whatever you say, I won't question a thing you tell me, I'll follow all of your advice—honestly, you tell me what to do and I'll do it . . . I want an eight-week training camp . . . I want you to teach me everything you know about boxing," he added.

Once Curtis started talking, he couldn't stop. His plea sounded desperate and I could sense a genuine humility in his voice. He'd rehearsed his pitch to my father, I think.

As I sat on the cinderblock wall, listening to the desperation in Curtis's voice, I felt more empathy for Curtis than I did back in Lewisburg.

"To hell with it, I'll just go to college," I thought as Curtis outlined his plan for redemption.

What else did I have to do? I was out of options. It was either the Smooth Coal Company, or climb into the ring with some other Noah Milton, or college. I chose college.

Setting on the cinderblock wall that lined our driveway, on that bright August evening, I let go of my jealousy and handed the makeshift boxing ring over to Curtis Wright. He needed it more than me.

***

I imagine the 12-year-old version of my father anxiously tearing away the red-and-green Christmas wrapping. I imagine him ripping through the tape that lined both sides of the cardboard box. My great-grandmother Virginia always wrapped Christmas gifts with way too much tape and with way too many ribbons and way too many bows and it took the Jaws of Life to get them open, but they were always worth the effort.

My great-grandmother Virginia once told me about the way my father's eyes lit up as he pulled those 12-ounce boxing gloves out of the cardboard box. She'd bought a pair for Steve and Rob too, but after a few backyard beatings, they gave their gloves to my father so he eventually ended up with all three pairs.

"Your daddy would walk all over town with those gloves over his shoulder, just looking for someone to box with him. They wasn't no boxing gyms around here in them days," she said.

The summer before I left for college, the two of us would set out on her rusted porch swing and talk. She'd tell me stories of the Great Depression years, and of her brother Carl and the Korean War, and of my father when he was little.

"Mike, and Steve, and Rob would get out there in the cattle rack and fight and a feud to beat all end."

I like imagining the 12-year-old version of my father boxing in the cattle rack behind the barn. There is something vulnerable about that version of my father.

"That's where I got the idea for the gloves. I figured the least I could do was buy them some gloves if they's gonna carry on like that."

My great-grandmother Virginia never watched my father box other than the backyard bouts with his cousins Steve and Rob. She did, however, play a key role in my father's maturation as a fighter.

"She was like a fight promoter," he'd say.

When the neighborhood kids were around, or when cousins came to visit, my great-grandmother Virginia played matchmaker.

"Bet you can't whip Steve, Mike," she'd say.

"Mike, Rob thinks he can whip you," she'd goad.

Before long, they'd all three be scrapping out in the cattle rack. Things were different back then, I suppose.

"Wasn't nothing else to do for fun, we didn't have Donkey Kong," my father once joked.

Virginia's husband, my great-grandfather Van Burton Snyder, likely sprang from the long line of German immigrants who found their way into West Virginia via the Potomac River during the early 1900s. He was a quiet and stern man. Van died when I was just a child so I have no recollections of him whatsoever.

"He didn't like sports. He didn't play much with us kids," my father would say.

And why should Van Burton Snyder be cheerful? Van spent much of his life down in the West Virginia coal mines. His consciousness was marked by the underlying tension that is symptomatic of a puritanical view of work. By the age of 50, Van's body was all used up and the coal mines tossed him to the side. That's how it often goes in coal country.

My father tells a gruesome story of how Van Burton Snyder lost his left eye down in the mines. I'll spare the gory details; a rock falls and Van looks up at the wrong time. The story of Van Burton's return home from the mines that evening is equally gripping. My father and his cousins Steve and Rob were playing under an apple tree in the front yard when the rusted Chevy truck pulled into the driveway. It was about two o'clock in the afternoon, nowhere near quitting time. Something was up. The three boys didn't think much of it until they heard my great-grandmother Virginia's scream.

"Grandpa's head was bandaged up, and the bandages were blood-soaked, and two fellas were guiding him into the house like he was a cripple," my father recalled.

"And I'll be damned if he didn't go to work the next day," he added.

Van Burton Snyder was a tough son-of-a-bitch—my father's words. He was the only miner at the Smooth Coal Company who refused to wear kneepads underground.

Van and Virginia Snyder had five children and adopted a sixth (my father's cousin Steve)—that's three boys and two girls in total. Lowell Snyder, my grandfather, was the second of the litter. Lowell dropped out of school in the eighth grade because he didn't have a winter coat. As a young man, Lowell worked as a mechanic, spent most of his time in the local bars, and eventually fell in love with my grandmother, Joy Short. My father came along shortly thereafter. Lowell was 18. Joy was 16. So like the rest of them, Lowell eventually took his post at the Smooth Coal Company. By the age of 50, Lowell's body was all used up and the coal mines tossed him to the side. Sound familiar?

Lowell's hands are what I remember most; they were mangled and largely without feeling. When I was a kid, my grandfather would pick up burning coals out of the campfire to impress my buddies and me. He'd squash hornets and wasps with his fingers. The younger version of myself used to think that sort of thing was noble. My grandfather was a tough, I figured.

"Dad was unhappy because nobody ever taught him how to dream. His whole life was work," my father once said.

"He didn't come to any of my ball games or any of my fights. That kind of shit was silly to him . . . he didn't see the point in it," he added.

As I write these words, my grandfather is dying of what the doctors believe is Lou Gehrig's disease. His mangled hands have lain dormant for some time.

"I'm the luckiest man in the world," Lou Gehrig said.

"Your papaw is still alive because he's too damn tough to know how to quit," my father says.

My father was born May 27, 1959. Back then, Lowell Snyder was low man on the totem pole at the Smooth Coal Company, and my grandmother Joy was only 16 years old, so the three of them moved into a 16-by-16-foot pink trailer parked on Van and Virginia's property.

"God, this is the little boy in the pink trailer," the adolescent version of my father used to pray when things were bad.

My father's childhood wasn't so great. Things weren't that rosy for my grandmother Joy either. She'd run off with Lowell in hopes of escaping her own unhappy home life but, in the end, Joy Short had only traded one purgatory for another. Being a Snyder was no easier than being a Short.

I know very little about the Short side of the family. I spent much of my childhood around Snyders and McCoys (my mother's side of the genetic fence). But I hear that my great-grandfather Denver Short was a storyteller; he had "one hell of a sense of humor," my aunt Michele once said.

"You found yourself physically leaning in to catch every detail of the story," she added.

Maybe that's where I get it. My great-grandfather Denver died when I was just a boy, so I'll have to take Michele's word for it.

Like most everyone else in Cowen, Denver Short spent his entire life down in the West Virginia coal mines. His father, John, had been a drinker and a gambler and had lost their first home in a card game when Denver was just a boy. Denver Short would never allow a deck of cards to come through the door of his home. He saved money with scrupulous paranoia.

"He liked to joke and carry on, but he was serious when it came to the subjects of work and money," my aunt Michele says.

Denver Short was just a teenager when he fell in love with my great-grandmother Carrie Ella Hammons.

"Grandma was quiet, serious, humble, a devout Christian woman," Michele tells me.

Apart from her warm smile and soft eyes, I don't remember much about my great-grandmother Carrie; she passed away on my twelfth birthday.

Denver and Carrie Short were good Christian folk, I hear. They minded their own business and didn't leave Short holler all that often. But there must have been something in the water. Their five boys were prone to raising hell.

"My love for fighting really came from the men on the Short side of the family," my father would say.

"The Short boys had a reputation," he added.

Drinkers.

Fighters.

Coal miners.

Tougher than a pine knot, all of them.

Dana broke his jaw in a mining accident. Victor lost his right hand in the mines.

"Vick still coon hunts, pulls the trigger with his right hand, and balances the barrel with his [prosthetic] hook," my cousin, Cody, tells me.

Alden Short was a tough son-of-a-bitch as well, they say. Uncle Sam shipped Alden off to Vietnam and he was subsequently shot by the Vietcong on Hamburger Hill. Alden is one of the rare few to receive both the Purple Heart and a dishonorable discharge.

"Alden ran off three times and they eventually stopped looking for him," my father once said.

When Alden eventually made his way back to Cowen, he fell back in line at the Smooth Coal Company just like the rest of his brothers.

Drinkers.

Fighters.

Coal miners.

Tougher than a pine knot, all of them.

But it was Joy's youngest brother, Donald, who served as my father's pugilistic muse.

Donald Short was about six-feet three-inches tall and weighed only about 170 pounds. He wore a straggly Charles Manson–style beard, had long ropey arms, and wild bloodshot eyes.

He looked like Alexis Arguello might look if Alexis Arguello had grown up in Appalachia and was hooked on elephant tranquilizers.

Donald didn't fall in line at the coal mines; he didn't fall in line anywhere. Donald was a drinker and a user and didn't care about much else.

"I swear to Christ that I watched Donald reach across a pool table and knock a guy out colder than a wedge," my father once said.

He grew up in the shadow of Donald's tough-guy reputation.

"Donald got shot off a motorcycle, he got stabbed . . . he must have got arrested 20 or 30 times," my father recalled.

"Schoolteachers would give me hell because I was kin to him," he'd add.

I've only met Donald Short a few times, but I can certainly vouch for his criminal record. During two of my undergraduate summers home from college, I worked as an intern for the Webster County prosecuting attorney. My aunt Nellie, my mother's oldest sister, was the prosecutor's secretary and helped me land the gig. I was the prosecutor's PS (paper shredder). It wasn't glamorous.

One day, while everybody else in the office was out to lunch, I snuck into the back room and read my uncle Donald's file. His criminal record was prolific, to say the least. His folder made David Bevington's *The Complete Works of Shakespeare* look like a paperweight. The most gripping selection from the folder was the one about Donald beating the Camden-on-Gauley town sheriff senseless, stripping him naked, tying him to a tree, and then driving around town in a stolen cop car. You don't have to believe me. I read the file.

"If there would'a been a Toughman Contest back in Donald's day, he would have won it," my father would often brag.

No such luck.

Donald Short spent most of his time down at Carpenter's Beer Joint looking for a chance to prove how tough a son-of-a-bitch he really was. In a town like Cowen, West Virginia, that sort of thing matters.

Our heroes are defined by their ability to take punishment, their willingness to grit their teeth through pain. Even Jesus Christ, with all his talk of peace, love, and forgiveness, would have never made it big in my town if not for that long ring walk to Calvary. He had to prove that he was one tough son-of-a-bitch or nobody in Cowen would have taken him seriously.

When I was a kid, my father used to wear a gray sweatshirt that read "Lord's Gym." The sweatshirt featured a picture of Jesus doing push-ups with a large cross on his back. I loved that shirt. Jesus's rippled deltoids were covered in blood; Jesus looked like a real badass.

Legendary heavyweight champion Rocky Marciano often joked, "I can't sing or dance but just to be gracious I'll take on any man in the house."[22]

My father loved that saying. He'd repeat those words as if they were his own. Rocky was from Brockton, Massachusetts, but his joke played well in Cowen, West Virginia.

I've only been in one street fight, but it really wasn't in the streets and wasn't much of a fight. In the fifth grade, John Boggs sucker-punched me in the boys' bathroom at Glade Elementary. I threw a few retaliatory punches, but none of them landed flush. Not my manliest moment, I'll admit.

Shipping off to Glenville State College in August 2000 didn't feel like a manly thing to do either. But there I was, setting in the back row of my English 101 course, surrounded by khaki- and polo-wearing college kids, listening to my toupee-wearing professor blather on about a whale named Moby Dick.

And a 100 miles away, there was Curtis "The Ice Man" Wright, training for small-town Toughman redemption in the back of a women's beauty shop, in a makeshift boxing ring that smelled of Paul Mitchell hair products, Mike "Lo" Snyder at his side.

And here I am, transferring these scattered memories into a laptop computer, sipping a macchiato in the back of a suburban coffee shop, surrounded by successful New York business types with their fresh pressed suits and leather briefcases, unable to escape the feeling that I could take on any man in the house, if need be.

Chapter 3

———

LO'S GYM

———

When I was 12 years old, my father brought me to the face of a coal mine, and walked me about 100 yards into the darkness. He made me wear an oversized yellow hardhat but, looking back, I imagine the accessory was for effect.

"How'd you like to get up at four in the morning and come to this?"

"I don't think I'd like it," the 12-year-old version of myself replied.

"Then I'd study those spelling words if I were you."

My father would say that sort of thing to me from time to time, but the educational impact always wore off a few days later. I was proud of the dangerousness of coal mining, proud of my father for facing it daily. At 12 years old, I'd already learned that real men *worked*, real men were providers.

"Ain't no such thing as Santa Claus."

"Your dad works at the coal mines . . . that's the only reason you get all them Christmas presents," a trailer park kid once told me.

In "Craving Coal Dust 'Like Nicotine': Why Miners Love the Work,"[23] a 2010 ABC News profile piece on the Upper Big Branch mining disaster that claimed the lives of 29 West Virginians, reporter Devin Dwyer explores the allure of coal mining for working-class Appalachian men. Dwyer begins with a familiar narrative, the story of uneducated workers who ignore the obvious dangers of the profession in search of a decent wage. Dwyer then transitions to a discussion of how the region's mining legacy impacts familial work histories, particularly for young men. Flags, bumper stickers, and pickup truck decals signal a regional passion for mining, Dwyer says.

Dwyer even cites a few locals who suggest, "when you get coal dust in your lungs, you want to go back."[24] One old boy even says he "craves coal dust like nicotine."[25]

"Your father still works in the coal mines?"

"How old is he?"

"Goodness gracious that must be dangerous work," my professor colleagues say.

I receive the same kind of response when I tell educated folks that my father used to be a boxing trainer.

"I don't know how any sane person can enjoy getting punched in the face."

"With all we know about concussions, I just don't see the allure of a sport like boxing."

"Goodness gracious that must be dangerous work."

Devin Dwyer has it wrong. It isn't the allure of a paycheck that gets the fighter into the ring. Fighters aren't adrenaline junkies. It isn't regional pride. It isn't family tradition. The tragedy lies in the fantasy. The fighter is never complete, never fully actualized. You are never a fighter. One becomes a fighter each time he climbs through the ropes and steps in the ring.

In Charles Bukowski's novel *Hollywood*, the protagonist, Henry Chinaski, likens prizefighting to the writing process. For Chinaski, both fighters and writers must have talent, guts, and conditioning. The mental and spiritual conditioning required in both activities, however, is what fascinates Chinaski the most, the reason for his comparison.

"You were never a writer. You *become* a writer each time you sat down to the machine,"[26] Chinaski reflects.

"What was hard was sometimes finding the chair and sitting in it. Sometimes you couldn't sit in it. Like everybody else in the world, for you, things got in the way: small troubles, big troubles, continuous slamming and banging. You had to be in condition to endure what was trying to kill you. That's the message I got from watching the fights,"[27] Chinaski adds.

As a writer, fighter, and child of Appalachia, Chinaski's analogy rings true to my life experience. Around my way, you have to endure the thing that is trying to kill you. It's a continuous process of proving you're a man. Some pick up the dinner bucket. Others strap on boxing gloves. Some do both. The tragedy lies in the fantasy. There *ain't no quitin' time*. Nobody cares what you did yesterday. When the sun comes up, it's time to prove it all over again.

We were born into extractive industry towns designed to harbor a very specific notion of manhood, purposefully isolated mono-economies built off the bravery of marginalized workers. This is how an 18-year-old coal miner musters up the nerve to crawl through a pitch-black coal mine to secure roof bolts. This is how the electrician rewires breaker boxes while standing waist-deep in stagnant acidic water. Around my way, there ain't nothing more important than proving you are a *man*, nothing more necessary for survival. The tragedy lies in the fantasy. The working-class Appalachian man is never complete, never fully actualized. You are never really *man* enough. This is the sociocultural pull that brings fathers and sons to the darkness of a coal mine, fighters to the squared circle.

This is the sociocultural pull that brought Curtis "The Ice Man" Wright and Mike "Lo" Snyder back to the Lewisburg Fair Grounds in November 2000, each seeking symbolic revenge.

***

Back at the Super 8 Hotel, Curtis was visibly shaken, sheepishly wagging his head back and forth in an awe-shucks disposition.

"Lo, I let you down tonight."

"Damn it, I didn't circle the ring, I didn't double my jab."

"I got hit with that first punch and just lost it," Curtis lamented from the edge of the mattress.

You'd have thought Curtis lost the fight.

"Friday night is always the hardest. You get that first win out of the way, advance to Saturday, and everything settles down," my father replied.

"You'll see," he added, after a moment of silence.

We made our way out into the hallway, next to the ice machine and the Pepsi machine. Curtis wanted to go over the game plan. It was almost midnight.

"Circle the ring one time before you even think about throwing a punch. Get the nervous energy out," my father instructed.

"Like this?"

"Yes, but keep that chin tucked, elbows in."

"Like this?"

"You know what to do, Curtis, you're ready."

Earlier that night, Curtis had been matched up with a local roughneck, who went by the nickname of Iron Head—the nickname was apt. Curtis and Iron Head fought three of the sloppiest, least disciplined rounds of boxing of the night. The bout was rife with haymakers, rabbit punches, clinches, pushing, and hitting on the break. If Iron Head hadn't been so out of shape, his hairy beer belly pink from body punches by the end of the fight, it just might have gone the other way. Curtis won a unanimous decision.

"I just wish you could have been in the corner with me, to settle me down," Curtis said after the midnight hallway rehearsal was complete.

Most Toughman boxers don't partake in training camps or even have trainers. They sign up, smack around a heavy bag for a few days, or not, and go fight. The folks who run the show provide stand-in corner men for the combatants, guys who offer basic advice between rounds, a few half-interested local boxing sages who are essentially there to offer fighters a sip of water when they need it.

My father didn't think of himself as a boxing trainer back in those days. He didn't have the nerve to ask promoter Jerry Thomas if he could work Curtis's corner. Instead, my father screamed himself hoarse from the cheap seats. Curtis, I'm sure, didn't hear any of those instructions.

"Chin up, Curtis. We got the first win out of the way."

My father placed his arm around Curtis, the same way he'd always do for me after a bad Little League game.

"Muscle memory is going to kick in tomorrow night," my father assured Curtis amid the glow of the Pepsi machine.

"You win fights in the gym."

"Tomorrow night, you'll go collect what you've already earned in the gym."

Until Curtis "The Ice Man" Wright came along, my father and I never referred to the spare room in the back of Classic Curl Beauty Shop as a boxing gym. Rather, we'd often say something like, "We're going down to the shop to box." This was a linguistic first and I instantly took note.

Yet, the small wooden sign, painted white with black cursive letters, that hung just above the top rope of our makeshift boxing ring had always suggested otherwise.

It came from the tin building that rested in the shade of a small poplar tree at the end of our trailer, the side furthest from the gravel driveway. The tin building was just big enough to house my father's homemade weight bench, welded by a few of the boys down at the Smooth Coal Company, a few weight racks, and a couple of dumbbells. In the winter, my father would warm the building with a small kerosene heater. No insulation. My father's hands would stick to the bench press bar if he didn't wear gloves.

During the summer months, the trailer park boys would crowd around the entry to watch the show. He'd play Bob Seger and Creedence Clearwater Revival on his portable cassette player until the batteries ran out. When my father would get up from the weight bench for a drink of water, the trailer park boys would always try to sneak a peek at his workout calendar, each page featuring a pin-up girl with big tits and a come-hither smile.

Above the weight bench was the small wooden sign, painted white with black cursive lettering. The sign read, "Lo's Gym."

Roger Frazier was constantly doodling dirty pictures down at the coal mines, Mickey Mouse with a large pecker, Donald Duck taking a swig of moonshine. A few of the miners got a kick out of it. My father always got a kick out of it.

"Draw me something, Roger," my father asked one sticky summer evening back in 1983.

"Hell, I'll paint ya something."

"Alright."

"What do ya want, Lo?"

"Paint me something for my weight building."

The next morning, Roger Frazier staggered into work with a small wooden sign, painted white with black cursive lettering.

Years later, my father hung Roger Frazier's masterpiece in the back of Classic Curl Beauty Shop to cover up a hole in the paneling. His gesture was somewhat satirical. The spare room in the back of my mother's beauty shop was no more a boxing club than was the tin building in Willoughby Trailer Park a Gold's Gym or Planet Fitness.

But that wasn't how Curtis viewed it. Before the tournament, he and his wife, Angel, had matching t-shirts made up for family and friends.

The t-shirts were gray with black lettering. The t-shirts read, "Curtis *The Ice Man* Wright" on the back.

On the front: "Lo's Gym."

***

The idea of Lo's Gym Boxing Club, or the proliferation of such an idea, at least for Webster County residents, has roots in Jimmy Utt's first boxing-themed newspaper article, printed one day prior to Curtis Wright's bout with Iron Head.

Jimmy Utt was a nice guy, the 4-H Club, church on Sunday kind of nice guy you meet in the Bible Belt. When Jimmy walked through the back door of Classic Curl Beauty Shop for the first time, he was probably in his early forties, was wearing a yellow West Virginia University polo, checkered blue-and-gold board shorts, a pair of thick-rimmed glasses, and an expensive camera around his neck. Jimmy was a freelance photographer and reporter for the *Webster Echo*, the only newspaper in our small mountain town. If you ever attend a Webster County sporting event, you'll likely see Jimmy on the sidelines, shooting pictures and getting the scoop.

"Dang, you've got yourself a little boxing gym down here, Mike."

"Yeah, it's not much, but it'll do."

"Don't be modest, this is real neat," Jimmy said, snapping shots of Curtis as he laced up his boxing shoes.

Curtis Wright had no idea Jimmy was coming to the gym that Friday. It was an unseasonably warm November evening, exactly one week until Curtis Wright's second crack at the Lewisburg Toughman Contest, and nobody, outside of a few hand-selected sparring partners, had been in the gym since the start of camp. Curtis looked unnerved.

Because I was over 100 miles away, off being a first-generation college student at Glenville State, I wasn't around for much of Curtis's training camp. Occasionally, I'd make it to a Friday evening workout, but that was about it. Sometimes my father would videotape sparring sessions and we'd watch them together when I came home on weekends. I watched so many of those sparring session tapes I sometimes feel as if I was a part of it all.

After about five minutes of small talk and photo snapping, my father finally came clean.

"Jimmy is going to do a story on you, Curtis. He's going to take a few pictures for the paper. He's going to let everyone in Webster County know that you are going to go to Lewisburg next weekend to win the whole damn thing," my father said, standing next to Lo's Gym's first beat reporter.

Mike "Lo" Snyder had once been a fighter himself. He understood the fantasy that lures fighters to the squared circle. He understood the hypermasculine cultural impulse.

This was a crude piece of psychological gamesmanship on my father's part, his first real gamble as a boxing trainer. Embarrassment had fueled Curtis Wright's ambition and my father wanted to ensure that Curtis did not lose sight of his motivation.

***

Philip Cochran came into adulthood during one of Appalachia's countless waves of urban migration, then, some years later, found his way back to the mountains. He was from the era when all of our great-grandfathers migrated to Cleveland, Baltimore, and Detroit looking for work. Philip wound up in Detroit, and through a series of circumstances that are unknown to me, wound up in a boxing gym. It wasn't Detroit's legendary Kronk Gym (the gym that produced Thomas "The Hitman" Hearns), but it was one of the many boxing gyms born out of the Motor City's post–Joe Louis years, a boxing renaissance for a city that was, at one time, one of the nation's most important boxing towns.

Philip wasn't the only West Virginia boy in Detroit back in those days. Hall of Fame boxing trainer Emanuel Steward, a native of Bottom Creek, West Virginia, was just one year removed from winning the National Golden Gloves bantamweight championship when Philip arrived in the Motor City. Those familiar with Detroit boxing lore know how the Emanuel Steward story goes. Despite amassing a dazzling amateur record of 94 wins to only 3 losses, Steward struggles to find managerial representation as a professional; his only serious offer comes from a group that demands he leave his mother and two sisters behind in Detroit. Steward abandons his professional dreams and takes a job as a journeyman electrician at the Detroit Edison Company. During the summer of 1969, Steward's younger brother moves from West Virginia to Detroit, begs his big brother to teach him how to box, and the two desperate and displaced West Virginia boys end up at a boxing gym called The Kronk. The rest, as they say, is history.

I never had the pleasure of meeting Philip Cochran so I don't pretend to understand his passions and motivations. But the Philip I know from my father's Beowulf stories isn't all that difficult to read. Philip Cochran learned to box in Detroit in the 1960s and, I would imagine, returned to Webster County an older man, with dreams of becoming Webster County's Emanuel Steward, in search of Appalachia's Thomas "The Hitman" Hearns. It wasn't long after Philip Cochran's return to West Virginia that he and Freeman McCourt came up with the idea of starting Webster County's first boxing club. Freeman was a local scrapper who had learned to box in the navy; he'd already secured the old Webster Springs High School gymnasium as a venue. All Philip and Freeman needed was a boxing ring.

***

Charlie Cummings,[28] by my father's estimation, was a *dope-smoking hippy*, the black sheep of a family of local extractive industry barons who owned *the* timber company in our neck of the woods. Charlie was Webster County's Falstaff but with Hal's bank account; he was propped up by a family of millionaires but chose to spend his days mingling with Appalachia's social underbelly.

I never had the pleasure of meeting Charlie Cummings but he, like Philip Cochran and Freeman McCourt, lived in my father's Beowulf stories. Charlie Cummings always showed up as a comic-relief bit character. Charlie was always one of my favorites.

"Lo, you think you can beat this colored fellow?"

"Yeah, Charlie."

"Good, I put $100 on you."

"Okay, Charlie."

Charlie Cummings always put $100 on my father. He'd mill around the crowd and find someone to take that wager. Those bets turned out to be a good investment.

"Fuck 'em up, Lo," Charlie would say.

"Yeah, Charlie."

"You gotta fuck 'em up, Lo, I got $100 on it."

"Okay, Charlie."

"Fuck 'em up, Lo," was Charlie Cummings's catchphrase in the Beowulf stories.

According to local legend, or at least my father's unreliable version of the story, Charlie Cummings attended the Larry Holmes vs. Kevin Isaac fight at Cleveland Arena on November 28, 1973, and became so impulsively enamored with the sweet science that he bought the boxing ring off of the promoter after the fight. It must have been one hell of a fight.

Charlie Cummings may have been under the influence of drugs and/ or alcohol when he bought that boxing ring; he stored the boxing ring in the basement of his two-story Webster County home and had it, along with the other contents of the room, painted cherry red. His painting the entire room cherry red probably had something to do with his being under the influence of drugs and alcohol.

From what I can gather from the Beowulf stories, Charlie didn't do much with the boxing ring other than buy it, have it shipped to his two-story Webster County home, and painted cherry red. I never had the pleasure of meeting Charlie Cummings so I can only speculate as to whether or not he experienced buyer's remorse.

And, in case you were wondering, the little-known Kevin Isaac knocked the future heavyweight champion of the world on his ass in the second round of that fight. But Larry Holmes got back up and finished him off in the subsequent round.

The living room was blanketed by the stench of marijuana. A psychedelic bong proudly rested on the glass coffee table like a Martha Stewart centerpiece. Charlie's wife was running around the house shirtless and his kids wouldn't stop screaming in the back. My father likened his wife to Yoko Ono, but that wasn't as much an ethnic characterization as it was a commentary on the early 1970s hippy vibe she gave off. Charlie had called my father the previous evening, said he had something to show him, something my father had to see; it was a surprise.

Charlie Cummings, like most people from around town, knew my father as Mike "Lo" Snyder, number 22 coming out of the backfield. Charlie loved high school football; he'd been to all of my father's games, something my father's father had never bothered to do. Charlie, of course, had an ulterior motive for inviting my father over to his two-story Webster County home that evening. Philip Cochran and Freeman McCourt were looking to find some local man-boys to move the cherry-red boxing ring from Charlie's red room to the old Webster Springs High School gymnasium. Mike "Lo" Snyder, number 22 coming out of the backfield, was being recruited for the Webster Springs Boxing Club and he didn't even know it.

As Charlie unlocked the basement door, my father began second-guessing his decision to indulge the mysterious invitation.

"Gotta keep the fucking pigs out," Charlie barked as he opened the door and slowly lumbered down the wooden basement steps.

My father had never been to Charlie Cummings's two-story Webster County home before and worried that hanging around Charlie Cummings's two-story Webster County home was a good way to establish a criminal record. He'd been nervous since the moment he arrived, second-guessing himself since the moment he agreed to Charlie's request over the phone.

"I call this the red room," Charlie shouted through the darkness, fumbling for the light switch.

After what seemed like an eternity of darkness, Charlie Cummings said, "Let there be light" and revealed a secret that would forever change my father's life.

Charlie broke the silence by saying something like, "the color red . . . it really gets me going, man."

As my father surveyed the red brick walls, red heavy bag, and red speed bag that decorated the exterior of the basement, the trepidation he had experienced on his way from the front door, through the living room, and down the wooden steps was long gone.

"Where in the hell did you get it?" my father mumbled, as he climbed through the ropes of a professional-style boxing ring with a bright cherry-red canvas.

A boxer never forgets his first time climbing through the ropes—it's something like a first kiss; the experience sticks with you. My father was an 18-year-old warehouse technician at the Smooth Coal Company, just a few months removed from his high school graduation, when he stepped into a boxing ring for the first time and it was Charlie Cummings's red room. He climbed through the ropes one person and climbed out another.

***

The bleachers were packed; everyone in Webster County was there. Cousin Steve, cousin Rob, Rick Cogar, and the rest of my father's buddies had a Spike Lee view of the action. An 18-by-18-foot professional-style boxing ring was erected on the 50-yard line of the Webster Springs Elementary football field. If you believe the local sages, it was the first amateur boxing card ever held in Webster County.

There were 29 fights that night and my father was scheduled for the third bout. My father's opponent looked like David Hasselhoff, if Hasselhoff were cast in a biker gang movie. After the weigh-in, Hasselhoff was Baywatching around the locker room in a black leather jacket that said "Hell's Angels" or something like that on the back. Hasselhoff had an entourage of biker-gang-looking fellows with him that night.

I never had the pleasure of meeting Philip Cochran, but I would imagine he viewed my father as the perfect client for his first foray into training. My father was young, athletic, competitive, tough, poor, hard-working, angry, and, most important of all, responded well to ridicule. Philip made a big deal about some prefight trash talk from the Hasselhoff biker gang. He wouldn't let it go. He stayed on my father about it, buzzed around the locker room in my father's ear.

"Lo, he's going to try to embarrass you in front of all your friends," Philip said, stoking the fire.

"He called you a pussy, Lo."

"Did you hear that, Lo?"

"He called you a pussy."

When the opening bell rang, my father shot out of the corner low to the ground, like a running back breaking his three-point stance.

Smack!

Down went Hasselhoff.

It was the first punch of the fight.

Hasselhoff was down, but he wasn't out. The Knight Rider made it to his feet by the count of six.

In the neutral corner, waiting for the referee to administer the mandatory eight count, my father glanced over the top rope and out into the crowd. Cousin Steve and cousin Rob were expressing their gratitude by shadowboxing invisible opponents. At ringside, Charlie

Cummings's ZZ-Top beard was flopping up and down with excitement. Philip gave my father the thumbs-up, followed by the sign language equivalent of "finish him"—a closed fist pounding an open hand.

The 17-year-old version of my mother was somewhere out there in the crowd that night, sitting with her sister Shelia and Shelia's eventual husband Kurt. The 17-year-old version of my mother was impressed, I imagine.

"Your dad beat that guy up pretty good," she once recalled when I asked for blow-by-blow replay of the events. My mother wasn't exactly of the Bert Sugar variety of boxing historians.

"That was a long time ago, Todd. All I remember is that he beat that guy up pretty good," she added.

"Box," the referee shouted.

My father shot out of the neutral corner just as violently and recklessly as he had done the first time. His straight right-hand jab served as the range finder for what would soon be a devastating uppercut. Cheers erupted at the old Webster Springs High School football field.

The Knight Rider was down again.

One—two—three . . .

My father gets another taste of the feeling he thought he'd given up.

Four—five—six . . .

It is difficult to explain the sense of accomplishment sports offer those who have little else to celebrate in their lives.

Seven—eight—nine . . .

The Knight Rider was down for the count.

I've studied my father's boxing scrapbook more than a few times. I've read the news clippings. The fight lasted only 82 seconds.

The ref counted to ten and Charlie Cummings was $100 richer.

***

Curtis Wright was matched up with Bruce Frank in the semifinals. Bruce boxed under the moniker "The Boxing Preacher."

"Is he a real preacher?" Curtis asked.

"Hell if I know," my father replied.

"I'd hate to hit a preacher," Curtis joked.

My father and I knew Bruce Frank from our dealings at Simon's

Gym. Bruce ran a small boxing gym just outside of Lewisburg; he'd occasionally bring two or three kids to the amateur shows in Morgantown. More often than not, his kids could fight. Bruce Frank was the defending Lewisburg Toughman champion; he didn't have much of a punch, but he knew how to box. He and Curtis, from what I could see, were the only two guys who had really trained for the tournament. Bruce Frank didn't look like a boxer. He looked like the Ned Flanders character from *The Simpsons*. He had a bushy mustache, a church-on-Sunday haircut, and wore thick-rimmed glasses when he wasn't boxing. Bruce was originally from Blacksburg, Virginia, and talked with what I thought at the time was an urban accent. Bruce couldn't let go of his glory days in the ring. He was in his mid- to late-thirties and was still boxing in Toughman Contests; he couldn't give it up. Bruce Frank didn't look intimidating, but he'd get in there and box circles around the maulers and sluggers he faced. His experience and boxing know-how made us a little nervous. His being from the Lewisburg area made us more than a little nervous.

You had to be a real boxing fan, someone who understands the little nuances of boxing, to enjoy the first two rounds of the fight. Curtis would jab Bruce, duck out of danger, and circle the ring. Bruce would double up on the jab, feint with the right, and escape from the corner.

Jabbing.

Dodging.

Ducking.

Both guys glided around the ring, never standing still for more than a moment. The drunken Lewisburg crowd booed like hell. In between rounds, somebody spilled a protest beer on my mother's jacket. Half the crowd was pulling for Bruce Frank. The other half of the crowd was just pissed off.

The third round was probably Curtis Wright's shining moment of the tournament. Curtis landed a solid one-two-three combination that sent Bruce Frank sprawling into the ropes. Frank was dazed, but quickly regained his footing. Curtis used his jab to back Bruce into the corner; he cut off the ring just like my father had taught him. Curtis kept Bruce trapped in the corner for the final 30 seconds of the bout. It was a crescendo of left- and right-hand combinations. Bruce blocked most of Curtis's punches, but the punches were loud and showy and Bruce wasn't throwing back. When the fight was over, I was confident that Curtis had won, but wasn't confident the hometown judges would give it to him. Waiting on the decision felt like waiting on the results of a biopsy. Bruce Frank was pacing around the ring, playing to the crowd a bit, looking desperate for reassurance.

"Alright, ladies and gentlemen, let's give a big round of applause for Curtis "The Ice Man" Wright and Bruce "The Boxing Preacher" Frank," Jerry Thomas announced to the crowd of 3,000-plus.

"The judges' scorecards are in and here is how they have it."

"Judge Tom Garrison scored the bout 29–28."

"Judge Cathy Rodgers has it 30–27."

"And, finally, judge Robert Watkins has it 29–28."

"All for the winner by unanimous decision . . . Curtis 'The Ice Man' Wright."

It was a mix of cheers and boos. Bruce acted like a wise ass, refusing to leave the ring before Curtis. He shoulder-shrugged his way around the arena, trying to stir up the hometown crowd. The Boxing Preacher didn't set a very good example for the congregation.

"I love you, Lo," Curtis said to my father back in the crowded locker room. Curtis had won four fights in a row and was quickly becoming a believer in whatever pedagogical wisdom my father possessed.

"I love you too, Curtis," my father replied, offering a brief victory embrace.

"Hey, none of that in boxing," an off-duty referee joked, overhearing the conversation.

"This last one is for you, Lo," Curtis said, ignoring the referee's comment.

"We've got one more guy's ass to kick," my father answered, glaring across the locker room at Tom "The Butcher" Butcher.

Tom "The Butcher" Butcher[29] didn't stand a chance. Tom was an ex-Fairmont State College football star who worked at his father's grocery store; he wasn't really a butcher or a boxer. The Butcher had won three fights on his way to the championship bout. There was an odd number of contestants in the tournament and he scored the luck of the draw and was given a bye in the first round. Tom wasn't all that impressive, but he had scored a few KOs.

"He's greener than grass," my father assured Curtis while Tom was still within earshot.

"Go collect what you earned in the gym," he added.

Curtis landed a lead right hand, the first meaningful punch of the fight. Tom staggered from one end of the ring to the other. Most Toughman fights are at least metaphorically over in the first 30 or 40 seconds. It doesn't take long to figure out that you can't box. Tom offered a few counterpunch haymakers, but nothing landed. Curtis circled the ring, just as he had practiced in front of the Pepsi machine, landed a stiff left jab, followed by a shotgun right hand. Curtis took his time, consistently landing straight left- and right-hand combinations. There was very little resistance to the beating Curtis was administering. One minute into the fight, Tom "The Butcher" Butcher found the canvas. The Butcher made it back to his feet and Curtis showed him the canvas one more time before the end of the first round.

Ding!

On his way back to the corner, Curtis gestured in my father's direction, as if to say, "We're doing it, ol' boy."

When the bout resumed, Tom was too exhausted to offer any substantial offense. But Curtis circled the ring anyway, and took his time. The Butcher offered up a weak jab, but Curtis slipped the punch and countered with a lead right and whipping left hook.

One—two—three . . .

The Butcher isn't knocked unconscious, but he isn't getting up either.

Four—five—six . . .

Curtis Wright gets to be "The Ice Man" once again.

Seven—eight—nine . . .

Flat on his ass, his knees slightly bent, his gloves resting on the canvas, Tom "The Butcher" Butcher gives the ref an "I've had about enough" nod and the ref calls it.

It was something akin to catching the biggest catfish in Summersville Lake, killing a 12-point buck up on Point Mountain. You'd have to be from around my way to understand the significance of what took place that night at the Lewisburg Fair Grounds. Curtis "The Ice Man" Wright was the first Webster County resident to win the whole damn thing (he'd gone 5–0, with three knockouts, in the tournament). It's hard to explain the significance of his achievement to someone from a large city. Curtis paraded around the ring in his nylon jacket, holding his two-year-old son in his arms like a trophy. We all met up back at the Super 8 Hotel and celebrated by ordering Domino's Pizza.

And come Monday, Curtis "The Ice Man" Wright was back at Columbia Forest Products, my father back at the Smooth Coal Company. I found myself back in my dorm room at Glenville State College, the nearest academic feeder system for Webster County first-generation college students. The three of us had allowed ourselves a little dream and the dream came true and getting back to small-town reality wouldn't be easy.

And a few days later, Jimmy Utt came down to Classic Curl Beauty Shop and shot the sequel to his Curtis Wright cover story.

The caption read, "Curtis Wright, of Lo's Gym Boxing Club in Cowen, Wins Lewisburg Toughman Contest."

Just as the coal mines were beginning to consolidate and close down, Curtis "The Ice Man" Wright restored Cowen, West Virginia's, masculine ethos. We were champions. We were Tough Men. Pugilistic alchemy transformed Classic Curl into Lo's Gym Boxing Club, a middle-aged coal miner into a highly sought-after local boxing trainer, and Curtis "The Ice Man" Wright back into what he was supposed to be all along—the toughest man in town.

When the *Webster Echo* hit newsstands out at Y-Mart and Foodland, everything changed. The floodgates were open.

Chapter 4

FLEX AND THE RUMBLE ON THE HILL

On June 16, 1983, welterweight journeyman Luis Resto shocked the boxing world by upsetting undefeated prospect Billy Collins Jr. at Madison Square Garden. The bout was featured on the undercard of the Roberto Duran vs. Davey Moore fight and was televised on *CBS Sports Spectacular*. For those interested in the profession of training human beings for fistic combat, the Resto vs. Collins Jr. fight can be read as a cautionary tale. Here's how it goes.

After the fight, Luis Resto attempts to shake Billy Collins Jr.'s hand when Billy Sr., his son's chief second, discovers that deception is afoot; Resto's gloves appear much thinner than normal. Billy Sr. raises hell and the New York State Boxing Commission impounds the gloves and a high-profile investigation ensues. Long story short, the commission concludes that Resto's trainer, Carlos "Panama" Lewis, intentionally removed padding from the gloves before the fight; both gloves were found to be a full ounce lighter than normal. The bout is eventually ruled a "no contest," but poor Billy Collins Jr. suffers a torn right iris, has blurred vision for the rest of his short life, and never boxes again.

Three years later, Resto and Lewis are both put on trial and found guilty of assault, criminal possession of a weapon, and conspiracy; Panama Lewis is also found guilty of tampering with a sports contest. The New York State Boxing Commission subsequently hands both Resto and Lewis a lifetime ban from boxing.

In 2007, filmmaker Eric Drath made a documentary detailing the Luis Resto-Billy Collins controversy. My father and I are in that documentary. A few hours into our first visit to New York City, we ended up on HBO.

"Damn, son, that's Panama Lewis," my father barked as we made our way from the Zab Judah-Miguel Cotto weigh-in at Madison Square Garden and out onto the busy sidewalks of New York City's Eighth Avenue.

Panama didn't look so great that day. His arms were frail and his potbelly protruded through his oversized black t-shirt. At first, I didn't think it was Panama. He had on a pair of white Oakley sunglasses and a silver *Jesus piece* that hung halfway down his protruding potbelly. He looked just like the guy who tried to sell us knock-off Gucci wallets earlier in the day.

"That can't be him," I quickly replied.

Panama had on a white do-rag, a gold Rolex watch, and was looking downward as he texted on his flip phone at the crosswalk. I couldn't see his face clearly at first. Then Panama flashed a crooked smile and I caught a glimpse of his trademark gold teeth.

"Go get a picture with him," my father urged.

I did.

"Hey Panama, can we get a quick picture?" I asked over the ambience of bypassing New York City traffic.

"Yeah. Gadda in, Poppa you get in da picture too," he replied in a surprisingly jovial tone.

We didn't see the cameras until after the photo op; we didn't see Drath's documentary on HBO until a few years later.

"Despite all he's done to harm the reputation of the sport, Panama Lewis continues to receive adulation from some boxing fans,"[30] Drath narrates during our three seconds of screen time with Lewis.

And there we were, grinning and palling around with one of boxing's most notorious bad guys, for a good three Mississippi's of HBO airtime.

"Son, you just got your picture with one of the greatest trainers in boxing history," my father smirked as Panama, Derth, and the rest of the film crew disappeared into the busy Manhattan crowd. I was more in awe of my father's enthusiasm than I was in awe of Panama Lewis.

"Dad, he's probably the dirtiest son-of-a-bitch in boxing history," I speculated.

"No. He's just the dirtiest son-of-a-bitch to get caught," he replied.

In the sport of boxing, *chief second* is the official title given to the person who oversees a fighter's corner. When two fighters enter the center of the ring for final instructions from the referee, the ring is cleared of all the peripheral characters. Only the boxers, their chief seconds, and the referee are permitted to take part in this obligatory ceremony. It is a moment that will soon be forgotten after the first punch has landed; it is the moment when a boxer stands side-by-side with the person most responsible for his or her failure or success, as if to pay public homage to the person who looked out for his best interest along the way.

It means something to be standing by a boxer's side at this point in a fight. More so than the referee, the state athletic commission, or the ringside doctor, the chief second is responsible for the well-being of a boxer—perhaps more so than a boxer is responsible for his or her own well-being. If you are the one wearing the gloves, you trust that your chief second has given you sage advice, prepared you for all the hardships that will soon come, and cares about you enough to save you from taking any undue punishment. For overly sentimental thinkers, such as me, this stage of a fight is an act of love, the last symbolic occurrence before painful realities show themselves to the crowd. It is at this moment when the combatants stand on the cusp of success, failure, and certain physical pain, all but alone in the world.

The chief second's presence in the ring is something of a public metaphor. A chief second can tell you what to do, he can walk you to the ring, he can introduce you to the referee, but when the bell rings, you will be the only one taking punches. When the referee has given his final instructions, the chief second is forced to walk back to the corner, climb out of the ring, and become a spectator—the corner man, the man in the corner. To be a chief second is to live vicariously through others. It is to believe you've figured something out about life worth sharing with another human being. It's a high-pressure job that will drive you to do desperate things if you let it.

Just ask Carlos "Panama" Lewis.

My father was the talent scout, not me. He had an eye for talent. His talent was seeing other people's talent. I've never met anyone like him, not in boxing or in life. He had the ability to take a kid with no ability and teach him how to succeed. He would find the one thing a fighter was capable of doing and accentuate that particular trait. I watched a lot of subpar boxers win fights under his tutelage. I didn't inherit this sort of vision from my father. I would never have made it as a boxing trainer. In spring of 2001, I learned my lesson. Jeffrey "Flex" Lemasters was my first and only boxing pupil.

***

Flex was a muscle-bound redneck. I don't think he would mind my saying so. He drove a jacked-up Ford truck with a lift kit. He wore Harley-Davidson bandanas. He wore thick, black steel-toed boots every day of the week. He rolled up his sleeves or went sleeveless eight out of 12 months a year. It had to be blizzard conditions for him to cover up his biceps. Flex wanted to be a body builder. His idol was Arnold Schwarzenegger. Flex walked like the Terminator, even when he was just walking to class. His 80s-style blond buzz cut was of the Dolph Lundgren/Ivan Drago variety.

Flex was a West Virginia country boy—the guns, the hunting, the tattoos, and the chaw of tobacco—all of it. He drank like a fish, skipped class on a regular basis, flirted with almost every girl who looked in his direction, and, most of all, loved to fight. That's probably why he took a liking to me. Boxing was all that I cared about back then. The walls of my dorm room were covered with boxing posters.

"You box?" Flex asked, after peering into my dorm room—he and I were fourth-floor neighbors in Pickens Hall.

"Yeah, I boxed a little. My dad has a boxing gym back home," I replied, leaving out the part about our boxing gym residing in the back of a women's beauty shop.

"Teach me some of that boxing," was Flex's swift reply.

I didn't know what I was getting myself into.

When I came back to campus after Curtis Wright's Toughman victory, I brought two pairs of 12-ounce boxing gloves and a pair of mitts with me. Every now and then, Flex and I would go to the lounge at the end of the dormitory hallway and push the furniture back against the wall. This was our ivory tower makeshift boxing gym. It wasn't much.

At first, Flex looked like Frankenstein with boxing gloves. Big and bulky muscles are typically looked down upon in the boxing world—they cause one's arms to get heavy in the later rounds and reduce speed. Long and lean muscles are what boxing trainers look for. Flex looked more like a Hollywood boxer than a real boxer. But after a few weeks, I started to feel better about my Frankenstein project. Flex was learning combinations, firing off shots from the shoulders, and seemed like he was limbering up a bit.

"I've got something here," I figured.

Flex was a gifted athlete, but didn't care much for athletics. I once watched him slam-dunk a basketball in a pair of Carhart boots.

"Basketball is a pussy sport," Flex replied, when asked why he didn't play basketball in high school.

Flex was at Glenville State College on a track-and-field scholarship, although I don't think he ever made it to track season. Flex was ruled academically ineligible after his first semester. Back in high school, Flex had been a West Virginia state champion in track and field. Boxing, however, seemed to suit his disposition much more than running circles on synthetic polyurethane surfaces. He was the type of guy who'd find a fight if one didn't come looking for him. Back in grade school, Flex had been a lanky introverted kid who was occasionally picked on by the older boys on the playground. In high school, however, Flex discovered weight lifting, body building, and his ability to outrun folks on synthetic polyurethane surfaces. If there had been a decent boxing gym in Martinsburg, West Virginia, he'd probably have become a Golden Glove State champion. But Flex took up boxing in the fourth-floor lounge of Pickens Hall, at 19 years old, a little late in the game, I suppose. Neither of us really knew what we were doing.

Near the end of the fall semester, I brought Flex to Cowen so that he could train in our makeshift boxing gym with my father and Curtis as they prepared for the upcoming Elkins Toughman Contest; winning it all in Lewisburg hadn't slowed them up much; a few weeks later the two of them were already back at it. They'd cooked up the dream of winning another Toughman Contest and turning professional.

"So, what do you think? Does Flex have potential?" I asked privately.

"He's strong . . . he hits like a mule . . . he's strong enough to take a good beating," my father joked.

That was it, my father's only diagnosis.

When I arrived back on campus for spring semester, I had it in my mind that I was going to turn Flex into a champion boxer. The Rumble on the Hill competition was only a few months away, so we signed him up.

"What in the hell is The Rumble on the Hill?" my father asked over the phone.

"It's like a generic Toughman Contest. This guy, Leon Ramsey, he runs The Dog House Gym here in town . . . he puts on an annual boxing event, part of the money goes to the football team, I think."

"Leon Ramsey. I've never heard of him."

Something about the idea didn't jive with my father and I could sense it.

"Dad, it's just like a Toughman but for college students."

"I'd be careful."

"Why? It's the same thing as a Toughman."

"I'd be careful about getting Flex hurt."

"Flex?"

"Yes."

After that phone conversation, Flex and I started training four days a week in the fourth-floor lounge in Pickens Hall. We trained more than we studied.

***

In February 2001, Curtis Wright hit a rough patch—my father's words. He and his wife, Angel, were having marital problems. Those marital problems limited the number of days Curtis was in training camp. I'm not blaming Curtis's loss in the 2001 Elkins Toughman Contest on his marital problems, or diagnosing his marital problems as the cause of his lack of conditioning in the final bout of the night, but the marital problems sure didn't help.

"Boxing will get you divorced quicker than shit," Charlie Handshaw, head trainer of the Handshaw Boxing Club in Ashland, Kentucky, once told my father.

"Quicker than shit," he repeated.

Angel wasn't a fan of the amount of time Curtis was spending down at my father's makeshift boxing gym. Curtis and my father worked long shifts during the day and sometimes trained long hours at night. My mother didn't like it all that much either, but she hadn't took to complaining about it yet.

Regardless, Curtis "The Ice Man" Wright lost a unanimous decision in the championship bout of the 2001 Elkins Toughman Contest. He'd gone 4–1 (with two knockouts) in the tournament, and still took home the $500 second-place paycheck, but his ego was, once again, bruised by the defeat. Oddly enough, Curtis's opponent in the championship bout was a guy named Mike Snider.

"That's the only guy you'd better worry about," my father joked before the tournament, upon looking at the bout sheet for the first time.

Curtis Wright's other Mike Snider was a college football player from Fleming, West Virginia, who was built like a linebacker but played running back. After the Elkins Toughman Contest, Mike Snider turned professional and is still doing that sort of thing part-time, I hear. There is no shame in losing to a guy named Mike Snider, spelled with an *i* or a *y*.

Back in February 2001, I'd hit a rough patch as well. I was homesick, ready to give up on the idea of college. Living in Pickens Hall was worse than living at Willoughby Trailer Park. I didn't like the dormitory toilets, the dormitory showers, or the disgusting cafeteria food. I didn't like my condescending professors, the excessive amounts of homework, or the anxiety all of it caused me. Most of all, I didn't like being away from "home." I repeatedly tried to talk my father into letting me quit school, but he wasn't having it.

"There isn't going to be no more coal miners in this family . . . I'm stopping the cycle with this one right here," my father would say while proudly telling folks that I was going to college.

"My boy is gonna get a degree . . . he ain't gonna have to put up with this coal mining shit," I'd hear him say on the phone.

My going to college made my father proud. But my going to college didn't make me proud of myself, not at first. I didn't understand what Glenville State College was going to do for my life. I wanted to be back at the gym, working with Curtis, helping my father.

"This will be the biggest regret of your life," my father told me.

I listened.

I returned to Glenville State College for a second semester.

But things didn't get much better, not a first. Back then I was an undeclared major, mostly taking general requirement courses, mostly boxing with Flex in the fourth-floor lounge of Pickens Hall, mostly getting drunk every night. The final month of my freshman year in college is something of a blur.

Back then I was pretty sure I knew a thing or two about boxing. I'd gym-hopped my way around the state of West Virginia, eavesdropped on more than a few of Curtis Wright's training sessions, and figured there wasn't much to being a chief second. My father was going to get Curtis back in line, they were going to win another Toughman Contest, they were going to turn professional, and I'd be there working Curtis's corner with my father. Schoolwork wasn't interesting to me. I was concerned with earning my BA in boxology. The 2001 Glenville State College Rumble on the Hill was to serve as my entrance exam.

***

"Ain't no way in hell we can let you boys fight," Leon said to Bill, looking mostly toward Flex.

The expression on Flex's face was that of a small child, his body-builder posture instantly deflated.

"Twenty pounds is too much of a difference, I won't allow it," Leon repeated for the third time.

Bill, from my recollections, seemed happy enough to let the whole thing go. He shook Flex's hand for whatever reason, and exited the locker room.

A few weeks before the Rumble on the Hill, Flex coaxed Bill Summers[31] into fighting him at the event. They sealed the deal with a weight-room handshake. Bill was a sophomore from Glenville, West Virginia, who lived on the fifth floor of Pickens Hall, and he and his brother Tyson were regulars at Leon Ramsey's gym. Bill Summers was the only guy in Pickens Hall brave or dumb enough to agree to get in a boxing ring with Flex.

Unfortunately, Flex's slim-waisted, body-builder frame was deceptive. You'd never have believed Bill Summers weighed a full 20 pounds more than Flex, who also carried broad shoulders and large biceps.

"Son, if you don't find somebody in your weight class, you ain't fighting tonight," Leon said, closing the door on the possibility of a Jeffrey "Flex" Lemasters vs. Bill Summers Pickens Hall mega-bout.

In nothing but his white Fruit of the Loom underwear, Flex stood in complete silence, brooding in front of the doctor's scales for what seemed like a good minute or two. Leon's stern tone let us know that he was serious.

"We're gonna wrap up the weigh-ins in 30 minutes," Leon added, glancing at his wristwatch, offering Flex one last ray of hope.

Outside the locker room, the crowd, a mixture of college students and Glenville townies, was beginning to fill the small gymnasium. It was one hour until the first bell.

"You've got 30 minutes, son," Leon instructed, as he finally arose from the folding chair and made his way to the nearest locker room urinal.

Flex took to the crowd like a door-to-door salesman. Guys with their arms around their sweethearts, guys waiting in line at the concession stand, anybody in the gymnasium who looked to be over 200 pounds received a pugilistic invitation to meet Flex in the middle of the boxing ring.

"Hey, you want to box me tonight?"

"My fight got canceled. You want to box me?"

When I'd watch Flex get rejected by the random college girls in the cafeteria, I'd laugh. This was embarrassing. I didn't have the nerve to accompany him as he picked his way through the bleachers, begging strangers to box him in an event they'd just bought a ticket to watch.

My father made the two-hour drive from Cowen to Glenville that night so that he could watch Flex's ring debut. He'd brought a pair of boxing shoes for Flex to wear as well; Flex didn't own anything remotely close to boxing shoes. When my father and I met at the entrance of the gymnasium, he could tell something was wrong.

"Where's Flex?"

"I don't think he's going to get to fight. Flex came in at 190 pounds. Bill weighed 225."

"Is there nobody else for him to fight?"

"All of the other bouts are matched up."

The Rumble on the Hill, like most spring formals, was a bring-your-own-dance-partner kind of affair. After the botched weigh-in, I was certain all of our fourth-floor training had been for nothing.

My father and I sat on the front row of the bleachers for a good 15 or 20 minutes before Flex emerged from the locker room with an ear-to-ear grin on his face.

"I found an ol' boy who's gonna fight me," Flex announced, pumping his fist in victory before extending a handshake to my father.

"You did?" my father and I replied in unison.

Flex didn't know what he was getting himself into.

"Buddy, I'll fight you. I box in the Marine Corps," Mr. Sweatpants answered when propositioned.

Flex's opponent was a tall and lanky redhead with a fair complexion and bright-green Nike sweatpants. Mr. Sweatpants looked like an easy draw, but looks can be deceiving. Legend has it that Mr. Sweatpants was a Wheeling boy, in town to visit his girlfriend, a sophomore history major at Glenville State College. He'd bought a ticket to the event just like everybody else, but ended up fighting Jeffrey "Flex" Lemasters in the second-to-last bout of the night.

I never had the pleasure of talking with Mr. Sweatpants, but I can certainly imagine the type of guy he was. Being propositioned in front of his co-ed girlfriend was probably too much for his hypermasculine ego to bear. He accepted the challenge, removed his oversized football jersey, stripped down to his tank-top undershirt and bright-green sweatpants, and weighed in on Leon Rasmey's rickety doctor's scales at just under 200 pounds.

I have no idea why Leon bent the rules for Flex; combatants were supposed to be registered students at Glenville State College. Maybe Leon had grown weary of Flex's persistent nagging. Maybe Leon was secretly hoping Flex would get his ass kicked by Mr. Sweatpants.

***

Flex's ring walk is something I'll never forget but would like to. It was the slowest ring walk I have ever seen or been a part of. Flex strutted from the locker room to the ring at a snail's pace, bouncing his shirtless pectoral muscles up and down to the beat of the entrance music. The crowd started booing halfway through the ring walk. Flex stopped to scan the crowd as they booed him. The boos intensified. Flex smirked, began bouncing his shirtless pectoral muscles more rapidly, and started walking again.

Flex's entrance was something straight out of the pages of WWE professional wrestling. The performance couldn't have been rehearsed. If so, my dorm buddies and me had no idea it was coming. Flex was Ric Flair, hamming it up to the dissatisfaction of a hostile crowd. He was taking his time, reveling in the moment.

During the ring introductions, Flex stood firm at the center of the ring and pointed his right glove at Mr. Sweatpants as if he were a bank robber with a pistol. He'd borrowed the intimidation technique from Aaron "The Hawk" Pryor, Carlos "Panama" Lewis's most famous pupil. I'd occasionally bring selections from my father's VHS fight collection back to college and watch them with my dorm buddies. Aaron Pryor's first bout with Alexis Arguello was one of Flex's favorite selections. Back then we did more fight watching than studying.

And like Aaron "The Hawk" Pryor peering across the ring at Alexis Arguello, Flex didn't move a muscle or even flinch. Flex just stood there pointing at his redheaded, sweatpants-wearing opponent. More boos. Showmanship is a character trait often looked down upon in working-class Appalachia. That night in Gilmer County, Flex was the bad guy. And I was Pickens Hall's Carlos "Panama" Lewis.

Ding!

Flex shot out of the red corner like a cannonball, got socked with a solid left jab, and instantly began bleeding from both nostrils.

Pap. Pap. Pap.

Flex took a three-four combination to his temple, forgot everything I taught him, and took another three-four combination.

Flex's legs looked like spaghetti strings.

Whack!

Mr. Sweatpants had been in a boxing ring before, his elbows were in tight, his chin was tucked, his punches straight and precise.

Whack!

Whack!

Whack!

Flex's knees buckled.

Whack!

Flex took a stiff uppercut.

Whack!

Flex staggered to the ropes and the crowd came alive.

Whack!

Flex was buzzed, swinging and hitting nothing but air, eating a consistent diet of double-jabs.

Ding!

Mr. Sweatpants had hit Flex with everything but the kitchen sink, to borrow a phrase from my father's generation. When Flex came back to the corner after the first round, he was drunker than I had ever seen him before. Me and my dorm buddies were seated in the bleachers that night so I'm not sure what Leon Ramsey's chief second stand-ins said to Flex between rounds one and two, but I'm sure he didn't follow their advice. The bell rang and Flex charged out of the corner just as recklessly as before.

Smack!

Flex walked into a lead right hand.

Smack!

Flex walked into a left-right combination.

Smack!

Flex took a one-two-three to the headgear.

Smack!

Sensing he had Flex on Queer Street, Mr. Sweatpants aggressively pursued the finish. Perhaps too aggressively. When the two fighters became tangled in a clinch, Flex's superior strength finally paid off. Digging my father's boxing shoes into the bloodstained canvas, and bulldogging Mr. Sweatpants into the Blue corner, Flex sandwiched Mr. Sweatpants into the padded ring post. Flex then wrapped his left arm around Mr. Sweatpant's neck, in a headlock motion, and desperately punched with his free hand.

Whap!

Flex punched his sweatpants-wearing opponent with a hard uppercut. Mr. Sweatpants went down like a ton of bricks. It was a beltline shot, but the ref ruled it a knockdown. I couldn't believe it. Mr. Sweatpants couldn't believe it. The crowd couldn't believe it. More boos.

You don't need to be a Gilmer County local, or even a student at Glenville State College, to guess that Leon Ramsey's Rumble on the Hill event didn't feature the cream of the crop in the refereeing world. Flex and Mr. Sweatpants were duking it out in the underworld of Appalachian boxing. The Marquis of Queensberry rules didn't apply in Glenville, West Virginia.

When Flex came back to the corner after round two, the cobwebs were starting to clear. He had mulled Mr. Sweatpants around the ring, landing a few haymakers, and scored an illegal but legal knockdown. Mr. Sweatpants looked visibly winded. He obviously hadn't trained for the fight. Mr. Sweatpants had perhaps spent all of his money in the first round. Flex's Frankenstein power punches were beginning to take their toll.

Ding!

Flex charged out of the corner once more, this time launching a sweeping left hook in the process. Flex missed.

Whack!

Mr. Sweatpants countered with a right uppercut and gravity pulled a rug out from underneath Flex.

Thud!

"One—two—three—four . . ." the ref counted.

Those of you who have witnessed a boxing match probably know that when a fighter is knocked down, he is given a mandatory eight count by the referee; his opponent is instructed to wait in a neutral corner before the fight begins again. The fight doesn't continue until the count has been given and the referee signals *box*. Well, that isn't how things worked out in the co-main event of the 2001 Rumble on the Hill.

When Flex hit the canvas, self-preservation kicked in. He immediately came off the canvas and sucker-punched Mr. Sweatpants as he was walking back to the neutral corner. Mr. Sweatpants went down with a thud.

I automatically assumed Flex was going to be disqualified for his off-the-canvas sucker punch. He wasn't.

The ref turned around and started counting for Mr. Sweatpants. The drunken crowd was in hysterics. Apparently they had seen a fight or two.

Mr. Sweatpants got up at the count of seven.

"Box!" the ref shouted.

Flex and Mr. Sweatpants collided in the center of the ring. Flex bear-hugged Mr. Sweatpants, lifting him a good five inches off the canvas, and both fighters went tumbling to the canvas. This was a rumble on the hill indeed.

The angry crowd once again made its displeasure known as boos echoed the gymnasium walls, beverages of all varieties soaked the gymnasium floor, and boxes of popcorn were tossed toward the ring.

Battered and weary, the two combatants got up and continued the fight. The ref didn't have any say in it; this wasn't his fight.

The final minute of the bout was a collective of headlocks, rabbit punches, kidney punches, brought to a crescendo by Flex's infamous kick to Mr. Sweatpants's shin. It wasn't pretty.

And, finally, the ding of a ringside bell brought it all to an end.

To this day, it was the dirtiest, least professionally officiated boxing match I've ever had the pleasure of witnessing. And my boxing pupil, Jeffrey "Flex" Lemasters, the pride of Pickens Hall, was the dirtiest son-of-a-bitch in the ring that night.

After a few minutes, the ringside judges handed down their verdict.

20–18. . . . Jeffrey "Flex" Lemasters

20–18. . . . Mr. Sweatpants

20–18. . . . Jeffrey "Flex" Lemasters

It was a split-decision victory for the Appalachian Terminator. It was an unpopular decision to say the least.

More boos.

More beverage tossing.

More popcorn spattering.

After the fight, Mr. Sweatpants returned to his girlfriend and his duties in the Marines Corps, if that line was even true, battered and bruised. Flex returned to the fourth floor of Pickens Hall, a humbled pugilist.

"I let you down, Snyder, I fought like shit," Flex said later that night, his speech slightly slurred, maybe from the beer, maybe from the fight. Mr. Sweatpants had rung Flex's bell pretty good. This was a different Jeffrey "Flex" Lemasters.

I was changed by the fight as well. Never was it more apparent that my decision to ship off to college would require a new identity, a new understanding of my own Appalachian manhood. College boys from around my way face quite the existential dilemma. We are born into communities and family work histories that demonstrate a very rigid pathway to becoming men. If we earn college degrees, we become the *Other*. There won't be work for guys like us after graduation. We'll become college boys. We'll never be able to come back home.

My short-lived career as a boxing trainer helped me understand this dilemma. I could never be my father and a college boy at the same time.

With one foot in the makeshift boxing gym and the other in academia, I had to finally choose. College was going to exile me from my hometown, alienate me from the working-class men in my family. This was a reality that was both terrifying and exciting.

A few weeks after the 2001 Rumble on the Hill, I packed my things and never returned to Glenville State College. Flex would do the same. I transferred to Marshall University in Huntington, West Virginia, the school I'd originally wanted to attend but didn't out of fear of *being too far away from home*. Flex quit school altogether.

Years later, after my wife, Stephanie, and I moved to New York, I reconnected with Flex on Facebook. We hadn't spoken to each other in almost seven years. He was different and so was I. Flex had a wife and I had a wife, and I had a baby on the way. He was working as a welder in a deep mine back in his hometown of Martinsburg, West Virginia. I was *professoring* in New York, worlds away from the person I used to be. Flex joked that he was still an undefeated boxer and that he was thinking about making a comeback. The joke was funny because we both knew the truth.

Flex was strong, he punched like a mule, but he was just strong enough to take a good beating.

Chapter 5

STREET
PREACHER

About two months before Stephanie Nicole's high school graduation, Stephanie's father walked out to his garage, lit up a cigarette, and suffered a massive heart attack. Stephanie was 120 miles away at the West Virginia State High School Drama Competition, which, ironically, was being hosted at the Joan C. Edwards Playhouse on Marshall University's campus, a facility located directly in front of the apartment complex in which we'd live together some years later. Right then and there, on 5th Avenue in Huntington, West Virginia, Stephanie Nicole stopped being a girl and was forced to become a woman. She was 18 years old.

A few weeks later, after all the food, flowers, and visitors stopped rolling in, Stephanie heard a knock at the door. It was about 7 p.m. in the evening; they weren't expecting visitors. Stephanie's mother peered out the blinds before answering the door. It was Mr. Arnold and Pastor Donne.[32]

"Becky, we are so sorry to hear about your loss."

"Thank you, Eugene."

"How are you?"

"I'm okay. Thank you."

Everyone shook hands.

"This is Pastor Donne, he's our new guy."

"Oh, nice to meet you, Pastor Donne."

"May we come in?"

"Oh, yes, of course. Please, come on in."

Stephanie was using her laptop computer, sitting on the couch, when her mother escorted Mr. Arnold and Pastor Donne into the living room.

"Stephanie, how are you holding up?"

Mr. Arnold had been Stephanie's computer science teacher the previous school year.

"I'm doing fine, Mr. Arnold. Thanks."

Becky made her way into the kitchen to fetch coffee.

"So, are you excited for graduation?" Mr. Arnold asked.

"Yeah, excited and nervous."

"Stephanie was one of my brightest students," Mr. Arnold said to Pastor Donne.

"Are you attending college, Stephanie?" Pastor Donne asked.

Becky made it back with the coffee. "Stephanie is attending Marshall University," Becky answered.

Stephanie had always been an academic overachiever, but the issue of her going ahead with the plans to ship off to Marshall University hadn't been completely settled since her father's passing. At first, she couldn't stand the thought of leaving her mother all alone.

"Marshall University! Ain't that something. Praise Jesus," Pastor Donne said, just before taking his first sip.

"Becky, Stephanie . . . Pastor Donne and I would like to extend an invitation to you. We'd love to see you down at the First Baptist Church of Cowen," Mr. Arnold announced.

Mr. Arnold was also a deacon down at the church.

"Ours is an awesome God. Jehovah Jireh," Pastor Donne chimed in.

There was a pause and everyone took a sip of coffee.

"We'd love to. It's just been crazy as of late," Becky finally answered, feeling a little embarrassed by the invitation.

Stephanie's family had never been a church-on-Sunday kind of family.

"There's no time like the present."

"Yes, I know . . ."

"There's no time like the present to experience God's grace and all of the good things he has to offer."

"Yes, I know . . ."

"With Stephanie going off to Marshall . . . it'd be good for you to have a strong church family," Pastor Donne added.

Stephanie and her mother were seated in the back pew the following Sunday.

***

All churches are different; they all have different dress codes, holy books, and price ranges. But most of the small-town Appalachian churches I attended as a child were essentially the same. You've got the gossip ladies, with their dyed hair and their oversized pocketbooks and their grandkids. You've got the recovering alcoholics who are just as fanatical about Jesus as they were about the bottle. You'll find a few army men who've shot and killed foreigners and vote Republican and tuck in their dress shirts and eat at The Hilltop Diner. You'll find a few zealots too, the fire-and-brimstone crowd. But you'll mostly find good, hard-working, Appalachian folks. You'll find retired schoolteachers who give back to the less fortunate, organizing grassroots solutions to poverty and inequality. They raise their young'ns to do their chores and to have good manners and to respect their elders and to say, "yes sir, no sir."

You'd find those kinds of folks in the bars and on street corners as well. That's how my father saw it. Or maybe that's just how I saw it as a child. God is real; church is a club. I couldn't tell you whether or not my father planted that seed of an idea in my mind or if I came up with it all on my own. The church house, as I came to understand it as a young person, was just a building, a few rows of pews, a few stained-glass windows, a couple of collection plates, and some fancy pictures of white Jesus. Cowen didn't have Joel Osteen–style mega-churches, but churches were fancy. Church folks were fancy. I was a trailer park kid.

Back in high school, I went to church on and off, but it was never because my parents took me. I was always chasing some church girl, some beautiful young girl whose father watched her like a hawk. My religion began and ended with those beautiful young church girls. I chased those girls religiously.

But then again, we'd pay it lip service. My father could give you the Cliff Notes version of the Bible; he knew the basic plotline. He'd been baptized. He'd been saved. His spirituality, however, had more to do with a moral obligation to help the poor than it did with anything that ever happened in Egypt. My mother, on the other hand, grew up in a staunchly conservative household—church every Sunday morning, Sunday evening, and Wednesday night. Her affiliation with my father killed her Christian ethos. We all *believed*, but none of us talked about it much. I didn't know Peter from Paul, Bathsheba from Beth.

But in the spring of 2004, the church "came calling." They got us under the tent and we'd stay there for just over five years.

We were eating supper when the silver minivan pulled into our driveway.

"Go see who that is. If it's for me, tell them I'm not here," my father said with a mouthful of food.

I opened the door and saw Mr. Arnold walking down our cinderblock steps toward the front porch; he had a well-dressed old man with him.

Mr. Arnold had been my computer science teacher back in high school; he'd been my basketball coach back in the sixth grade as well.

"Hello, Todd. Is your dad home?"

"Uh."

"We'd like to chat with him a bit."

Mr. Arnold was smiling ear-to-ear.

"Just a second."

My father was going to kick my ass for not running them off. In the kitchen, my father cussed me underneath his breath before putting on his shirt and walking to the front door; I'd left Mr. Arnold and well-dressed old man out on the porch.

"Mike, I'd like for you to meet Pastor Stanley Donne."

"Stanley. Nice to meet you."

They shook hands.

"Mike, we'd like to make a little proposition to you."

I was listening in the other room.

"Okay. Come on in. Have a seat on the couch."

They all sat down. My mother fetched coffee. Everyone crossed their legs and drank their coffee and finally Mr. Arnold got to it.

"Mike, you and Curtis Wright still boxing?"

"No. Not lately."

"Mike trained this fellow named Curtis Wright. They won back-to-back Lewisburg Toughman Contests," Mr. Arnold informed Pastor Donne.

Two years had passed since Curtis Wright's second straight Lewisburg Toughman Championship. After Curtis's loss in the championship bout of the Elkins Toughman in 2001, he and my father were more determined than ever to show everybody in Webster County they could do it again. During their third training camp together, everything fell into place. The distractions were minimal and the workout sessions were intense. My father and Curtis even took a few sparring field trips to Tommy Franco Thomas's gym in Clarksburg. Curtis eventually found himself in the ring with Tommy, trading punches with a man who'd went to war with Leon Spinks.

Long story short, Curtis "The Ice Man" Wright dominated the 2001 Lewisburg Toughman Contest, going 5–0 (with three knockouts), beating Bruce Frank, once again, by a lopsided unanimous decision in the final bout. This time around, Jerry Thomas invited my father to serve as one of his stand-in corner men. My father paid his dues, working a few of Jerry's shows leading up to the Lewisburg event. His days of screaming from the cheap seats were over. Winning the whole damn thing for a second straight year did little to slow them down; a few weeks later Curtis and my father were right back at it. They'd cooked up the dream of turning professional and getting a shot at the big dance, as my father called it. During his 12 months of training with my father in the back of Classic Curl Beauty Shop, Curtis compiled a record of 14–1 (with seven knockouts), capturing back-to-back Lewisburg Toughman Championships, with a runner-up finish at Elkins sandwiched between those victories. Jimmy Utt's third Curtis Wright cover story, featuring a color photograph of my father and Curtis standing in the makeshift boxing ring holding up two Toughman jackets, had the entire county believing Curtis was on his way to becoming a professional boxer. Boxing, like the coal industry, can be defined as a "hope business."

No such luck.

Harold Johnson, my mother's landlord, sold the brick building that housed Classic Curl Beauty Shop to Chip Dawson.[33] He'd offered to sell the building to my folks, but they were in no position to buy. Rumor had it that the Smooth Coal Company was shutting down in the spring and my father didn't have the guts to dip into his savings account. Chip bought the building, opened a barbershop, and my mother was out of a job and my father was out of a makeshift boxing gym. Curtis Wright went back to being the toughest guy at Columbia, my father went back to being the best boxing trainer down at the Smooth Coal Company, and the makeshift boxing ring lay piecemeal, under a thick blue tarp, on our back porch.

"I've seen the pictures in the paper. That's really something. Sounds like Curtis is a real good boxer," Pastor Donne said.

My father started rattling off all of Curtis Wright's accomplishments.

"Mike was a real good boxer too. I watched him knock some old boy for a loop back when he used to box," Mr. Arnold chimed in.

"Yeah, I was 5–0, all five wins by the first round knockout," my father bragged.

"If they don't get to the point, he'll go on like this all evening," I thought.

"Eugene and I think you have something special. We think you have a talent," Pastor Donne said.

"A talent?"

"Yes, a God-given talent."

"How so?"

"Mike, just look what you did with that Wright boy," Pastor Donne said.

"God wants you to use your gift," Mr. Arnold added.

"Just imagine if you were given the opportunity to use that gift to bring young men and young women to Jesus Christ."

Mr. Arnold was a better slick talker than he was a computer science teacher or a basketball coach.

"How so?"

"The First Baptist Church of Cowen has just purchased Doc Hinkle's old place on Main Street. We want to turn it into a youth center. We want to use the youth center as a catch net, we want to catch some of these kids who are falling through the cracks," Pastor Donne announced.

"I think that sounds great, fellas. Lord knows, these kids around here don't have any positive outlets."

My father started talking their language.

"Here's the deal. We want you to become a youth minister," Mr. Arnold said.

"Fellas, I'm just an old sinner. I don't think you want me trying to teach Bible school."

"No. No. No. That's not it. We want you to use the gift God has given you. We want you to be a leader of young men."

"Boys, I don't know . . ."

"Mike was the guy who started the Cowen Little League . . . he coached the Junior High Football team as well . . . he's a leader . . . look what he did with that Wright boy . . . Mike is a leader of men," Mr. Arnold said to Pastor Donne.

Pastor Donne extended his hand across the coffee table.

"Mike, we want you to be a leader of men for Jesus."

They shook hands again, for whatever reason.

"Boys, I'm no teacher."

"No, you're not. You're a coach. You're a leader of men. We want you to give that talent over to Jesus Christ."

"Come again?"

"Mike, we are going to call the community center The Edge. It's going to be a place for kids who are on the edge, about to fall through the cracks."

"Yeah, like I said, that sounds nice."

"All we need is a draw. We want to give you the upstairs portion of the building. We want to give it to you to open a boxing gym."

Leaning back in his recliner, shying away from it all, my father looked visibly skeptical. He was.

"It's four times the size of that little room in the back of Cheryl's beauty shop. Do whatever you want with it."

"Set up your boxing gym."

"Be a leader of men. Win these kids over to Jesus," Pastor Donne said.

"Help us save these kids," Mr. Arnold added.

***

My father didn't know where to start so he phoned Jerry Thomas.

"Mike, you'll need to become a certified USA Amateur Boxing trainer. And you'll need to file paperwork for the club as well. Your insurance is covered under USA Boxing," Jerry said.

"Um. Okay."

"Oh, and the kids, if they are actually going to spar or compete, they'll need to pay their registration fees, they'll need an amateur boxing license . . . like the one Todd had when he boxed at Simon's Gym. I'd recommend charging a small gym fee to cover the cost."

My father followed all of Jerry's advice closely, aside from the gym fee.

"I'll get you in contact with Gary Toney. He's the former national president of USA Boxing. Gary was an Olympian. He works closely with Tommy and Larry Davenport out of Charleston. These are the guys you'll need to know to get started."

"Um. Okay, Jerry."

"Oh, and do you know Bill Hopkins?[34] He is the man you need to speak to about getting certified as a trainer."

"Um. Okay, Jerry."

"And, I'd recruit a few trainers to work alongside of you, Mike. You'll need a few helping hands. Running a boxing gym isn't a one-man job," Jerry instructed.

Curtis "The Ice Man" Wright and Todd "Touch Down" Snyder would have been my father's first and most obvious choices for assistant trainers, if not for the fact that Curtis and I were preoccupied with more important matters at the time. Curtis had left Columbia for a higher paying job in the coal mines. His wife, Angel, had also drawn a metaphorical line in the sand when it came to boxing. I, on the other hand, was about to enter the student teaching portion of my senior year as an English education major at Marshall University. Curtis and I had moved on, it appeared.

The first invitation went to Jeff Dean. Jeff had been my father's sidekick throughout all of Curtis Wright's training camps, fetching water from my mother's mini refrigerator and videotaping sparring sessions. When I was 12 years old, my father received a warehouse job at the Smooth Coal Company (a sizable promotion) and moved my family out of Willoughby Trailer Park and into a two-story fixer-upper on Mason Street, just outside of town. I had plenty of friends back at the trailer park, but Mason Street was bereft of kids. So, it goes without saying, that first summer was pretty lonely. Jeff Dean was my first Mason Street friend.

Jeff lived just down the street from us in a small two-bedroom house with his aging grandmother, and, for reasons I didn't understand when I was 12 years old, didn't have to go to school or to work. Jeff was large in stature, probably six feet one inch and 240 pounds, but was as gentle as a mouse. Years later, I'd read Steinbeck's Lennie and think of him. Even though Jeff was a good 15 years older than me, the two of us were inseparable that summer and many summers to come. As the years went by, Jeff Dean was always there when my father needed him—he'd help mow the yard, carry heavy objects, whatever was necessary. My father was always good to Jeff; he'd take Jeff shopping, buy him things, treat him like part of the family. We'd always have Jeff over to the house on Christmas Eve and for birthday parties. Jeff Dean was part of our Mason Street family, which my father sometimes jokingly referred to as "the Mason Street gangsters."

"You want to get certified to become a boxing trainer, Jeff?"

"I'll pay for your certification and you can help me with this new gym?" my father asked later that evening.

"Hell yeah, old buddy," Jeff enthusiastically replied.

"I'm gonna call you Jeff 'Bundini' Dean," my father declared.

"You are gonna be our voodoo man, our good-luck charm," he added, Jeff chuckling, not quite getting the Drew Bundini Brown[35] reference.

Jason Bragg, our neighbor from directly across the street, was my father's second and perhaps most convenient choice for a helping hand. Looking back, it was probably Jason Bragg who tipped Curtis off about our hidden boxing ring (the two men had been good friends back in high school). The week before Curtis Wright's unannounced visit to Classic Curl, my father had invited Jason down to the makeshift gym to spar his son. Jason was seven years older than me but was exactly 135 pounds, within the parameters of my weight class. After the sparring session, I imagine Jason Bragg running home to phone Curtis, spoiling our secret.

To the Mason Street outsider, I imagine both Jeff Dean and Jason Bragg were odd selections. My father could have easily found a more intimidating posse. Jeff was a gentle giant with a rosy face, spent most of his days piddling around the Cowen Volunteer Fire Department, a habitual giggler who wouldn't hurt a fly. Jason Bragg, on the other hand, had always been the smallest kid in his class, weighing in at a mere 103 pounds his senior year of high school. Jason wore a constant Cheshire grin. He was a good-looking but undersized country boy, handsome but hardly intimidating. Back in the day, Coach Woods had made it abundantly clear what folks around Cowen thought of guys like Jason Bragg.

"Jason, you're just too damn little."

"I don't have room for a guy your size on this basketball team."

Jeff and Jason were drifters of sorts, scattered leaves blown around town and finally settled onto Mason Street. Jeff didn't know all that much about his biological father, rarely lived with his biological mother, and, as an adult, wound up living with and taking care of his aging grandmother. After high school, Jason worked a few construction jobs, spent a year working at a ski resort in Snowshoe, West Virginia, before winding up at the Smooth Coal Company. When Jason moved in with Tiffany Williams and her two girls, our neighbors from the other side of Mason Street, he and my father became both neighbors and coworkers.

As was the case with Jeff Dean, I instantly took a liking to Jason Bragg. Jason loved to talk sports, loved to laugh and carry on. He'd sometimes hang around our house and come over to watch boxing on Saturday nights. During Curtis Wright's time at Classic Curl Beauty Shop, Jason often served as a sparring partner for his high school buddy, despite being much smaller and never having boxed before. Jason took a few beatings on those sparring session VHS tapes.

"Dad, you're going to get Jason killed. Curtis is twice his size," I argued.

"Jason can take it," my father flatly replied.

At the time, I didn't know what my father was up to.

Jason Bragg's love of boxing came from his father, a railroad man who spent much of Jason's childhood away on work, often living in motels for weeks at a time. Jason's father wasn't much of a sports fan, but he'd spent some time in Youngstown, Ohio, working on the railroad, developing a strong admiration for the pride of Youngstown, Ray "Boom Boom" Mancini. Maybe that's who Jason Bragg always wanted to be. Perhaps those were the sports figures Jason admired most—little tough guys like Ray "Boom Boom" Mancini.

"What do you think about becoming a certified amateur boxing trainer, helping me out with this new boxing gym?" my father asked one morning down at the Smooth Coal Company.

Jason Bragg had no real firsthand boxing experience, but he'd long been in love with the sport of boxing, never missed one of Curtis "The Ice Man" Wright's Toughman events. It didn't take much convincing to get him on board.

"Hell yeah, I'd love to help you out at the gym, Lo," Jason replied.

A few months later, the four of us found ourselves across the table from Bullet Bill Hopkins, of Bullet Bill's Boxing Club in Fairmont, West

Virginia. I'd been spending most of my time studying and taking tests, and my father, Jeff Dean, and Jason Bragg were a little out of practice.

Bullet Bill Hopkins was a textbook curmudgeon. He had snow-white hair, always wore a look of disapproval, and had long droopy cheeks that flapped when he voiced his disapproval. He looked like an aging bulldog. He'd spent some time with Uncle Sam and you could tell it. He didn't talk, he barked.

"Alright, here's the skinny, fellas," Bill said as he tossed the test booklets down on the table.

"I don't know you fellas. Hell, you might know more boxing than me. You might. You might not. How the hell should I know?"

Bill was wrong, of course. My father was the only one of us at the table who'd ever won a boxing match. We each grabbed a booklet.

"This test is bullshit. That's right. Bullshit. A test can't teach you boxing."

He sat down at the table and pulled out the answer key.

"I'm going to give you boys the answers. We need good trainers in this state. The amateur system is shit. Less than shit. We need more boxing gyms . . . okay, you fellas ready?"

We weren't.

"Number 1 . . . C."

"Number 2 . . . B."

It took us a second to realize he was giving us the answers.

"Number 3 . . . C."

"Number 4 . . . that's C."

"Number 5 . . . A."

Jason Bragg looked like a first-time SAT test-taker—he was nervous as hell.

"What was number 2?" he leaned over and asked my father.

I tried to fend off the laughter. Jeff couldn't hold it back.

"Shit, Jason, he's giving us the answers and you still can't pass."

"Problem, boys?"

"No sir."

"Okay. Number 6 . . . that's B."

The four of us walked out of the room certified USA Amateur Boxing trainers, Lo's Gym Boxing Club an official USA Amateur Boxing Club. We hadn't even opened the test booklets.

***

It was a large two-story brick building, located directly beside the church down on Main Street in Cowen, just a half a mile up the road from the building that once housed Classic Curl Beauty Shop. The two-rung parlor-style sign that hung from the metal pole out front read "The Edge" on tier one and "Lo's Gym" on tier two. The first floor was complete with a kitchen, bathroom, and worship service area. The first floor played host to yard sales, church meetings, church dinners, and the like. Fighters entered through the back door. The stairway was narrow, a steep climb up the wooden steps. It was beautiful and ragtag all at the same time. My father's makeshift boxing ring found its new home in the far-left corner of the upstairs room, heavy bags and uppercut bags hanging from each homemade ring post. Three large mirrors lined the wall closest to the ring, four sets of speed bags, four heavy bags, and a few double-end bags dangled from the ceiling. Hand wraps and jump ropes lined the back walls, setup benches and slip bags decorated the perimeter. A few rows of metal folding chairs lined the corner closest to the stairway. The floors were wooden and creaky. No air conditioning.

Black-and-white boxing posters and photographs were the motif—photos of Jack Johnson, Jack Dempsey, Willie Pep, Rocky Marciano, and Sugar Ray Robinson. Posters and photographs were scattered throughout, accenting important areas of the gym: images of Muhammad Ali, Joe Frazier, George Foreman, Roberto Duran, and other fighters from my father's day. My contribution to the décor was fold-out posters from *Ring Magazine*, the fighters I admired most: Pernell Whitaker, Mike Tyson, Roy Jones Jr., and Floyd Mayweather. Boxing history covered the plywood walls and the kids would stand and admire like art aficionados. They'd ask questions and we'd tell stories.

When Lo's Gym Boxing Club officially opened its doors to the public in March 2004, my father gave himself to Mr. Arnold and Pastor Donne's vision for The Edge. Because Lo's Gym was housed in a church-owned building, my father felt obligated to make the gym a positive influence in the community. He did not, however, feel obligated to attend church on Sundays. I was happy to take up the slack in the church department. Stephanie Nicole attended Sunday service with her mother, mostly during summers and winter breaks. After my father moved his makeshift boxing ring into the vacant upstairs room in The Edge, I began tagging along with Stephanie and her mother.

By the time I showed up on the scene, all of the church boys had already taken their best shot at Stephanie. I can't say that I blame them. I've never seen a woman as classically beautiful as my wife. Stephanie's bright-green eyes, her sandy red hair, the beautiful curves of her lips— they belong on the silver screen or in a poem. Every line, every curve of her body, is far more alluring than she'd ever give herself credit for. Stephanie is the kind of woman who makes men nervous, but doesn't have a clue that she is doing it; hers is an innocent seduction. I'd known Stephanie all of my life, but didn't fall in love with her until Huntington, West Virginia. Stephanie and I were first-generation college students at Marshall University, a long way from home, we thought. Perhaps we were country bumpkins who simply gravitated to *the familiar*. Maybe each of us was more homesick than we would have liked to admit. Maybe we were running from the past, couldn't imagine a future in Cowen, West Virginia, but were attracted to "home." Six months into our Marshall University romance I began saving up for an engagement ring. I'd found the beautiful church girl who was going to save me from myself. It had been a long road to finding Stephanie Nicole.

Beautiful women were a necessary component of manly identity. As an adolescent, I didn't possess the imagination to dream up a scenario where men didn't want or need beautiful women to validate their worth. I'd never met an openly gay man in my life. Thus, to be a man, for the younger version of myself, was to dunk basketballs, catch touchdowns, score knockouts, and have sex with beautiful women, all before finding your place in the coal mines, all before choosing that one beautiful woman you wanted to have sex with for the rest of your life. You weren't a man until some beautiful woman proved you were. My closed-minded notions of Appalachian manhood fell squarely into the ideological category my colleagues in queer studies refer to as heteronormativity, a world view that promotes heterosexuality as the preferred norm. In my community, anything queer would have been in direct opposition to the ideological framework established by the coal industry. Our isolated extractive industry town was built off of heteronormativity, an economic setup that required folks to settle down early in life and start having *young'ns*. Fooling around with beautiful girls was just part of becoming a man, I figured.

I started fooling around with girls when I was 13 years old, lost my virginity at 14. The poor girl wasn't my girlfriend or even a friend. She was a wild child from the other side of the county with a roughneck boyfriend who was a few years older than both of us. I was a rookie, but she'd been at it for a while. There was no dating or courtship process between wild child and me. Rather, she simply passed a folded note underneath the desk during study hall. The note read:

"Do you want to fuck me?"

A week later we found ourselves on her mother's couch. After about ten minutes of bad sex, I was a man.

"You are lucky Mike Snyder is your father . . . or I'd kick your fucking ass, you little prick," the roughneck cuckold whispered into my ear after he'd cornered me in the gymnasium a few weeks later.

The beating that never happened didn't do much to slow me down. Aside from boxing, beautiful girls were all I thought about during my high school days. This isn't to suggest I was a *ladies' man*. I was more Romeo than Don Juan, always convincing myself that I was damaged beyond repair when some high school girl broke my teenage heart. I was too short. Too skinny. Not handsome enough. Not ambitious enough. Not popular enough. Not smart enough. Not *man* enough. What the *wild childs* had to offer was fickle and the beautiful church girls were saving themselves for the godly men they were preordained to be with. I was practice. Until Stephanie Nicole came along, this side of my masculine ethos was just as bruised and shaky as the boxing side of the equation.

For whatever reason, Stephanie saw something in me that I simply didn't see. She'd convinced herself that I was different and it was in those differences that I would find whatever greatness I possessed. She had convinced herself that I was worth whatever it would take to bring it out of me. Maybe that's how love works—to love someone is to see and understand the person they want to be.

"If you asked me, I'd marry you right now," Stephanie said one humid September evening, sitting along the famous memorial fountain at Marshall University.

"I wouldn't even hesitate," she added, batting those beautiful doe eyes.

I'd already bought the engagement ring.

It was easy with Stephanie. She wanted to peel back the layers of my insecurity. She wanted to understand my imagination, wanted to tag along for the daydream.

"If you want to be a writer, be a writer," she'd say.

"I believe in every single one of your crazy little dreams, Todd."

"That's your problem. You weren't meant for back home."

Stephanie was right. I didn't fish. I didn't hunt. No turkey season. No deer camp. No tree stand. I didn't ride four-wheelers. I didn't drive a jacked-up Ford truck with a lift kit. I didn't chew Skoal or score touchdowns. I didn't fit. Maybe she didn't fit either.

After one year with Stephanie at Marshall University, I was born again—saved. Hallelujah! I proposed marriage.

When I graduated from Marshall University in May 2004 with a degree in English education, I decided to keep at it and go for a master's degree. The plan was to increase my earning potential before becoming a high school English teacher. At least that's how I sold the plan to my parents. My father would have welcomed my return to Cowen, welcomed my presence at his new boxing club. I'd fallen in love with the idea of college, with the idea of becoming a writer, with Huntington, West Virginia, and with Stephanie Nicole. Truth be told, making it out of Cowen, West Virginia, made me feel like a big man. College was my father's dream, but I lived it. I was an expatriate back then. I was Hemingway. Setting in the Drinko Library coffee shop, setting out on the college green, I was Willoughby Trailer Park's Ernest Hemingway; distance changed everything. My parents, my grandparents, my sister, my cousins, my uncles, my aunts, and my hometown friends—they'd all lost me. They'd lost me to a world beyond the Appalachian Mountains and it was only a matter of time before I'd be gone for good. Cowen, West Virginia, would never lay a glove on me again.

I was running from the small-town fisticuffs of Appalachian manhood yet in some strange way it was boxing that had saved me from drowning in hostile academic waters. My love affair with the sport of boxing was the gateway to finding my own ambitions as a writer and scholar. Louis vs. Schmeling taught me about World War II, the Nazis, and the fickleness of patriotism. Muhammad Ali was my introduction to the American civil rights movement. James Braddock's "Cinderella Man" story was a lesson on the Great Depression. Boxing turned me into a scavenger of history and culture; the first book I ever read cover to cover was my father's 1975 edition of Ali's biography *The Greatest*.[36] My first college essay dealt with Maya Angelou's treatment of Joe Louis in *I Know Why the Caged Bird*

Sings.[37] Boxing was my literacy sponsor, to borrow a term from scholar Deborah Brandt.[38] I eventually learned how to use boxing as a conversational bridge, a way to mask my first-generation college student anxieties. I'd chat about Azumah Nelson with my education professor from Ghana, listening to a story of Ghanaian warriors. I'd write compositions on Julio Cesar Chavez for my Spanish 101 instructor from Mexico City and essays on Acelino Freitas for my Spanish 102 instructor from Brazil. With my graduate school English professor from Arkansas, I'd check in on hometown boy Jermain Taylor. Folks love talking *home*, I came to learn, and I was good at talking boxing.

During my graduate school days at Marshall (two years in total), I would come home for winter and summer breaks to train with the fighters down at The Edge. I'd always find myself holding the mitts. Sometimes I'd spar. My father and I worked corners together. We developed fighters together. Stephanie would occasionally visit the gym, taking photographs of the fighters as they trained. She would also attend amateur boxing competitions to document the small-town triumphs on a WordPress website she built for the club. My father, Jeff Dean, and Jason Bragg were constant fixtures in the gym. Stephanie and I came and went.

***

The second reincarnation of Lo's Gym was a big deal in our small town, a stark contrast to its predecessor down at Classic Curl Beauty Shop. My father found himself with a gym full of 30 to 40 kids a night, mostly teenagers. He'd work each kid three rounds on the hand pads, sometimes doing 15 or 20 rounds in a row before taking a break—this after working a 4:00 a.m.–5:00 p.m. shift in the coal mines each day. He'd even get in there and spar with the kids when necessary. Jason would spar, I did my part as well, and others would join in on occasion, but it was mostly my father up in the ring.

Members of the church would sometimes show up and watch the workouts, but they mostly got in the way, standing around with their hands in their pockets, occasionally passing out flyers with Bible verses on them.

Curtis Wright was, at first, enthusiastic about the new boxing gym; he brought along his 14-year-old nephew Craig on opening day. But

Curtis's disappointment was obvious; the ring was crowded with teens and preteens. Heavy traffic. This wasn't Curtis Wright's Lo's Gym. Things were different. My father was different.

Before each workout, fighters and trainers would stand in a large circle, holding hands, taking prayer requests. The circle wouldn't break until after saying "The Lord's Prayer." The prayer circle, as it came to be known, was as far as my father took it with the religious rhetoric. Most of our kids were from the bottom—welfare kids from broken homes. These were the tough guys, the first to try cigarettes and marijuana, the first sexually active kids in their class, etc., etc. They'd ask for prayers for their sick parents, grandparents, and siblings. They'd pray for their fathers to find jobs, pray for their parents to get back together. Those public declarations were both sad and beautiful. We'd say "The Lord's Prayer" in unison and then it was time to box.

There were, of course, other noticeable changes in my father's training routine. First, he stopped playing the rap music I supplied him with for Curtis Wright's workouts. He couldn't risk a deacon or pastor catching wind of a *motherfucker*. So, per my father's orders, Stephanie and I would occasionally venture into the Christian bookstore in the Huntington Mall and buy some of the worst rap CDs known to man. My father wanted the beats, the rhythm, but not the cursing.

Community service also became an integral part of Lo's Gym. My father paid for each and every fighter's USA boxing license out of his own pocket. He also paid for each and every fighter's boxing uniform, satin Ringside boxing trunks (black with red trim) and a matching black tank top. The only catch was that active fighters had to take part in community service to earn their license fee and boxing uniform. The community service activities ranged from trips to visit nursing home residents, to car stops for needy families, to an annual winter coat drive. My father wanted his boxers to understand they were connected to and could be a positive force for change in their troubled communities. Many of the kids took part in the community service activities, but never actually competed as boxers. Few, if any, attended Sunday church service.

"Mike, how many of these kids are saved?"

There'd occasionally be a deacon or church figurehead in the gym, asking my father such questions.

"I can't answer that," he'd say.

"Mike, we gotta get some of these kids in church," they'd urge.

"That's your department," he'd answer.

Lo's Gym Boxing Club was a safe haven for troubled kids in our town and the surrounding communities, a place to come in from the storm, my father imagined. He didn't pretend to know the way to heaven or the mysteries of the universe. My father knew how to teach discipline, respect; he knew how to make poor kids feel special.

"Mike, you need to get some of these kids to sign up for Vacation Bible School."

"Do you think so and so has found Jesus?"

"Do you think so and so's parents have found Jesus?"

When the kids started piling in, my father convinced himself the gym would be his life's work, his greatest contribution to Cowen, West Virginia. He actively sought out the worst of the worst, recruited the alternative school kids, the castoffs. He even began visiting kids at the Salem School for Boys, writing letters to kids he'd never met. The Sermon on the Mount was his creed and, for those five years, he practiced what he preached.

Yet, tensions remained between my father and the church.

"You really need to get these kids in church, Mike."

"Boy, we'd really like to see these kids on Sunday."

"Mike, how many of these boys do you think are saved?"

***

I begin with Bobby "Wild Boy" McCartney[39] for it was Bobby who most clearly exemplified the clientele of Lo's Gym Boxing Club. Bobby was poor. Not poor in the sense that he was unable to purchase Nikes. Poor. Painstakingly poor. Dirt poor. White trash poor. From the sour stench to the hand-me-down clothing, he was poor. When Bobby McCartney arrived at Lo's Gym on opening day, he was 13 years old.

"Sir, is this the boxing gym?"

"Sure looks like it," my father replied.

Bobby was the first to put on the gloves, the first boxer in the ring. He was a scrawny trailer park mess, couldn't crack an egg with his punches, but my father put it on real thick.

"Wow. You've got a great right hand, Wild Boy."

My father nicknamed most of the kids because there were so many he couldn't, at first, remember their real names.

"Can I do some more of that boxing, sir?"

"Sure thing, Wild Boy."

"All right, old buddy."

Bobby McCartney's conversations with my father would amuse me to no end.

"Wild Boy, you won a free t-shirt this week," my dad would say.

"Hey, Wild Boy, I have a pair of shoes I want you to try on."

"Heck no, you don't have to pay to get in, Wild Boy . . . you are our only undefeated fighter."

Bobby McCartney loved being loved. He loved belonging to something more than poverty. For all five years the gym was open, he attended every training session. Bobby never competed, nor could he. But Bobby was always there. He would lead us in "The Lord's Prayer" before every training session and would be the first guy in the ring to work the hand pads with my father.

The talent pool wasn't all that impressive those first couple of weeks. I wasn't sure if the idea was going to pan out. Lo's Gym was packed full of Bobby McCartneys—kids in need of a haircut and a hot meal, kids who walked in smelling like cigarettes and marijuana. Jimmy Utt had shot a two-page story on Lo's Gym's new location, but I doubt any of those kids had parents who read the *Webster Echo*. We had the townies and the streetwalkers. We had the alternative school kids and the unemployables. We had the Bobby McCartneys, the kind of folks Jesus was referring to when he said, "Remember the least."

Bobby's biggest contribution to the gym, in my opinion, was his giving my father the nickname that would carry him through his second act as a small-town big shot.

"You the preacher?" Bobby asked during that first week in the gym.

"No, Wild Boy, I'm the Street Preacher."

From that point forward, the nickname stuck. My father wasn't interested in outlining who was going to hell and who was not. He wasn't even interested in talking about heaven or hell. He wasn't even interested in talking about the Bible. He was, however, interested in reaching the Bobby McCartneys of the world.

One humid May evening, a few of the members of the church showed up to see if their investment had panned out.

"Show us your toughest fighter," one church member joked.

When the clergy was around, my father was a man of few words. He nodded his head and called for "Wild Boy." Bobby dutifully began his routine on the hand pads. The routine consisted of simple jabs, lead right hands, a few uppercuts, and one or two hooks. To the boxing novice, it just might look impressive.

"What did you think?" my father asked as he stared into the eyes of the four church members.

"Mike, that was really good."

"You're doing a great job with these kids."

"No," my father murmured as they began to turn and walk away.

"Excuse me?" Pastor Donne asked.

"I meant, what do you think of his shoes," my father replied.

I watched as Pastor Donne's eyes lowered and focused on Bobby's tattered, worn-out, pair of soleless tennis shoes.

"That's sad, Mike," one church member said.

"No, that's why I'm here," my father replied.

***

In *Appalachia Inside Out*, scholar Robert Higgs refers to the social phenomenon as "muscular Christianity," a brand of Christian rhetoric, particularly common in the Appalachian region, one that suggests sports are "the bridesmaids of religion."[40] Beginning in the 1920s, with the formations of The Young Men's and Young Women's Christian Associations, organized links between sports and religion began to form in the Appalachian region. As a young person, I remember saying the "Lord's Prayer" before football and basketball games. I remember robust support for the Fellowship of Christian Athletes Association in my high school. In my neck of the woods, folks lived by the creed of faith, family, and football.

Appalachian extractive industry towns are full of such spiritual breeding grounds for masculinity, churches that promote the importance of physical activity as a means of tapping into the working-class psyche of potential members. Yet, the idea of a church-sponsored boxing club was odd to more than a few folks in our small town. The congregation was half curious, half appalled by the idea.

"What would Jesus say about the violence?"

"What would Jesus say about the blood?"

"Jesus wouldn't have double-jabbed anyone, right?"

I'm paraphrasing again.

My father knew that it was just a matter of time before the whole thing came crashing down. Yet, he was dedicated to making the most of an imperfect situation. "Smokin' Lo" finally had a real boxing club; Lo finally had his gym. Mike Snyder was doing something important with his life.

Mr. Arnold and Pastor Donne did their part to validate my father's ethos with the rest of the congregation. Other churches in the county sponsored summer basketball leagues and bowling teams, so why not try something different? The idea that sports could bring young men to church, win them over to Jesus, was one that largely went unchecked in the community. My father had proven himself as a coach and boxing trainer; he could get kids under the tent.

"Let's give this boxing stuff a try," they'd say.

My father's financial contribution to the church, and to The Edge, came in the form of an annual boxing show hosted in conjunction with the Cowen Railroad Festival each July. Ever the romantic, my father named the event The Marvin Gothard Classic, in an attempt to honor his high school football coach. Most folks in our town had never been to a boxing match so the event would be a great way to win new recruits to The Edge. All of the proceeds would, of course, go back to the church. Pastor Donne was on board with the idea. Mr. Arnold was supportive as well.

Leading up to the first Marvin Gothard Classic, Pastor Donne began working boxing-themed sermons into the mix. I don't think my father would have enjoyed any of them. He never attended so I can't be sure.

One Sunday Pastor Donne preached about winning and losing, playing on the life-is-a-fight metaphor.

"If you don't have Jesus, you are a loser."

That got a big "A'men" from the congregation.

"The real victory is victory through Jesus."

A'men!

"When you get knocked down, look to Jesus."

A'men!

"When life has you on the ropes, look to Jesus."

A'men!

"Jesus is the truth, the way, and the life. And, he is working miracles here in Cowen, West Virginia."

A'men!

After the sermon, on our way out to the car, I caught a glimpse of Bobby McCartney riding his bike down Main Street, a lit cigarette perched between his 13-year-old lips.

***

My mother isn't the storyteller in the family, but she does spin this one particular story on occasion. It takes place at Go-Mart in Webster Springs, back in 1980.

"Put that back, Wesley . . . we came here to get milk and that's it."

The little boy in the dirty Captain America t-shirt gives his mother a sad-eyed look and puts the ring pop back on the shelf.

After placing the gallon of milk on the counter, the heavy-set Appalachian woman removes a handful of coins from her purse. She spreads the coins out on the counter for the Go-Mart cashier and begins counting dimes and nickels one at a time.

My father is standing with the 18-year-old version of my mother, two customers removed from the sad exchange of words.

As the heavy-set Appalachian woman parcels out the pennies, nickels, and dimes, my father steps out of the checkout line, picks up the ring pop and places it back into the hands of the boy in the dirty Captain America shirt. He then proceeds to give the boy a $10 bill.

"Get some bubblegum too," my father whispers in his raspy voice.

"The money looked so big in that little boy's hands," my mother said.

"It was the first time I realized that I loved your father," she'd always add.

This was the story of my father's religion. This was what he understood and knew of Jesus Christ. My father started Lo's Gym's annual coat drive because his own father had never owned a new winter coat as a boy. Bobby "Wild Boy" McCartney was the first kid to receive one of those coats.

"Hey, Wild Boy, see if this coat fits."

The kids in Lo's Gym called my father Street Preacher, and treated his advice as if it were the gospel. Jesus turned water to wine, but my father turned Curtis "The Ice Man" Wright into our community's first Toughman champion. The young Appalachian man-boys of Cowen, West Virginia, all wanted my father to turn them into Curtis "The Ice Man" Wright. When the first Marvin Gothard Classic was announced in the *Webster Echo*, the town was abuzz with excitement.

From my Hemingway "college boy" vantage point in Huntington, West Virginia, it all seemed sort of silly to me. I knew my father wasn't going to attend the church on a regular basis and I knew the fire-and-brimstone crowd would eventually call for his eviction. I knew that my father, at his age, couldn't endure the day-in-day-out rigors of both coal mining and boxing, and figured my mother would eventually tire of it as well. I frequented the gym, on and off, leading up to the first Marvin Gothard Classic. The gym was mostly filled with Bobby McCartneys; there wasn't an "Ice Man" in the bunch.

Yet, I couldn't shake the feeling that Lo's Gym was the beginning of a new version of my father. The situation was ridiculous, but my father's enthusiasm was palpable and infectious. My father was *born again*, it seemed. He'd graduated from the Toughman world to something bigger, more significant.

The next five years of Mike "Lo" Snyder's life can be categorized as an inexplicable journey filled with both heartache and triumph, one that would take an old West Virginia coal miner from the Smooth Coal Company to Washington, D.C., to be honored by the United States Government for his Sermon on the Mount service to a poor Appalachian community. It would be a journey that turned poor trailer park kids into state champion boxers, a journey that would turn amateurs into professionals.

And in the end, my father did get the phone call he'd always dreamed of, a chance to take a local boy to the big dance, an HBO Pay-Per-View in Atlantic City.

The revival down on Main Street was a sight to behold. All of my Mike "Lo" Snyder's fantastic corner man dreams came to life.

My father wasn't perfect, certainly wasn't without sin. He wasn't an expert on the King James and was far too foul-mouthed to be a Sunday school teacher.

But he was Cowen, West Virginia's, Street Preacher; Lo's Gym Boxing Club was his miracle.

PART II

——

COUNTERPUNCHERS

——

Parables of Coal Country Pugilism

——

Chapter 6

THE UNLIKELY REINCARNATION STORY OF RICK COGAR

The Cowen Hotel *sure was something*, a beautiful three-story building located just off Main Street. The Community Market was located just *a piece* down the road. There was a movie theater and a bowling alley. There was a drugstore that sold comic books and Coke floats. There was an Odd Fellows Lodge and Lloyd Sims's Exxon Gas Station and the Cowen Quick Shop and the J. M. Barger & Son Fix-It Shop. The B&O Railroad Station was booming. You couldn't get a table at Dyer's Restaurant on Sunday. Cowen had its own grade school and high school back then. An old boy named Lee Rapp even had a taxi service, kept it going for a good 20 years. Once upon a time there was Tenny's Department Store, Pizza Depot, and Brenson's Furniture.

"There was a job for anybody who had the backbone to work," my grandfather Lowell once said to me.

"Back in them days, you had everything you needed right here," he added.

Cowen was born a railroad town, the offspring of King Coal's promise of hope, prosperity, and industrialization. West Virginia, the largest coal producer east of the Mississippi River, was built off such promises. An extensive network of railroads transported the coal away from Cowen and off to power plants located in important places, feeding the appetite of an energy-hungry nation. The rugged mountain terrain fostered a certain degree of physical isolation, but the locals didn't mind the isolation all that much. Those were the good old days. No reason to leave a town like Cowen, they said.

On May 6, 1968, a tragedy occurred at a coal mine owned by the Gauley Coal Company in Hominy Falls, West Virginia.[41] A continuous miner drilled into an unmapped adjacent mine that was, unbeknownst to the miners, filled with acidic water. When the continuous miner drilled through the wall, water suddenly rushed through the mine, instantly killing four men and leaving 15 men trapped underground; six of those men were trapped for ten days. My grandfather Lowell was part of the rescue team that saved the lives of the 15 men stranded underground. He was also part of the recovery team that discovered the bodies. Lowell was 29 years old.

I grew up on my grandfather's Hominy Falls campfire stories; they were brave, heroic, but at the very same time they scared the hell out of me. Ask any old coal miner and he'll spin a few mining tragedies for you. There are certainly enough of them to go around.

In December 1907, an explosion occurred at the Fairmont Coal Company's number six and number eight mines.[42] The Monongah Mine Disaster claimed the lives of 367 West Virginia men, the largest mine disaster in our nation's history. The benchmark.

Seven years later, an explosion of coal-seam methane took the lives of 183 men in Eccles, West Virginia.[43]

Ten years later, an explosion at the Benwood Mine in Marshall County, West Virginia, claimed the lives of 118 coal miners.[44]

Fast forward a few decades and you've got the Buffalo Creek flood, a disaster that occurred as the result of a burst in the Pittston Coal Company's coal slurry impoundment dam, four days after having been declared "satisfactory" by a federal mine inspector.[45] The flood released 132 million gallons of wastewater on 16 communities along Buffalo Creek Hollow.[46] One hundred and twenty-five people were killed, 1,000 people were injured, and over 4,000 were left homeless.[47]

Talk to the right folks and they'll tell you about the days rural coal towns were booming. They'll tell you that coal mining, as an industry, has come a long way. It is as safe as it can be now, both for the environment and the people. They'll tell you the EPA needs to stop meddling in King Coal's business. Coal keeps the lights on. It puts food on the table. This is the gospel of West Virginia politics. When the coal is booming, we ain't got it too bad around here.

On January 2, 2006, an explosion occurred at the Sago Mine in Sago, West Virginia.[48] The blast collapsed a wall that trapped 13 miners underground for nearly two days. The incident received extensive media coverage worldwide. Mass media bigwigs came to town to get the scoop. In the rush to be first, an erroneous report told the world, and the families of the trapped coal miners, that all of *our* boys had been found alive and well. Only one coal miner survived.

Seventeen days later, a conveyor belt explosion took the lives of two men at the Aracoma Alma Mine in Logan County, West Virginia.[49]

Four years later, a gas-related explosion occurred at the Upper Big Branch Mine in Raleigh County, West Virginia, and 29 coal miners lost their lives.[50]

The Sago and Upper Big Branch incidents, remixes of an all too familiar tune, foster a renewed national focus on an industry long criticized by outsiders and environmentalists. Unsafe conditions are exposed. Mining officials are given a litigious slap on the wrist. Anxious and defensive days for our fathers and grandfathers. Anxious and defensive days for West Virginia. Our regional identity, the encomium of King Coal, exposed as propaganda. Yet, West Virginia clung to the past, its defensiveness toward outsiders never more apparent.

"Them damn environmentalists won't stop until we are all out of work."

"The EPA is gonna end coal mining."

"What are we gonna do for work around here?"

By 2007, it was all gloom and doom around my way. The Smooth Coal Company remained standing, be it on wobbly legs. But every other month, the rumors would pick back up.

"They're gonna shut Smooth down in the spring."

"I heard Smooth is shutting down after Christmas."

"Buddy, when Smooth shuts down, they won't be no work here."

"When Smooth shuts down, it won't never come back," folks would say.

Scholars argue that the collapse of the American steel industry in the late twentieth century reduced demand for the metallurgical coal that is prominently found in Appalachian states such as West Virginia. Increasing air quality concerns over thermal coal, used in power plants across the country, didn't help the industry all that much either. Before the Sago and Upper Big Branch mine disasters, the coal industry had been in a steady decline for decades. The economic struggles of the manufacturing industries that burned coal for power found their way to towns like Cowen and settled in. Trickle-down poverty.

And in the end, King Coal's biggest rival emerged in the form of cheap, cleaner-burning natural gas. It was obvious to all those outside the hometown fan base who was gonna win this one. In a span of just over five years, King Coal went from champion to underdog, a *tomato can* with no future. Yet, the details unearthed by the media coverage of the Sago and Upper Big Branch mining tragedies baffled outsiders.

"How can locals defend such a dangerous and exploitive trade?"

We're the faithful congregation of the Church of King Coal, we answered.

When I was in the second grade, my friend Samantha Cochran lost her father in a mining accident; Samantha's father was the brother of Philip Cochran (my father's boxing trainer at the Webster Springs Boxing Club). My wife's close friend Crystal lost her father to a mining accident in the second grade as well. All of us Cowen kids made it a point to pray for the coal mines at our bedsides each night. We'd pray that the right person would win the election. We'd pray that all these new *hippy* regulations didn't put the mines out of business. We'd pray for the jobs. We'd pray for King Coal. When a coal mine shuts down, *it don't come back.*

***

My father's Beowulf stories were entertaining but predictable. They could be separated into three distinct categories: (1) revenge stories in which my father takes on a schoolyard bully who has picked on someone who is a nice guy or a pussy or didn't deserve it; (2) football stories in which my father plays hurt but saves the day, despite the small-town politics and favoritism that put the team in jeopardy in the first place; and, my personal favorites, (3) boxing stories in which he takes on bigger, stronger, and more experienced opponents who just don't have as much heart as he does. If you sat there long enough, you'd get one of the three, or a combination of the three, or all three.

The Pete Whomsley[51] story was my favorite. It begins in the commons area of the newly consolidated Webster County High School. Pete is walking through the commons, books in one hand, brown bag lunch in the other, minding his own business. Tony Clevenger[52] is hiding around the corner, with a sucker punch waiting for him.

Whap!

Tony nails Pete right between the eyes, sending him sprawling on the floor.

"I think it was over a girl, but I can't remember. . . . either way, it was a cheap shot and Pete never fought nobody."

"When Tony came back to school the next week, me and Rick had it all planned out," my father would say, always smirking.

All of my father's high school fight stories began this way, Rick Cogar by his side egging on the schoolyard justice. My father told me this particular story about 20 or 30 times; each time it changed just a bit, but the general principle of the story stayed the same.

"That's the old Trojan gift horse move, Dad," I said on about the twentieth retelling of the story.

He didn't understand the reference and proceeded to his favorite part.

Tony is walking up the cement hallway that leads to the vocational portion of the high school. Rick approaches him, smiling ear-to-ear.

"What'd-ya say, old buddy," Rick shouts, hand extended in the traditional handshake position.

Tony looks confused.

"Where ya been?"

"Got suspended."

"No shit. What for?"

"Shocked the shit out of Pete Whomsley."

"Yeah, I heard about it . . . well, this is for Pete," Rick says mid-handshake.

My father is waiting around the corner with a vicious sucker punch. Tony's right hand is encased in Rick Cogar's firm grasp. Tony is less than helpless.

Whap!

Tony learns that sucker-punching people isn't nice.

Rick Cogar was the meanest, orneriest, rowdiest little bastard the Webster County school system had ever seen, at least that was my father's version of the story. He was a scrawny little shit, mouthy too. I've seen a few pictures and Rick looked the part. He was muscular but skinny, had a floppy Beatles-style haircut, wore form-fitting tank tops, and bell-bottom jeans. According to legend, he'd pick fights with guys twice his size, would drive teachers absolutely bonkers, and was the class clown to end all class clowns. Rick was the guy who made the football team, but never got in the game because he wouldn't listen to a damn thing the coach told him. He'd drive Coach Marvin Gothard absolutely crazy.

Coach Gothard was my father's Cus D'Amato, constantly trying to get my father to walk the line, teaching him life lessons, helping him realize his own potential. My father loved Coach Gothard like a father, but it sure sounds like he and Rick gave Gothard hell on a fairly consistent basis.

Coach Gothard wasn't from Webster County, as was the case with most of the staff back then. He was from just outside of Huntington, West Virginia, a place that seemed *big city* to all of the folks around Cowen. Coach Gothard was a pioneer; there was a teaching college in Glenville, West Virginia, and Coach Gothard had gone to it, earned a degree in secondary education, and eventually found work at the newly consolidated Webster County High School. My father and Rick Cogar were members of the first incoming crop of WCHS students; a Cowen Bulldog and a Webster Springs Wildcat, small-town sports rivals turned best friends.

Legend has it that Rick Cogar was my father's biggest boxing advocate. He'd show up at the Webster Springs Boxing Club just to watch him train, and never missed a fight.

"You hit like goddamn Howard Davis. You've got one hell of a punch," Rick would always brag.

"Howard Fucking Davis, baby. That's what you are going to be. The next Howard Fucking Davis."

Rick knew how to compliment my father; comparing him to the

recently crowned U.S. Olympic Gold medalist was the right way to stroke my father's ego. Howard Davis was Rick Cogar's favorite boxer. My father would tell all of this to Howard Davis himself some years later.

Rick and my father were brothers of sorts. They both had problematic relationships with their fathers, didn't have any biological brothers, and found something in each other's ignorance and bravado that was endearing. Rick kept my father in trouble and got him out of it a few times. I grew up on Rick Cogar stories, hyperbolic street fight stories, most of them only halfway believable.

There were two sets of Rick Cogars in those stories. There was the Rick Cogar who is always getting my father into street fights fueled by drunken rebellion, and then there is the Rick Cogar who finds Jesus. The beer-drinking, cigarette-smoking, lunchroom-fighting Rick Cogar was always my favorite. Stories of the Rick Cogar who finds Jesus always killed the vibe; his stories were told with a different rhetoric.

"Rick got Shirley pregnant the summer after graduation, and let me tell you, it changed that man," my father would say.

"Todd, when he found out that he was having a little girl, he straightened the hell up, married Shirley, stopped drinking, stopped smoking, started going to church with Shirley and her family . . . he was a different person," he said sadly.

"I thought Rick was bullshitting at first, trying to get in good with Shirley's folks, but it wasn't no bullshit, he got baptized, started working for J. T. Sullivan's logging outfit, started growing up."

"If Rick hadn't straightened up, I doubt I would have either. I think his daughter saved us both."

I knew a few Rick Cogars back in high school; they found Jesus after graduation, put down the booze and picked up the Bible. In my hometown, people tend to find Jesus after high school. They find Jesus when they start families and have children, when they find their way into the mines, when life gets serious. I'd probably have found Jesus that way too if I'd stuck around.

My father was driving down Main Street when he spotted Rick's car parked outside the bar. Rick's wife was eight months pregnant, he'd been walking the line the whole eight months, but my father feared the worst. My father pulled a U-turn at the top of Cowen Hill and went back. He parked his truck across the street, took a deep breath, and walked across the road to the bar. Before he could open the door, a voice called out to him.

"Lo, hey, over here."

It was Rick's wife Shirley.

"I saw you drive by. You were going after Rick weren't you?" she chuckled.

"Yes, yes, I was, Shirley," he admitted, a little embarrassed.

"He's just buying bread, Mike. Foodland is already closed," she smirked, rubbing her belly.

"How you feeling, Shirley?"

"Oh, my back hurts, but I can't complain."

About that time Rick came out of the bar, brown paper bag in his hand, a loaf of Wonder Bread peeking out of the top.

Shirley immediately told on my father.

"Mike drove up the hill, came back, and was going in there after you, Rick."

"He was? Lo, were you about to thump my butt for going to the bar?"

"Yeah, I was, Rick," my father answered, still embarrassed.

"All of that is over, Lo, in the past," Rick said, wrapping his free arm around my father's neck.

It happened on a Sunday.

Rick was working for a contractor, cutting a road that was going to eventually lead to a deep mine. When the tree kicked out, the saw cut Rick's throat and the tree landed on his head. Rick Cogar died up a holler, in the middle of the Appalachian wilderness, in a town named Cherry Falls.

Shirley called my father.

"Rick's dead, Mike, we lost Rick."

Six weeks later, she'd have a baby girl named Rachel.

That is how my father would always end the final tale of the legend of Rick Cogar. He'd always end the story with that line.

***

If we'd been playing tackle football in the schoolyard, I would have picked Craig Wright first. Craig was Curtis "The Ice Man" Wright's nephew. Craig looked like a little Curtis; he looked like a playground scrapper. I would have bought stock in Craig right from the start. Boxing was in his blood,

I figured. But then again, that's probably what people incorrectly assumed about me. Boxing bloodlines are funny like that. You just never know.

Craig was 14 years old, was just about to enter his freshman year at Webster County High School, when his uncle brought him to the gym. Craig was already making a name for himself as a football player down at the grade school; the kid had a ripped six-pack, bulging biceps, and a thin teenager mustache to match. I'm guessing the 14-year-old girls loved him.

Craig took to it fast. He was a good recruiter for us. I don't ever remember him coming to the gym alone. Every now and then he'd bring us a kid who could fight. Craig Wright brought his buddy Chris Short, also 14 years old, with him to the gym a few weeks after it opened. Chris Short was a tough kid to read. He was big and strong and looked the part, but not in the same way Craig looked the part. Chris Short was farm tough. He baled hay with his daddy, and worked on car engines, and piddled around with motorcycles, and hunted, and fished, and didn't seem that interested in anything that didn't resemble work. Chris was shy, had sandy blond hair, pale skin, looked at the floor when he talked; he hadn't learned how to fake it like Craig had. Sports weren't his thing, but they were about to be. After feeling Chris's southpaw straight left hand on the pads, I knew my father would bring it out of him. Craig Wright and Chris Short appeared to be our best shot at actually winning a fight at the first Marvin Gothard Classic. It was our debut event as a boxing club and all of our kids were boxing virgins, matched up with heavily experienced opponents. If Craig and Chris could win their fights, we could save face. The other guys looked to be in way over their heads.

I'd never seen my father so nervous. It was 3 p.m. and Tommy and Larry Davenport hadn't made it to Webster County with the boxing ring; the show was supposed to start at 7 p.m. Fighters and trainers from Ashland, Kentucky; Huntington, West Virginia; Charleston, West Virginia; Fairmont, West Virginia; and Ironton, Ohio, were milling around in an empty gymnasium, probably wondering if this new trainer had any idea what he'd gotten himself into. Fifteen bouts were scheduled and we'd sold over $3,000 worth of tickets, but the boxing ring had yet to arrive. My father was livid.

"If this show doesn't come off, I'm finished with this shit. I'll tell Pastor Donne and the rest of them to stick it up their ass."

"Did you call Tommy or Larry?"

"They won't answer their phone."

Tommy and Larry Davenport ran a boxing club out of the Charleston Recreation Center in South Charleston. They also made a few bucks on the side by transporting their boxing ring around the state for amateur and professional events. Back in the day, both brothers had been Golden Glove champions, but Tommy was the bigger name; he'd fought briefly as a professional boxer and once challenged for the IBO title in Paris. They were good boxers and good trainers, but punctuality wasn't their strong suit. They'd do this sort of thing to my father every year. Panic and paranoia was the only way my father knew how to react to stressful situations.

The Davenport brothers made it to Webster County just in time. They were tightening the turnbuckles while paying customers began filing through the doors.

"Hey, Big Mike," Tommy yelled as he strolled through the door at 5:30 p.m.

Everyone called my father "Lo," but Tommy decided to brand him "Big Mike." Tommy behaved as if he wasn't even late.

"Let's make this thang happen," Larry chimed in, my father almost speechless with panic.

Tommy and Larry's lateness threw my father off, I think. He was a mess that night.

To the outside observer, everything was going according to plan. The gymnasium was packed with fight fans; Webster County hadn't hosted a boxing match in 22 years. Our fighters looked the part in their shiny new red-and-black uniforms. The corner men looked the part in their shiny new red-and-black jackets. The boxing ring, although a little late to the venue, looked the part as well. Most of the people in attendance had never seen a boxing ring before. Everything appeared to be in order, but my father was coming apart at the seams. Everyone and everything was bothering him. My father was sweating profusely by the start of the show.

Bobby "Wild Boy" McCartney said the "Lord's Prayer" over the microphone, Pastor Donne said a few words about The Edge, Larry Davenport's daughter sung the national anthem, and just like that we were underway. Four fights into the card Lo's Gym Boxing Club was 0–4. It was apparent to anybody who was watching that our kids were nervous, overmatched, and simply outclassed. With each loss you could hear the steady rumblings of the crowd intensify. Craig Wright and Chris Short were both matched up against boxers from the Brick House Boxing Club in Ironton, Ohio. Craig's opponent had nine fights under his belt; Chris Short's opponent had 15. The lanky kid from Ironton did a number on Craig. Straight rights. Uppercuts. Hooks to the body. The lanky kid from Ironton hit Craig Wright with every punch in his arsenal. And, to his credit, poor Craig took it like a man. Craig's uncle, Curtis, had a hard time watching it, I think. Curtis laid it on Craig pretty thick back in the locker room. With one bout remaining on the card, the score was West Virginia Tri-State Boxing Association 5, Lo's Gym Boxing Club 0.

"Man, they're putting it to us," Jason Bragg said to me back in the locker room. He and I were both a little embarrassed for my father.

"Chris, you gotta win this one for Lo," Jeff "Bundini" Dean desperately urged.

"We gotta win at least one fight," he said, hoping to motivate Chris. None of us knew how to stir the emotions of a stoic kid like Chris Short. He hadn't been raised on halftime speeches like the rest of us. My father largely remained silent.

Chris Short was matched up with Cody Scarburry, a pug-nosed kid with a squared jaw and thick, unkempt, shaggy brown hair. He didn't look like much, but the passbook had him listed as 11–4 and, at that point in the night, my optimism had already left the gymnasium; a kid with 15 fights was about to climb in there with a kid with zero fights.

"You ready to go, Chris?" my father asked, breaking the locker room silence.

"Yessum."

"You're our last hope, give 'em hell," Jason Bragg added.

"I'ma try."

Chris Short's voice was timid and soft and made him seem smaller than he was. Chris acted as if he was on his way to a poetry reading or to pick out socks at Wal-Mart. You could easily misread his demeanor. During the prefight announcements, Cody Scarburry started pounding his chest and mouthing to Chris. He was *talking shit*, but it was too loud in the gymnasium to hear what he was saying.

"Whuts he doing?" Chris said to my father in the corner, slobbering from his mouthpiece.

"He's making fun of you, Chris," my father answered unenthusiastically.

Ding!

Chris circled the ring twice before throwing a punch. Chris landed his southpaw jab with ease. He turned Cody Scarburry whichever way he wanted. Chris landed solid combinations and ducked out of the way and began circling again. It was almost boring. Chris was gliding around the ring just as Curtis "The Ice Man" Wright had done back in Classic Curl Beauty Shop years ago. I couldn't believe my eyes. I knew Chris could fight, but I'd never seem him so calm and in control. In the second round, Chris landed a brutal one-two-three combination that staggered Cody Scarburry, causing him to wobble from one side of the ring to the next. Most kids jump on their opponents and *go to town* when that sort of thing happens, but that wasn't Chris Short's disposition. He circled the ring, set his feet, landed more combinations, and got back to circling again. The third round was easiest of all. Chris probably landed ten unanswered punches, shots with textbook precision, shots demonstrating the beautiful choreography of the sweet science. I don't remember Scarburry landing a single meaningful punch in return.

And just like that, my father's first victory as a trainer in three years, his first since Curtis "The Ice Man" Wright.

When the Marvin Gothard Classic concluded, a few bouts later, the panel of USA Boxing judges awarded Chris Short the first-ever Rick Cogar Fighter of the Night Award. My father had named the award, bought the trophy, but relegated the responsibility of selecting the winner to the USA Boxing judges working the event. Rick Cogar's mother and father and sister were in attendance to give the award to Chris Short. At first, I wasn't sure if it was a pity vote because they felt sorry for our hometown gym or if Chris had truly fought that well. Either way, we were all in need of a confidence boost.

"Hey, Lo . . . can I ask you something?" Chris calmly said, wiping the sweat from his brow back in the locker room.

"What is it, champ?"

"Who is Rick Cogar?"

"Chris, I named that award after my best friend, Rick. He was one hell of a fighter."

Chris smiled that bashful smile, his eyes diverting to the floor.

"I'm proud that it went to a guy like you," my father added.

"He still alive, Lo?"

"No, buddy. He died when he was just 18 years old—logging accident," my father said.

"I'm real sorry about that."

It was the most I'd ever heard Chris Short say at one time.

"I tried to do what you asked me to do," Chris added.

The other kids from our gym crowded around Chris Short and gawked at his trophy.

***

My father bought an oversized brown teddy bear at Tenny's Department Store on his way over to Webster Springs Memorial Hospital. When he arrived at the hospital, he tried to give the teddy bear to a nurse, but she insisted he go back and see Shirley. My father entered the room cautiously. Shirley was asleep, her hair disheveled, one foot sticking out of the blanket covering the bed. My father didn't wake Shirley; he quietly sat the teddy bear on the chair beside Shirley's bed. He gently kissed Shirley on the forehead and, on the way out, covered up her foot.

I never had the chance to meet Rachel Cogar but my father used to hang pictures of her in the hallway where he kept his dinner bucket. My father would kneel down in that hallway for an early morning prayer before picking up his dinner bucket and heading to the mines. Sometimes he'd touch Rachel's picture before picking up his dinner bucket. I caught him doing that sort of thing on more than a few occasions.

Rachel and her mother, Shirley, ended up in North Carolina, I think. Before social media hit, she and my father would write letters to each other. Rachel would send pictures and my father would update his homemade altar. I'd study those pictures. Rachel was perpetually beautiful, most certainly out of my league. I grew up with Rachel, in a way. Back when I was an awkward teenager, I'd daydream that one day we'd meet and fall in love and start a family and somehow the entire thing would come full circle. Some beautiful young church girl would break my insecure teenage heart and I'd daydream about Rachel.

Rachel and her mother, Shirley, never made it to any of our Marvin Gothard Classic events, four events in total. She never had a chance to present the award named after her father. Perhaps she didn't grow up on the Rick Cogar Beowulf stories like I did. Maybe still, to this day, she doesn't know that her father was the meanest, orneriest, scrawniest little bastard the Webster County school system has ever seen. Rick Cogar never competed as a boxer so maybe Rachel didn't understand why such an award was named after her father in the first place. Maybe Rachel didn't know that her old man once whopped T. J. Boggs, the tallest guy on the Braxton County basketball team, in the Go-Mart parking lot. Maybe she didn't know Rick gave it to ol' Tommy Shoemaker at the Webster County Fair.

My father almost gave it to Billy Rogers[53] at Rick's funeral. Billy had the nerve to approach my father and a few of his buddies out in the parking lot of Adam's Funeral Home and ask, "Do you boys know if Rick was saved?"

My father grabbed Billy by the throat and slammed him against the side of the funeral home. It took three pallbearers to get my father off of Billy.

My father almost gave it to Rick Cogar himself the first time they met. It was a sweltering July evening on Baker's Island, the summer before the consolidation of Webster County High School. Rick was talking to a few long-legged girls from Webster, over by the diving board, when my father approached.

"You got something to say to me now, you cocky little prick?"

"Buddy, I don't know you," Rick replied, taking a few steps backwards.

"Yeah, I heard you were running your damn mouth about wanting to kick my ass," my father said, making up the distance between him and Rick.

"Buddy, I don't know how I could want to kick your ass if I don't even know you."

"Well, I'm here now if you want to try, you rat-faced Webster Springs suck."

"Buddy, I'm from Bolair, I ain't no Webster Springs suck."

"You're Randy Prayter,[54] ain't you?"

"Hell, no. I'm Rick Cogar."

"You ain't Randy Prayter?"

"Hell, no. I hate that little mouthy shit, too."

"You ain't shitting me?"

The long-legged girls relax and start to laugh about the whole thing.

"I ain't Randy Prayter, but listen here . . . if you want to kick that little mouthy shit's ass, me and you are gonna be good friends," Rick replies, his hand extended.

"I'm sorry, I thought you were Randy," my father said, finally apologizing.

"Hell, if you hate Randy that much, I'm'a buy you a beer," Rick says.

"I'll take you up on that offer, buddy," my father replies.

They'd do that sort of thing from time to time, mostly down at Doc Hinkle's Beer Joint. Coach Gothard caught my father and Rick down at Doc Hinkle's Beer Joint one night. My father and Rick were both under 21 years old, but they'd been throwing back beers all night long. Gothard strolled into the bar, instantly spotting the two underaged football players.

"The next beer is on me, boys," Gothard said, approaching the table.

"And you are gonna pay like hell for it come practice on Monday," he added.

As a punishment for their underaged drinking, Rick Cogar and my father ran 25 laps around the track after football practice each evening. They'd do that for the next two years.

"That beer still cold, boys?" Gothard would call when Rick and my father passed by each time.

Doc Hinkle's Beer Joint went out of business around the same time the coal industry took its first big hit in the early 1980s. The building was vacant for much of my childhood, a rickety skeleton that my father would bring back to life with Rick Cogar stories. Some 20 years later, Doc Hinkle's Beer Joint would be purchased by the First Baptist Church of Cowen and renamed The Edge; the second floor would be home to a boxing club called Lo's Gym.

Reincarnation?

***

A few months later, they matched Chris Short up with Cody Scarburry again, this time in Charleston, West Virginia. The boys in Ironton must have been sore about it. That didn't matter; Chris won another lopsided decision. In October my father took Chris and a few guys to Ashland, Kentucky, for a show. They matched Chris up with Scarburry for a third time. That didn't matter; Chris won that fight easiest of all, knocking

Scarburry down in the final round. Chris was 3–0, all three wins coming against the same pug-nosed kid from Ironton. At first, I wasn't sure if Chris was a great boxer or just a greater boxer than Cody Scarburry. Either way, Chris Short was, during the early days, Lo's Gym's only undefeated fighter. But you'd have never known it by the way he behaved. Chris didn't brag or boast or strut around the gym like most of the guys. He wasn't even that interested in socializing with the other kids. Chris would show up and almost instantly get to work, hitting the bag, shadowboxing, jumping rope. Getting him to talk, or sign the bout sheet for an upcoming fight, wasn't easy.

A few weeks before a boxing event, my father would bring a blank piece of paper and place it on the table in the far-left corner of the gym. He never asked kids if they wanted to fight, nor did he ever coax them to do so. He would announce the presence of the bout sheet during the prayer circle, announce the date and location of the boxing event, collect the sheet at the end of the week, and call the promoter with the names and weights of his fighters. More often than not, the bout sheet was full of names that had no business being there.

Chris Short, despite being our only *ringer*, signed up for only three out of the first seven bout sheets my father presented to the gym. It drove me, and Jason Bragg, and Chris Short's father, Rodney, absolutely crazy. My father didn't seem to mind.

"Lo, try to talk Chris into fighting in that Boone County event," Rodney would say, always in private.

"He's looking good. He's ready," he would add.

Chris Short fought only when he wanted to and my father was fine with that. Chris trained like he was about to get a shot at the title regardless of whether or not his signature graced the bout sheet. He and my father held an unspoken agreement on the issue. The rest of us played Don King.

In December 2004, Chris Short signed my father's bout sheet for the West Virginia Silver Gloves. Chris easily won the tournament, adding yet another accolade to go with his Rick Cogar Fighter of the Night trophy. That's when the USA Boxing folks started joining in on the Don King action.

"Lo, you've got something with that Chris Short boy."

"That Short boy is a real talented kid."

"You ought to send him on to the Regional Tournament."

My father talked to Chris about it, but Chris didn't seem all that interested, and that was the last of it. Chris Short took a few weeks off from the gym after winning the West Virginia Silver Gloves. Then one dreary March evening, Chris showed back up and started training like a son-of-a-bitch. Chris signed the bout sheet for the Golden Gloves tournament in Charleston in March 2005. As an under-16 nontournament participant, Chris Short won both of his fights by knockout. After the event, Gary Toney, president of the West Virginia chapter of USA Boxing, announced the following:

"The prestigious Governor's Cup Award goes to most outstanding fighter of the tournament . . ."

"This year's recipient is the first boxer under the age of 16, in the history of West Virginia amateur boxing, to win the award . . ."

"I am proud to present the 2005 Governor's Cup Award to Chris Short, of Lo's Gym Boxing Club in Cowen, West Virginia."

Chris and Rodney were already on the road, heading back to Cowen. My father climbed into the ring and accepted the award on Chris's behalf.

My father didn't tell Chris about it until the following day. He did, however, call Rodney to ensure his boy was going to be in the gym. The Governor's Cup was a two-tiered trophy with a bronze base. It looked like the kid of the trophy big-time college football players win just before they are drafted into the NFL. When Chris walked into the gym, the trophy was waiting in the middle of his makeshift boxing ring. Chris was embarrassed by the whole thing and asked his father to take his trophy to the truck before the rest of the guys showed up. My father had to almost beg Chris to pose with that trophy for a Jimmy Utt cover story.

I don't remember Chris Short ever saying a curse word. I don't remember him ever bragging about a victory, or taunting an opponent. I don't remember him ever arguing with my father. He was a quiet kid, a good kid. Chris had a chiseled body for a boy his age, but wasn't in the least bit interested in showing it off. He didn't even seem all that interested in the hormonal young girls who hung around the gym. Chris mostly palled around with Jason Bragg, his father, and his uncle Charlie, who'd been paralyzed from the waist down in a mining accident. My father saw to it that the church built a wheelchair ramp for Chris's uncle Charlie or anyone else who might need it. When Charlie was in the gym, Chris trained like hell.

In December 2005, Chris Short successfully defended his Silver Gloves State Championship and took yet another extended break from Lo's Gym. None of us really knew what to make of it. He was our gym's best and least active fighter, our greatest prodigy and our most puzzling enigma. The Rick Cogar Fighter of the Night was everything my favorite version of Rick Cogar was not.

***

Rick Cogar's untimely death ended Mike "Lo" Snyder's amateur boxing career back in 1978. It was the beginning of a hard realization. Life in Cowen is "no fair fight." You work till you die, be it the early or late rounds of life.

"My only fear of death is that hell might be coal powered," my father often joked.

"The devil will have a coal mine down there in hell . . . heating things up . . . and I'll have to be a damn coal miner the rest of eternity," he'd add.

For my father, boxing was an escape. He didn't think boxing would make him rich or even get him out of Cowen; that ship had long since sailed. Boxing could, however, prove to folks around town that he was more than a damn coal miner. It could show the world there was something beautiful in his toughness.

"I didn't want the coal mines for Chris Short," my father once reflected.

"I didn't want him to fight either, not if he didn't want to."

"But I did want to show him the world outside of Cowen," he added.

My father tells only one Beowulf story where Rick Cogar loses a fight. Stevie Walker,[55] two heads taller, and a good 50 pounds heavier, tumbles down a steep hillside with Rick, ends up on top, and lands a few good ones just before my father jumps in. My father, of course, gave it to Stevie pretty good afterward, so the Beowulf story goes.

When I was a kid, my father used to bring Rick Cogar back to life on a fairly consistent basis. He had a cassette tape, made by Rick and a few of their buddies during a drunken camping trip the summer before senior year of high school. My father would play that tape while lifting weights, often taking long breaks between sets to laugh, cry, and reflect. I've listened to that tape with my father a few hundred times. Rick was funny, foul-mouthed, and certainly inebriated—his Appalachian accent identical to my father's. He'd bring Rick back to life with that cassette tape; bring him back to life with a few Beowulf stories afterward.

And, for just over four years, my father brought coach Marvin Gothard back to life, resurrected the legend of Rick Cogar via a boxing trophy, one given to the toughest fighter of the night.

Or maybe it was the other way around, for it was Chris Short, the first recipient of that trophy, who brought Lazarus back from the coal mines.

When my father was in Chris Short's corner, he was boxing trainer once again, something more than a damn coal miner.

Chapter 7

JEREMIAH AND THE THREE BEARS

In the first bout of the 2004 West Virginia Silver Gloves tournament, Chris Ledsome hit Mitchell McCallum with a poleax uppercut that completely removed the loosely fastened Everlast headgear from Mitchell's head and launched it into the air and out of the boxing ring. The headgear landed squarely in my lap at ringside.

For a split second, I hesitated to look down, fearing the sweat-soaked Everlast headgear resting in my lap might actually include a severed human head.

At the Summersville Armory a few years later, Chris Ledsome hit Justin Novaria, the number two–ranked heavyweight amateur in the country (under the age of 16), with a six-inch punch that cracked like a .22 shotgun. Novaria collapsed as if he were a West Virginia buck that'd unknowingly found his way into the crosshairs of a gunman. The kill shot was delivered during the breaking of a clinch, and because of my position at ringside, I didn't see the punch land. But it was, without question, the most impressive punch I've ever heard.

Chris Ledsome, at 15 years old, could have easily passed for 20. He was already six-foot-something, had tree-trunk forearms, stocky shoulders, bowling-ball calf muscles, and deep ridging-fleshy bags underneath his wild linebacker eyes. Even as a teenager, Chris looked and sounded like a coal miner; his vocabulary was full of obscenities and his hands were callused and his forearms and shins were always bruised from this or that.

When Chris first started coming around, I fashioned him as a playground monster—the kind of guy who steals your lunch money, blacks your eye, or pulls your ponytail, the kid who is a good head taller than everyone else in the school picture. His teachers were just as afraid of him as were the kids on the playground, I figured.

Chris was the middle of the three Ledsome Bears. Nate, 18 years old at the time, was the oldest of the bunch. Well over six feet tall and over 300 pounds, Nate looked more like a professional wrestler than he did a boxer. His bald head, occasionally sprouting bright-red stubble, was the size of an NFL football helmet, his rust-colored goatee always shaved in a well-maintained chinstrap design. We figured Nate would hit like a mule and he did. But once you got to know him, Nate was more Gentle Giant than Andre the Giant. The oldest Ledsome Bear was really just a teddy bear. Nate lost his first amateur bout and never fought again.

Matthew Ledsome, 11 years old at the time our gym opened, was the youngest Ledsome cub. There was no way my father would be able to get Matthew a fight; he was already five-feet six-inches tall and well over 150 pounds—just too damn big for the 11-year-old age bracket. Matthew lost interest in boxing before my father could find anyone big enough to fight him.

The middle Ledsome Bear, however, was just right. Chris liked fighting and hated his opponents. He hated their personalized satin boxing trunks, their Nike gym bags, their Jordan brand boxing shoes, their hometown cheering sections—all of it. Chris was equally brutal with sparring partners; my father had to keep a close eye on him in the gym. Chris wanted to embarrass his opponents just as much as he wanted to hurt them. He was a playground boogeyman. Chris would dare you to give him his comeuppance.

Unlike many of the boxers at Lo's Gym, the three Ledsome Bears had unwavering support from their parents. Poppa Ledsome, always sporting a Harley-Davidson bandana and handlebar mustache, was literally the driving force behind it all. He'd load the three Ledsome Bears into the back of his rusted pickup truck and bus them down to Lo's Gym each evening. Perfect attendance.

Poppa Ledsome didn't have a job. He was on medical disability or welfare or both. I never asked. So, like Craig Wright, Lo's Gym's playground boogeyman never came to the gym alone. It was always Chris, his older brother Nate, his younger brother Matthew, and Momma and Poppa Ledsome. Looking back, I don't think any of the Ledsome Bears ever came to the gym alone. If Chris was in the gym, you could count on seeing the rest of the family. Lo's Gym was likely the most exciting part of their day.

The Ledsome Bears fashioned themselves good ol' country folk, West Virginia hillbillies, perhaps. They'd give a stranger their last dime; change a fella's tire if he were broke down along the side of the road, and so on. But they were certainly rough around the edges, counterculture by the ethical standards dictated by the American Right. Such families, I've come to believe, are the by-product of a uniquely Appalachian socioeconomic system, one that lacks access to both economic and educational opportunity; families both freed and imprisoned by a culture birthed by the extractive industries. Such families are often poor in equity but rich in spirit. The Ledsome Bears always seemed miles happier than members of my family. You'd simultaneously feel sorry for them, laugh at their social awkwardness, and be frightened by their disregard for social etiquette and societal standards of acceptable behavior.

Poppa Ledsome, rumor had it, once stuck a pistol in his neighbor's mouth because the man didn't want to pay Matthew for mowing his yard because the job, by the neighbor's lawn-care standards, was not satisfactory.

"It wasn't loaded, he was just scaring him," they said.

The Ledsomes were a calculated risk that my father was willing to take. Those were *his* people. *The Least*. He could talk their language. Like the naive teenager who thinks he can change a cheating lover, my father believed in the reformation project that was the three Ledsome Bears. When they bounced through the door that first day, my father instantly pegged each brother a champion boxer. But it was Chris who emerged as the true talent; there was no mistaking the hierarchy of the Ledsome entourage. Chris quickly became *the fighter*, everyone else the cheering section. Unlike his older brother Nate, losing his first amateur bout did little to diminish Chris Ledsome's playground bravado—Chris was never in a fight that he, at least outwardly, didn't think he'd won. Once my father convinced him that fitness was just as important as toughness, things took off.

Six months into it, the middle Ledsome Bear became Lo's Gym's second *Chris* to win a state championship.

***

The rumor was that Jeremiah's mother had checked into a chemical dependency center in southeast Ohio and that he would be staying with the Ledsome Bears until she got her act together. Jeremiah's father wasn't in the picture, they said.

Momma and Poppa Ledsome took in Jeremiah without hesitation— six people living in a two-bedroom home located in the closest thing to *the projects* we have in small-town Appalachia. During the warm months, Jeremiah and Nate would sleep out in the pop-up camper in the driveway. At least that was the word around the gym. I never asked.

Jeremiah Harris was a first cousin to the Ledsome Bears, from Momma Ledsome's side of the family. He was kin, but he sure as hell didn't fit the mold. Jeremiah wasn't big, brash, or intimidating. Jeremiah was pathetic, a gangly mess. He probably weighed a buck twenty soaking wet—when he removed his shirt, you could count each and every one of his protruding ribs.

Jeremiah Harris was 18 years old when Poppa Ledsome first bused him down to Lo's Gym with the rest of the Ledsome Bears; Chris Ledsome had just won the first of his back-to-back state championships. Jeremiah was quiet that day. I remember him mostly setting in the back of the gym with Momma and Poppa Ledsome. It was like that for a while. Jeremiah sat and watched.

"Hey, Jeremiah, let's hit the mitts for a little bit. C'mon, it's no big deal," my father said, breaking the tension.

It took a little nudging from Poppa Ledsome, but my father finally got Jeremiah off the metal folding chair and into the makeshift boxing ring. My father loved working the mitts with guys like Jeremiah.

Pap! Pap!

"Hey, you've got one hell of a left hook, Jeremiah."

Pap! Pap!

"We might have another state champ right here."

Pap! Pap!

"You see that Chris? Your cousin can bang a little bit too."

Ding!

"I'm gonna call you 'Left Hook' Harris," my father said after the third and final round, slapping Jeremiah on the back with one of the mitts, knocking Jeremiah forward slightly.

Jeremiah's painfully crooked teeth revealed themselves to me for the first time, his Coke-bottle frames steadily sliding down the sweaty slope of his thin, pointy nose. Jeremiah Harris had gone three rounds on the mitts, was completely exhausted, and was damn proud of it. He had caught the bug, just like the rest of us. Before Jeremiah "Left Hook" Harris came along, Chris was typically the only member of the Ledsome entourage doing any work. Nate and Matthew were there because they didn't have anywhere else to go. They'd hit the mitts with my father and then stand around and talk with the rest of the boxers—or flirt with girls if there were any in the gym. Jeremiah, on the other hand, gradually started flirting with the sport of boxing.

At first, Jeremiah wanted to learn how to hit the heavy bag. Next, Jeremiah wanted to learn how to hit the speed bag. Jeremiah wore the same black pleather jacket day in, day out, regardless of the weather; the same worn-out Ohio State Buckeyes cap with the severely bent brim. When he would work out, which wasn't much at first, he trained in dusty blue jeans and wore tan hunting boots while he hit the mitts with my father. I never took him for a serious fighter, despite the fact that he gradually began training seriously. About three months into it, Jeremiah asked if he could spar. It must have been eating at Jeremiah somewhere behind his withdrawn demeanor.

Jeremiah's early sparring sessions were a sad sight. There wasn't a single guy in the gym Jeremiah could whip. He had no punching power. He had horrible defense. A strong gust of wind could knock him over. Jeremiah was Popeye before the spinach. It wasn't pretty.

"Hey, you did good in there today, Jeremiah."

"You're getting better, I tell ya."

"One of these days, you're gonna land that left hook on someone's chin and knock 'em cold," my father would say after sparring sessions, trying to pick up the pieces of Jeremiah's fragile psyche.

Like most things in life, my father was cautious about sparring. A bad sparring match would run a kid off—he'd get whipped and you'd never see him again. My father wasn't in the business of running kids off or getting them hurt. At this point, he mostly viewed the gym as a community center, a safe haven for poor and troubled kids. He didn't care if any of the guys competed or became champions. Rarely would he let fighters take part in what trainers call "live sparring." The only exception was, of course, Chris Ledsome.

Back then Chris was the unofficial bouncer of Lo's Gym Boxing Club. When townies, or bullies, or drunks found their way into the gym, my father would shepherd them into the ring with the middle Ledsome Bear.

"I got this teenage boy that needs taught a lesson. You need to get in there and show him a thing or two," my father would say.

Chris would pound the townies, bullies, and drunks into the ropes or bludgeon them into submission in less than a round. My father had no tolerance for townies, bullies, or drunks. He couldn't risk having them around. The church was going to throw us out eventually, he figured. He was simply trying to delay the inevitable.

Roger Hatfield[56] probably got it the worst. Roger showed up one evening, just before closing time, smelling like a fifth of vodka, slurring his speech, ranting about *goddamn pussies.*

"I got this teenage boy that needs taught a lesson. You need to get in there and show him a thing or two."

Roger was probably a tough customer back in the day, but at this point he was just a few years shy of 50, looked 60, and was emaciated from the drinking, drugs, and poverty. As my father gloved up Chris, who'd already completed his daily workout, Roger began stretching and shadowboxing in the mirror. It was Otis Campbell meets Richard Simmons. The routine sparked laughter from a few of the boxers who'd stuck around to see the familiar show.

"Roger, you're not going to kick him, are you?" Jason Bragg asked, leaning over the top rope, trying to mask his amusement.

"Fuck 'em!" Roger belted out in an inebriated southern drawl, as he continued the shadowboxing and staggering.

The sparring session didn't last 20 seconds. Chris landed a one-two combination that further sent Roger Hatfield off the beaten path of sobriety.

"Damn, we outta burn those things. They've probably got hepatitis

C all over them," Jason whispered into the earhole of the headgear as he unfastened Chris Ledsome's bloody boxing gloves.

Jeremiah and I had a ringside seat for that one. As I glanced away from Roger's contorted frame, trying not to laugh, I caught a glimpse of Jeremiah beaming with pride, wearing a grin that stretched for what seemed like a country mile, his elbows resting on the canvas as he peered into the elevated boxing ring from underneath the bottom rope.

We didn't say a word to each other. We didn't need to. I could read his mind.

Jeremiah Harris wanted to be a big man, just like his little cousin.

***

The large portrait of professional football star Randy Moss that hangs in the gymnasium at Dupont Middle School serves as something of a shrine to the local sports hero. Every time we brought fighters to a show hosted at the old Dupont High School in Bell, West Virginia, our guys would stop and stare at the portrait upon entering the gymnasium. They were in awe of the Randy Moss mythology, inspired and suspicious of the idea of a local boy making it all the way to the big time. Other than the oversized picture of Moss, the gymnasium wasn't much—folding metal bleachers, outdated basketball hoops, a rickety boxing ring decorated with a plastic red tarp that hid the undercarriage of the ring from spectators. The shows were sparsely attended; fight cards of ten bouts or less. We'd often regret the one-hour pilgrimage to Randy Moss's hometown. For whatever reason, things always turned out badly.

Things turned out badly for Jeremiah "Left Hook" Harris in his first amateur bout. He was matched up against a dark-skinned Italian kid from Ironton, Ohio, with a record of two wins and one loss. It was the fairest fight my father could find for Jeremiah; most of our guys had to make their debuts against boxers who'd already had more than a handful of bouts. That's West Virginia amateur boxing, I suppose. You fight or you don't. If you wait around for an even fight, you'll likely do more waiting than fighting.

The Dupont Middle School show opened with Chris Short going up against the kid from Ironton who'd whipped Craig Wright at the Marvin Gothard Classic. Chris fought a smart but overly defensive fight, and lost a close decision. Chris Ledsome was next up for our gym; he was matched up against Joey Summers for the second time in three months. Once again, that's West Virginia amateur boxing. If you stay active, you'll likely end up fighting the same guy four or five times a year. If you wait around for a new opponent, you likely do more waiting than fighting.

Joey Summers was a hulking young man, an ogre-sized teenager, whom Chris would always pummel but just couldn't knock out. In their previous bout, Joey had defenselessly extended his left glove to Chris after the ding of the opening bell. The touching of gloves before a fight is a time-honored tradition of sportsmanship established by the Marquis of Queensberry rules during the early 1800s. Chris extended his left glove as well, but it was not to take part in boxing's answer to a gentlemanly handshake. When fighters tried to touch gloves with Chris, he'd use his left hand to intentionally blind his opponents from the thunderous overhand right that quickly followed.

Whap!

Poor Joey Summers.

The Chris Ledsome vs. Joey Summers rematch at Dupont Middle School was more of the same; Chris pounded Joey and Joey took it beautifully. Lo's Gym was one for two on the night when Jeremiah Harris got the call that he was next up.

Jeremiah hadn't said much since we arrived at the gymnasium. He was a quiet kid so I didn't think much of it. In retrospect, I'm certain that Jeremiah was rendered mute by fear. I stayed back with Jeremiah in the locker room while Jason Bragg and my father worked the corner for Chris's fight. I warmed Jeremiah up on the mitts, offered some rudimentary boxing advice, and tried my best to keep him loose. After the ring announcer declared Chris Ledsome the winner of the bout, I led Jeremiah out of the locker room and out onto the basketball court. Jeremiah's headgear looked far too large for his tiny Q-tip-shaped head, his skinny arms dangling at his side, as if his boxing gloves were too heavy to lift.

The dark-skinned kid from Ironton, Ohio, made his way to the ring first. Jason Bragg ushered Chris Ledsome back to the locker room and my father met Jeremiah and me at the three-point line. I was watching the dark-skinned kid from Ironton climb through the ropes, waiting for the ring announcer to call Jeremiah's name, when I heard my father ask, "You okay, champ?"

Jeremiah had scurried from my side. He was heading in the wrong direction, away from the ring and toward the large plastic garbage can located directly below the oversized portrait of Randy Moss.

"And, fighting out of the blue corner, from Lo's Gym Boxing Club in Cowen, West Virginia . . . Jeremiah Harris," the announcer called over the microphone.

Silence followed by a steady murmur from the crowd.

With his gloves helplessly clinging to the rim of the plastic garbage can, half of Jeremiah Harris disappeared from my sight. The mouthpiece was the first to go. The sounds of projectile vomiting, followed by disgusting grunts and moans, echoed the walls of the trash can. I remember my father rubbing Jeremiah's back with soft comforting pats. I remember the referee, the ring announcer, and the dark-skinned kid from Ironton, Ohio, all peering out of the ring with looks of concern and confusion. I remember the wide-eyed stares of the folks in the crowd. I remember standing alone at the three-point line, wide open. I remember Jeremiah's slow emergence from the plastic trash can, the discoloration and bewilderment on his hairless face. The mouthpiece was long gone. I remember glancing upward from the scene, taking in the large portrait of a teenage football legend from Rand, West Virginia, perched on one knee, his furrowed eyebrows stern and determined.

My father refused to let Jeremiah go through with the fight and the referee granted the dark-skinned kid from Ironton, Ohio, victory by disqualification. Jeremiah "Left Hook" Harris lost his amateur boxing debut without even stepping into the ring. He was 0–1 before ever climbing through the ropes.

***

Jeremiah was back in the gym on Monday. The poor guy had to hear about the Dupont incident for weeks, with most of the teasing coming from the three Ledsome Bears.

Behind my father's back, guys started calling Jeremiah "upchuck."

"Show us that famous upchuck punch, Jeremiah," they'd tease.

I never called Jeremiah Harris "upchuck," but I did think it was a more appropriate nickname than "Left Hook" Harris.

Much to my surprise, Jeremiah signed up for the Charleston show a few months later. Signing his name on the bout sheet took some nerve.

The Charleston show was a large pro/am card—with boxing clubs coming from as far away as the famous Kronk Gym in Detroit. Every serious boxer in our gym wanted to be on that card. Ten days before the Charleston show, the promoter called and said he had matches for Chris Short, Chris Ledsome, Claudia Cline, Dustin Wood, Jennings Barger, Brandon Holcomb, and Jeremiah Harris. That's West Virginia amateur boxing—you never quite knew if you were going to get a fight until the bell rang.

The lights were just as bright as I thought they'd be, the setup impressive. It was a crowd of fancy dressers—blazers and blue jeans, floral prints and pearls. There were well over 1,000 paying customers in the Charleston Civic Center that night. Because the fight card was so large—18 amateur bouts and two professional fights—the show started at three in the afternoon. Lo's Gym had the second and third fights of the night.

Brandon Holcomb,[57] a Lo's Gym newbie, was first up. Brandon was matched against a kid from the Lexington Legends boxing club in Kentucky.

Brandon Holcomb, 17 years old at the time, was a strong puncher from a tough background. He had been training at Lo's Gym for about two months and was giving a few guys fits in sparring. I knew he was going to fare well, but apparently he didn't. After first laying eyes on his opponent, Brandon removed his mouthpiece with his right boxing glove, and disapprovingly glared at my father.

"Oh great, I gotta fight the guy with the robe?"

"What are you talking about, Brandon?"

Brandon's opponent was a stocky blond kid, decked out in Kentucky blue boxing shoes, matching trunks, and a matching robe. Most amateur boxers don't wear boxing robes into the ring. It was certainly the first time I'd ever seen an amateur boxer wear a robe before a match. Perhaps the ensemble came as a matching set. I didn't ask.

"Check this guy's shit out . . . he is wearing a robe . . . I bet this guy has 20 fucking fights," Brandon shouted at my father, violently stuffing the mouthpiece back into its rightful place.

"Brandon, the kid is 0–1, I checked his passbook. He's just as nervous as you are. Now settle your ass down," my father responded.

"Great! I gotta fight the guy in the robe," Brandon slobbered and complained, shaking his head in disapproval.

Fear made Brandon belligerent.

"Look, Brandon, they're not going to let him wear that robe during the fight. Don't worry about it," my father responded, looking increasingly unnerved.

When my father became unnerved, I'd usually fall silent or stay out of his way. Most of the boxers at Lo's Gym never got to meet this side of my father; guys would occasionally have to learn the hard way.

"I gotta fight the guy in the robe? That's my luck," Brandon continued to mutter to anybody who would listen.

The three Ledsome Bears made their way over to Brandon to check out the commotion. They teased and fueled the fire, confirming Brandon's fears that a guy wearing a boxing robe had to be something special.

"It's a setup, Lo. I bet that guy has 20 fights," Brandon slobbered.

A prefight panic attack was not all that uncommon for Lo's Gym fighters, but Brandon was striving for new heights. He began pacing back and forth, shaking his head rapidly, flinging his arms in disapproval. Brandon was the bewildered tourist who has just discovered his or her wallet is missing.

"I promise you that he isn't going to take the robe off and hit you with it," my father finally shouted in Brandon's direction.

The ring announcer called Brandon's name and he, my father, and Jason Bragg made their way to the ring.

The motivational speech didn't work. Brandon was on the bicycle for all three rounds. He ran and hid and ran some more. It was a performance straight out of a Jerry Lee Lewis comedy routine. The kid from Lexington wasn't all that impressive. The robe won a unanimous decision.

Jason Bragg worked the corner with my father for that one, so I can't be certain of what was said between rounds. What I do know is that when I escorted Jeremiah "Left Hook" Harris to the ring for his bout, we found my father stone-faced as Medusa. As my father held the ropes up for Jeremiah to enter the ring, he grabbed Jeremiah underneath his boxing jersey and firmly pinched the skin that connected Jeremiah's pectoral muscle to his underarm.

"You better fucking fight, Jeremiah," my father shouted in an angry and raspy tone, pinching and slightly twisting Jeremiah's skin further before finally letting go and allowing him to enter the ring.

I'd never heard my father talk to Jeremiah or to any of the boxers that way before. One of my father's biggest flaws as a trainer was that he almost completely focused on the positives, rarely getting on a kid and telling him what he was doing wrong. My father's formula was to build a kid up, give him as much confidence and self-respect as possible, occasionally nudging him about minor flaws in his technique. This was a different Lo, one I was more familiar with than were the boxers down at Lo's Gym.

Jeremiah's opponent entered the ring second. He was a tall, freckle-faced kid with a muscular build, fighting out of Buster Douglas's boxing club in Columbus, Ohio. The freckle-faced kid from Columbus's passbook said he was 2–2, but you never knew whether or not you could trust an out-of-state passbook. A kid would be 2–2 as Frank Jones in Kentucky and 12–3 under the name Thomas Peck in Ohio. Even Jeremiah's 0–1 record was misleading, if you really wanted to get technical about it.

During the fighter introductions, I could faintly hear my father cursing underneath his breath. He was still heated over Brandon's fight. I didn't look in my father's direction, but I could hear the cursing.

"Afraid of a goddamn boxing robe."

"I've never seen anything like it."

"Who gives a shit about a goddamn robe?"

I was more nervous about working the corner with my father than I was about how Jeremiah was going to fare in the fight.

When Jeremiah returned to the corner after the referee instructions, my father gave him one last piece of advice before the bell rang.

"You'd better fucking fight, Jeremiah."

I didn't have high hopes for what was about to take place. But at least Jeremiah had made it into the ring this time. Moral victory?

Ding!

The freckle-faced kid from Columbus landed the first punch of the fight, a swift left jab.

Pap!

Then he feinted with the left and landed a lead right.

Pap! Pap!

I knew that any minute we were going to see the bottoms of Jeremiah's Chuck Taylor tennis shoes. He'd finally ditched the hunting boots.

Pap! Pap!

Jeremiah looked like something out of a 1920s black-and-white boxing highlight reel, his chest awkwardly puffed out, his elbows in tight, his gloves firmly planted in front of his face, his head cocked back, as to avoid damage via good posture.

Pap! Pap!

The freckle-faced kid from Columbus was a stick-and-move boxer—he'd feint and float his way around the ring. Jeremiah was, of course, the antonym to such artistry, dragging his right foot behind his left, inching his way toward and away from the action like a wounded dog with a hurt hind leg.

As the timekeeper smacked the apron, warning the boxers that ten seconds remained in the first round, Jeremiah finally threw his first meaningful combination—a jab and right hand that didn't land, followed by a left hook that did.

Smack!

The freckle-faced kid from Columbus staggered slightly, the punch landed flush and knocked him off balance for a few seconds. He quickly recovered and closed the round with a hard left jab that penetrated Jeremiah's 1920s-style defense.

Ding!

When Jeremiah came back to the corner, I figured he'd quit on the stool. He'd landed a good left hook, but lost the first round badly.

As Jeremiah sat down on the stool, my father violently yanked the mouthpiece out of his mouth.

"How many times did you throw the left hook?"

"Tell me!" my father repeated twice.

"One," Jeremiah muttered as he gasped for air.

"And it landed," my father urged.

"You hurt that kid. . . ."

My father was never big on Knute Rockne speeches. He was no Teddy Atlas in the corner. My father typically began his work by asking the fighter if he wanted to continue, even if the guy was winning big. He'd give the fighter a few sips of water; sometimes offer one or two comments. This was different. Brandon Holcomb had unhinged my father and my father was taking it out on poor Jeremiah Harris, who couldn't fight his way out of a paper bag, as the old folks say.

The timekeeper signaled for the chief seconds to exit the ring and Jeremiah rose from the stool.

"I want to win, Lo," Jeremiah said, as my father climbed through the ropes and out of the ring.

"Then throw that left hook like you want to win," my father responded from the other side of the ropes.

"My sister. I want to win this for her. My sister died," Jeremiah said through his mouthpiece.

It was the first we'd heard of it. We didn't even know Jeremiah had a sister.

My father paused, just for a moment, before walking down the wooden ring steps.

"Well, then throw your fucking left hook and win this for her," he replied.

The referee interrupted the conversation by tapping Jeremiah on the shoulder, Jeremiah's neck was sticking out of the ring as he continued to converse with my father.

Ding!

I was so caught up in the strange dialogue I almost forgot to sit down. I was lost in the pathos.

Pap! Pap! Pap!

The second round began just as did the first. The freckle-faced kid from Columbus landed a few jabs and feinted Jeremiah into a hard right hand. Jeremiah started firing back, but was landing only every other punch.

Pap! Pap! Pap!

I was looking downward, placing the spit bucket behind the stool, when it happened. As a corner man, I had a bad habit of placing myself in the wrong position, always missing the good stuff.

Whap!

You don't have to believe me. I wouldn't believe me either. But I'll be damned if Jeremiah Harris didn't throw a picture-perfect left hook that knocked the freckle-faced kid from Columbus flat on his ass.

When my eyes returned to the ring, the freckle-faced kid from Columbus was struggling to make it back to his feet. He was seriously dazed. You can always tell how seriously dazed a fighter is by the way a guy gets up from the canvas.

As the referee administered the mandatory eight count, Jeremiah looked to my father and pumped his fist in what appeared to be a victory celebration. I'd never seen Jeremiah do anything like that.

When the bout resumed, Jeremiah overwhelmed his opponent with a barrage of one-two-three combinations. Most of the punches were missing, but a few were landing.

Whap! Whap! Whap!

The freckle-faced kid from Columbus was covering up, wasn't fighting back. It went on like that for about 30 seconds or so.

Whap! Whap! Whap!

The referee called the fight. There was a roar from the crowd. It had been a fairly quick plot twist and the crowd apparently enjoyed surprise endings.

Jeremiah's long skinny arms stretched toward the heavens, in the same pose Muhammad Ali made famous over Cleveland Williams.

Jeremiah's celebration over his vanquished opponent was more shocking than the left hook that did the job. Of all the people in the world to have a moment like this, Jeremiah deserved it.

Jeremiah never boxed again. And why should he? That night in Charleston, West Virginia, he was champion of the world.

And I stopped calling him Jeremiah.

It was Jeremiah "Left Hook" Harris from then on.

***

Imagine an entire mountain, which in the late 1970s supplied Georgia Power with one million tons of coal annually, being traded to a company agent for a hog rifle.[58] Picture the locals who refused to sell their land being jailed and bound for refusing to sign on the dotted line.[59] Post–Civil War America brought about an age of industrial plundering. The captains of industry raided the mountains, acquiring the land they needed, acquiring the mineral rights to the surface land they didn't.

"That's the kind of thing you need to know when you buy property in West Virginia. The kind of thing that ought to be in the deed."

Those mineral rights are "heaven high and hell deep," my father's mining supervisor once told me.

In West Virginia, King Coal always had the political upper hand. Back in the old days, it was loopholes such as Johnson's Law, "a statute that exempted corporations from consequences of accidents that occurred on their property."[60] Hence the familiar Appalachian cultural adage "the company gets the profits; the miners get the shaft."[61] When economic times get tough, so do the coal company lawyers. They'd shut down the mine, file bankruptcy, and cheat the workers out of their retirement money. It's the oldest trick in the book.

In 2015, for example, Patriot Coal Co., a spin-off of St. Louis–based Peabody Energy, filed bankruptcy, its second bankruptcy in three years. After filing bankruptcy, the company revealed a plan to divert money that had been set aside for health care benefits for 969 retired coal miners to pay "bankruptcy lawyers and other costs."[62] Now you see them, now you don't. Hocus pocus. No more health care benefits.

Over the years, hill folk got wise to the fact that crooks and thieves ran the show. Somewhere along the way, families began sticking it right back to the system, finding ways to make the system work to their advantage. If you believe the mass media's stereotypes of outsiders, you'd say welfare culture, or entitlement culture as it is often called, has run amuck in rural Appalachia. Folks are too damn lazy to work. They want a handout. Those hillbillies want a government check just for being poor and lazy. There are plenty of Appalachian outsiders who'll sell you this version of Appalachia, and a few insiders who'd promote such an idea as well.

In the *New York Times* best-selling memoir *Hillbilly Elegy*, the author J. D. Vance offers up a tough-love critique of an Appalachian culture in crisis. Kentucky born and Yale educated, Vance's bootstraps narrative garnered a healthy share of mainstream popularity during the 2016 election, one in which rural working-class Appalachians were given much credit for Donald Trump's political success. "Forgotten America," the pundits called it. Vance's rhetorical strategy takes a page out of the conservative Reagan-era playbook of personal responsibility—a repackaged version of the "culture of poverty" argument that blames Appalachian hillbillies for their own poverty. The memoir, as Sarah Jones of *New Republic* correctly diagnoses, "is little more than a list of myths about welfare queens repackaged as a primer on the white working class."[63] Throughout the text, Vance provides personal examples to back his cultural diagnosis. He tells us of shiftless coworkers who get fired for not working and then take to social media to blame the government for a failing economy. His stories demonstrate the shortcomings of the mountain folk mindset, the value systems of hillbillies who spend their way into poverty, blaming outsiders for Appalachia's continuing struggle. The problem with the culture of poverty explanation is that it fits nicely within the propaganda narrative that the extractive industries give to outsiders. We, the captains of industry, brought economic opportunity to Appalachia, but these hillbillies are just too damn stupid to take advantage. The workers' comp cheats are simply quitters; they've given up. Such a narrative leaves little room for the stories of fighters. It suggests that everything Appalachian folks need to *make it* is actually within reach. It ignores the fact that our world views and value systems have been heavily conditioned by extractive industry culture.

That was never how my father saw it. He'd been a coal miner his entire adult life, but he didn't judge the guy who stuck it back to the system. He didn't look down on the guys who lived a carpe diem, almost fatalistic, lifestyle either. That wasn't the life my father wanted for his family, but he certainly understood folks who'd been conditioned to see it that way. The trailer park hustlers lived a life that was, in some ways, closer to the truth. When a country boy had the chance to stick it back to the coal mines, or the government for that matter, the chickens were simply coming home to roost.

In Cowen, West Virginia, folks don't spend their way into poverty. They are born into it. They know the judges aren't gonna give them a fair shake when it goes to the scorecards. They know a fixed fight when they see one. Working with Jeremiah and the three Ledsome Bears down at Lo's Gym was an education in cyclical poverty. It was a college course on Appalachian cultural value systems. These guys were from the other side of the coal mining coin, so to speak. Their fathers didn't toil away in the mines, didn't give themselves to the Appalachian American dream. Their folks saw it all for what it was and said *fuck it*. But don't call them quitters; these guys are fighters too. Tough as hell, I came to learn. To those who are quick to call for personal accountability as a solution to Appalachia's socioeconomic problems, I offer this Webster County fairytale, the story of Jeremiah and the Three Bears. It is the story of a fleeting moment of happily ever after. It is the story of fighters born into unfair and unforgiving circumstances. Rather, it is a story of chickens coming home to roost.

Chapter 8

RING GIRLS

In *Strategies for Survival: Women's Work in Southern West Virginia Coal Camps*, Janet Greene positions the role of coal miner wife as an "integral [and often unrecognized] segment of the mining community" during the early days of West Virginia coal mining. As one might suspect, "women of the southern West Virginia coalfields had few employment opportunities outside the home between 1900 and 1950."[64] The primary work of coal miner wives was, however, "critical to coal production: they fed the miner, washed his clothes, took care of him when sick or injured, and raised the children who would become the next generation of mineworkers."[65] These women didn't sack and lug coal, but they sure as hell worked.

And that's how it was for most of my childhood in Cowen, West Virginia. Very few of my friends had mothers who worked outside the traditional domestic duties outlined in Greene's study. I had a few friends with teacher moms. I had a few friends with nurse moms. My own mother was a hairdresser. I didn't know anybody who had a coal miner momma. Toughness isn't a virtue found only in the darkness of a deep mine. Our mothers were miracle workers during tough times, portraits of endurance and perseverance. Our mothers canned food and hoed the garden. They picked the beans and strung the beans and boiled the beans. They cooked the venison. They added just the right amount of spices to the deer jerky. Our mothers made sure that we ate well enough to forget we were poor.

Our mothers were portraits of humility. They clipped coupons. They balanced the checkbook. They faced the embarrassment of standing in line at the WIC[66] office, spent food stamps at Foodland. Our mothers were adept at *finding a way*. They were the caretakers of miners and miners-to-be. They were sometimes our only source of love and affection. Our mothers wrapped the Christmas presents and baked the birthday cakes and helped us with our spelling words. They loved us; they protected us. We could cry to our mothers but no one else.

Our mothers accepted their lot in life and didn't much complain about it. They rolled up their sleeves and went toe-to-toe with patriarchy and misogyny on a daily basis; our towns were built of such thinking. *A woman's place is in the kitchen. A woman should stay home and raise the young'ns. A woman should stand by her man.* Janet Greene has it right. Our mothers were an important piece of the puzzle. If not for our mothers, the whole extractive industry shebang would have fallen in on itself.

Our mothers were strong and beautiful. I'm not talking Daisy Duke, or Elly Mae, or Grandma Clampett in her rocking chair. They were financial planners. Tomato canners. They were gardeners and teachers and doctors and nurses and preachers and psychiatrists. Their endurance was the by-product of the material circumstances of their being. Our mothers weren't coal miners, but they were goddamn tough.

And, every now and then, they'd have daughters.

***

Claudia Cline was Goldilocks if Goldilocks had a tremendous right hand and the bears didn't mind having her around. Curly blond hair. Dangling turquoise earrings. Sweetheart dimples. Pearly whites lined up like a Hollywood starlet, the work of some overpaid Summersville orthodontist. She was everything that a boxer is not. Claudia was Cinderella if Cinderella had TKOed her evil stepmother, a feminine paradox. Our wives, girlfriends, and significant others found her just as intimidating as did her opponents.

Claudia Cline arrived at Lo's Gym at the age of 17. Folks around Cowen knew her as the Nicholas County Potato Festival Beauty Queen. Claudia ran in all of the local pageants. She won them too. On several occasions, I caught guys taking it all in, sneaking secret glimpses in the mirror of our upstairs boxing gym.

For the most part, there were two kinds of girls who hung around Lo's Gym: (1) fighters—young girls who were a little rough around the edges, born into problematic family situations; and (2) fans—scantily clad hormonal teenage girls looking to pick up man-boys—ladies with their minds on the back-road pleasures of rural nightlife. When Claudia Cline showed up that first day, I figured she fell into the second category.

Things people likely said to Claudia during her first day at Lo's Gym: "You're too pretty to box."

"You're going to ruin that pretty face with this boxing stuff."

"Stay from away from my boyfriend."

But I digress.

Claudia was from Nicholas County, Webster County's slightly more affluent neighbor to the south. She was one of the few boxers in our gym who came from *money*. When I was a kid, I thought everyone from Nicholas County was a Romney—an Appalachian Rockefeller. She had it pretty good, we figured. Claudia drove a nice car, had nice clothes, and lived in a nice house. Her looks. Her gender. Her socioeconomic background. None of it fit.

"Hey Todd, climb in here and go a few rounds with Claudia on the mitts," my father shouted across the noisy ebb and flow of the gym, smirking ever so slightly.

"And see what you think," he added.

Claudia had just gone two rounds with my father, her curly blond hair ringed with sweat, her doe eyes shaded by the Everlast headgear, her dimpled cheeks flushed.

Claudia was in shape, but she was a pageant girl. She was a rich girl, a future Tae Bo instructor or fitness enthusiast, perhaps.

She'd never actually climb through the ropes and compete.

Smack!

When I felt Claudia's overhand right collide with the mitt, I instantly changed my opinion.

"Hold up. Have you boxed before?"

The Everlast heavy bag down in the basement belonged to Claudia's stepfather, but it was her therapy, a temporary release from the anger she hid like a teenage secret. Claudia hit the bag more than he did.

Claudia's biological parents divorced when she was just four years old, and her father remarried when she was six. Claudia began stockpiling the gunpowder that fueled her lethal overhand right during those formative years. When he'd miss her basketball games, when his new children took priority over his older ones, Claudia's father sparked the flame.

"One year my brother and I asked for a computer for Christmas . . . and my father wrapped up his old computer and gave it to us . . . he had bought a new computer for his family," Claudia once told me.

The popular girls at Nicholas County junior high school were equally to blame. They'd call Claudia "thunder thighs," insinuate that her muscular body denoted lesbianism. The teasing led to body image issues, the body image issues led to low self-esteem—more gunpowder. Claudia would take it out on the heavy bag after school each evening.

Beauty pageants were Claudia's mother's solution. Claudia was bright, well spoken, physically fit—she'd show well, Claudia's mother figured. She was right. Winning local beauty pageants helped Claudia become more comfortable in her own skin; the tiaras were a validation of sorts. I'm not sure how things would have played out if Claudia had lost those pageants. More gunpowder, I suppose.

But organized sports were Claudia's primary outlet. She excelled at softball, basketball, and track and field. Claudia played for her younger brother, Harrison, although she never told him as much. Harrison received his first kidney transplant when he was only 16 years old; he was in and out of the hospital for most of Claudia's teenage years. Harrison's medical condition required that he endure eight hours of peritoneal dialysis each night; sports were out of the question. Claudia played because Harrison couldn't.

So maybe the sounds of Claudia pounding the heavy bag down in the basement were too much to bear? Maybe the fit was just too obvious?

When Lo's Gym Boxing Club started gaining local notoriety, Claudia's stepfather recommended that she give it a try. Her mother reluctantly made the 20-minute drive to Cowen, watched cautiously from the back of the gym, suspicious of the idea.

"No, I've never boxed anything but a heavy bag," Claudia replied, in her soft southern accent.

***

Our gym's first boxing road trip was at the 2004 Sternwheel Regatta, an annual Labor Day festival that celebrates the river-town history of Charleston, West Virginia. The bouts took place outdoors, in a makeshift arena out on Magic Island, a five-acre island surrounded by the Kanawha River. The conditions were brutal. It was every bit of 90 degrees on Magic Island that day.

Claudia was matched up against a girl from Pikeville, Kentucky. Her opponent was tall and slender, with the legs of a track star. She held a sizable height and reach advantage, so my father stayed on Claudia about slipping the jab and getting inside.

"Slip and dip . . . slip and dip," my father repeated, shooting his left-hand pad toward Claudia's headgear as if it were a straight left jab, Claudia instantly dodging the punch and countering with a right to the body.

My father and Claudia worked magic on the hand pads. It was a kata, a dance, ballet even. My father believed in those mitts more than most trainers do. When working a fighter on the hand pads, he became a puppeteer. He could force fighters to do the right thing.

And Claudia Cline was quite the dance partner. She landed each punch with precision, she played the hand pads like a musical instrument—the ends of her blond cornrowed hair flapping up and down as she slipped punches and retaliated with force.

Pap! Pap! Pap!

A few 30-second intervals on the mitts, with a little pathos-heavy rhetoric in between, and my father would have a boxer ready to do battle.

Claudia played the hand pads out on Magic Island that day. A small crowd gathered to watch the prefight show. *Oohs and Aahs.*

There were no locker rooms out on Magic Island so the girl from Pikeville probably heard and saw the slip-and-dip hand-pad routine. Someone from her gym sent a spy over to our side of the ring. It was a real covert operation.

"How many fights that girl got?"

The spy looked to be in his mid-fifties—he was balding, double-chinned, a protruding beer belly covered by a University of Kentucky t-shirt—the shirt was a dead giveaway. You don't see many of those in my home state.

"She lost her first fight . . . about five weeks ago, that'd make her 0–1," I answered sarcastically, but honestly.

At this point, Claudia was one month removed from her amateur boxing debut at the Marvin Gothard Classic. She'd been in there with a 23-year-old police officer from Bullet Bill Hopkins's gym in Fairmont,

West Virginia. There wasn't a fair thing about that one so I understood where Kentucky Spy was coming from. Lady Cop was five years older and almost ten pounds heavier than Claudia. We'd been lied to about her ring experience as well.

But it had been the fight of the night. Both boxers scored standing eight counts, both left the ring with bloody noses and black eyes. Claudia lost the bout to Lady Cop, but it was a spectacular debut nonetheless. Claudia proved she had the *stuff*, as the old-timers say.

The very next day Claudia made a mandatory appearance at the Nicholas County Auditorium as the reigning Nicholas County Potato Festival Queen, the cornrows still in her hair, the shiner under her right eye covered by a thick coat of Maybelline.

"Really?" Kentucky Spy replied in a matter-of-fact tone.

"Yep. Really."

"This should be a good one then," Kentucky Spy said, his hands firmly planted in the pockets of his wrinkled cargo shorts as he slowly meandered away from the small crowd of onlookers.

Claudia was first in the ring.

The girl from Pikeville was called up next.

My father and I were perched on our stools in the blue corner as the referee offered instructions to the fighters at center ring; beads of sweat trickled down the backs of our necks as we peered up into the ring, awaiting the opening bell.

Those final moments before the opening bell feel the same for trainers as they do for fighters. After the first punch has landed, that changes, of course.

"You slide the stool in the ring, have the spit bucket ready. I've got the water bottle," my father instructed, quickly glancing in my direction.

Before fights, my father was a nervous wreck. Micromanaging was his way of dealing with the nerves. He planned everything that could be planned; he'd unnecessarily repeat those plans to me when he became nervous.

"What's going on?" I asked, noticing that Claudia, her Pikeville opponent, and the referee seemed to be taking part in an unusually lengthy conversation.

The two fighters and the referee stood center ring, heads bobbing in conversation, for what seemed like a good two minutes.

The conversation finally came to an end when the referee waved his arms into the air, as if he'd just stopped the fight on an injured combatant. The girl from Pikeville returned to the red corner with her headgear hung low. My father and I scurried up the wooden steps to meet Claudia on the ring apron.

"She quit," Claudia shouted through her mouthpiece, her eyes full of anger and disappointment.

It was the last time my father danced like that with Claudia before a fight.

A few months after the Sternwheel Regatta, we found ourselves in what appeared to be a hollowed-out Heck's Department Store, located at the end of a small shopping center in Ashland, Kentucky.

Mayfield Pennington, head trainer at the Pikeville Boxing Club, assured my father his girl was "trained up," ready to go through with the fight. My father had learned his lesson; it was all handshakes and *howdy-do*. He was Dustin Hoffman, an Academy Award winner. I don't play cards, but I can imagine the thrill poker players must get when they know they have a good hand.

At this point, Claudia had won more beauty pageants than boxing matches. Amateur boxing is hardly a thriving enterprise in the Mountain State; the women's boxing landscape is even more barren. More often than not, we had to *travel abroad* to get Claudia a match.

When the bell finally rang, the girl from Pikeville circled the ring, opening the bout with a lifeless jab that Claudia easily slipped and countered.

Claudia's thunderous overhand right landed squarely on the jaw of her opponent, the punch echoing off the walls of the hollowed-out Heck's Department Store like the first serve of a racquetball game.

The girl from Pikeville doubled over into the ropes and Claudia fed her a stiff left hook on the way down.

***

April 1989. Cowen, West Virginia.

Kathy Cochran was a 25-year-old bartender at a local watering hole, Red Gables. The bar, which featured a back room full of weights and workout equipment, was located just a few miles from Willoughby Trailer Park, where my family lived at the time. Every now and then, my father would spend evenings out at Red Gables, working out and shooting the shit with the local boys. The gym wasn't much. The bar wasn't much either. But Red Gables it was.

Kathy Cochran, by my father's account, was "tougher than a pine knot." She once wrestled a live bear to the amusement of a packed house of drunken Red Gables patrons. The bear had been declawed and was wearing a muzzle, but Kathy was half in the bag so I'm not sure if you could call it a fair fight either way. True story.

My father had seen Kathy mix it up more than a few times, drinks and punches.

"She'd hit a man just as quick as she'd sock a woman," my father once said.

But Kathy Cochran wasn't an athlete. She was bar room fit. It didn't take much convincing from drunkards down at Red Gables to talk Kathy into fighting in the upcoming Beckley Toughman Contest.

The week before the tournament, my father couldn't resist the urge to try Kathy out on the hand pads. He didn't fancy himself a boxing trainer in those days, but he showed Kathy a few things—how to jab, how to throw a few combinations, how to tuck her chin and bend her knees. Back then, Jerry Thomas's traveling boxing circus was just starting to take off; the newly created women's division was an oddity. Everybody down at Red Gables figured Kathy would win the whole damn thing.

But Kathy Cochran didn't win the whole damn thing. In the championship bout of the 1989 Beckley Toughman Contest, Kathy Cochran lost a close but unanimous decision. Her opponent was a 22-year-old Concord University basketball player from Mullens, West Virginia. Her opponent's name was Christy Martin.

If you watched any of Mike Tyson's Pay-Per-View cards in the mid- to late 1990s, you've likely watched Christy Martin fight. After winning the Beckley Toughman Contest, Christy graduated from Concord, moved to Bristol, Tennessee, turned professional, and fought her way to a promotional deal with legendary boxing promoter Don King. Boxing under the name "The Coal Miner's Daughter," a tribute to her father's occupation and to her home state of West Virginia, Christy went on to become a world champion, fighting on televised undercard bouts for ring legends such as Julio Cesar Chavez, Felix Trinidad, Evander Holyfield, and, of course, Mike Tyson. The first female boxer to grace the cover of

Sports Illustrated (March 1996), Christy compiled a record of 49–7 (31 wins coming by knockout) during her illustrious career; she is, without question, *the* pioneering figure of female boxing.

"Who was tougher, the bear or Christy Martin?" I once asked Kathy Cochran down at Lo's Gym, her two boys running around the gym like kids in a candy store.

"Ain't no doubt about it," Kathy replied. "Christy."

***

June 2016. Canastota, New York.

My father and I had just taken exit 34 off the New York State Thruway, parked our car on the museum grounds, when we noticed a large crowd of autograph seekers forming around the outdoor stage of the International Boxing Hall of Fame. After moving to New York in the summer of 2011, I began attending the annual Boxing Hall of Fame festivities regularly. When my father could get some time away from the mines, he'd drive up to New York and we'd go together. You never knew who you'd run into on the streets of Canastota—Oscar De La Hoya, George Foreman, Sugar Ray Leonard, Marvin Hagler, Thomas Hearns, Roberto Duran—we'd taken pictures with all of these guys over the past few summers. We knew that a flock of Canastota autograph seekers, especially one that large, meant someone of merit was on the premises.

"I think that's Christy Martin," my father said, as we made our way toward the crowd.

I caught a glimpse of Christy's trademark smile.

"Yeah, that's Christy."

Dressed in a white button-up shirt and khaki pants, Christy looked more like a schoolteacher than a world champion boxer. I'd read that after retirement, Christy had fallen back on her original career plan, the BA in physical education she had earned from Concord University. But even at 48 years old, Christy looked to be in fighting condition. Students beware. The girl can punch.

"Okay, folks. We've got to get Christy to the next event. Back up, please," said members of the Boxing Hall of Fame event staff to the crowd as they formed a semicircle around Christy.

Christy continued to sign boxing gloves and photographs for the impatient crowd, the event staff doing their best to give her room amid the chaos.

My father and I hung back for just a second, taking in the scene, pondering as to whether or not it would be sensible to join the mob.

"Okay, folks. That's the last one. There will be plenty of time for autographs and pictures this weekend. We've got to get Christy to the next event," the lead staff member commanded as Christy handed an autographed program back to a fan.

"How about a quick picture with an old West Virginia coal miner?" my father shouted over the crowd.

Christy's eyes lit up, as if she'd suddenly awakened. The trademark smile returned to her face.

"Who said that?" Christy called back.

"Right here, Christy," my father called in his raspy voice.

The sea of fans slowly parted and my father and Christy Martin stood face-to-face for the first time in 27 years. They posed for a quick picture.

"What part of West Virginia are you guys from?" Christy asked.

We said Cowen and Christy nodded her head, familiar grounds.

"Kathy Cochran, an ol' girl from our town, was your opponent in the championship bout of that Beckley Toughman Contest. I was there, ringside," my father said.

"That's where it all started," Christy smirked, anxious to engage in conversation about the night she found her passion.

Christy didn't remember Kathy's name, but she sure as hell remembered the fight. Boxers never forget a good tussle. I wanted to mention Kathy's tune-up fight with the bear, but better judgment carried the day.

My father and Christy went back and forth about the fight for a few minutes, ignoring the impatient looks of the would-be autograph seekers.

"Are you a boxing trainer?" Christy asked.

"I trained fighters for a few years. I had a little gym in Cowen," he replied.

There was no fooling Christy; she could pick a boxing trainer out of the crowd just as easily as she could a coal miner.

"I always fought for the state of West Virginia. No matter where I trained . . . Florida, Tennessee, wherever, I always requested that I be announced as The Coal Miner's Daughter from West Virginia," Christy said.

"Well, you were always an inspiration to the fighters at my gym," my father quickly replied.

"You gotta be tough when you come from where we come from," Christy smirked.

"Sorry, guys, we've got to get Christy to the next event," the Boxing Hall of Fame staffers called, tightening the circle.

"That's especially true for women," my father added, his raspy voice cracking.

The Coal Miner's Daughter flashed one last smile, extending her hand to the only coal miner in the crowd.

"Thank you."

***

Taji, a rural district located north of the city of Baghdad, was once the primary center for the manufacturing of chemical weapons under the reign of Iraqi President Saddam Hussein. It was also the location for Myria Gumm's first and only boxing victory. The series of events that brought Myria Gumm from Cowen, West Virginia, to the headlining bout of Taji Fight Night was more gradual than spectacular, a familiar story for folks around my way.

Myria Gumm was a party-up-a-dirt-road-with-the-boys kind of West Virginia girl—as country as they come. Long brown hair. Deep brown eyes. A big heart. A short temper. Myria's extroverted personality always made her seem larger than her five-foot six-inch frame. She didn't come from privilege, but we all knew she was going places. Cowen is much too small for girls like that.

After graduating from Webster County High School in 2002, Myria enrolled at Ohio Northern University in Ada, Ohio. Myria was the only member of her small graduating class to attend an out-of-state college. She was hellbent on doing something different, in love with the romantic idea of getting out of her Podunk mountain town and seeing the world. Like most first-generation college students from around my way, Myria Gumm found herself up against the ropes.

One semester into it, Myria realized ONU wasn't for her, college perhaps. Her grades were mediocre, money was tight, and she was more than a little homesick.

Not that home life had been that easy for Myria. She'd lost her father at a young age, grew up in a single-parent home, spent a good portion of her time feeling alone, swallowing the anger.

"Myria had to grow up too quick," my wife once said to me—the two Cowen girls were close friends.

"She was doing laundry, taking care of adult responsibilities, while the rest of us girls were playing with Barbie dolls," Stephanie added.

Myria enlisted in the National Guard during winter break of her first semester at ONU. Myria was lost and the National Guard is *always ready, always waiting*.

Myria finished out the year at ONU, completed her basic training requirements during summer break, and returned to school in the fall of 2003.

But everything felt out of step; the college routine had slipped away from her ever so gradually. Myria dropped out of school at semester's end and returned *holme*.[67]

When Myria Gumm first walked through the doors of Lo's Gym in the summer of 2004, she was 20 years old, living out of a one-bedroom apartment in Summersville, West Virginia, working at a local Pizza Hut. At this point, Myria had no illusions about her future. She was to become a fighter for country, for Uncle Sam, for the American flag, for eagles, and everything else that is patriotic. The Pizza Hut gig was just a stop along the way as she figured out which branch of service she wanted to enlist in.

As Myria escorted Stephanie and me to our table, Pizza Hut menus folded beneath her arm, the two high school friends played a quick game of catch-up.

"You guys home from college for the summer?"

"Yeah. I'm working at the bank in Webster. Todd's helping his dad out at the gym."

"What gym?"

"Mike opened a boxing gym, about five months ago. You haven't heard about it?"

She hadn't.

Stephanie offhandedly mentioned Claudia Cline and a few of the high school girls from around our way who boxed.

"I was down at Classic Curl with my grandma a few years ago and your mom let me into the back room, let me check out your dad's ring and all the boxing stuff," Myria said to me enthusiastically.

"I've seen Myria kick some ass before," Stephanie joked, embarrassing Myria just a bit.

Myria had been in a few well-known scraps back in her high school days. Most of her hallway scraps were the result of Myria standing up for someone else. Myria Gumm hated bullies. Her uncle, Junior Cobb, was the same way, my father tells me. Never starting the fight but always finishing it.

After a few grade school fight stories, Stephanie and I ordered breadsticks and extended Myria an invitation to Lo's Gym. She was gloved up and in the ring the following night.

***

Sergeant Aponte was short and stocky, about five feet six inches and 158 pounds. He'd been an accomplished boxer during the younger days of his military career. Taji Fight Night was Sergeant Aponte's gift to the troops, a temporary escape from the 15 rounder in Iraq. The company vs. company boxing event was for bragging rights, but it was as official as an amateur boxing match could be under those conditions. There was a regulation boxing ring, a thick professional-style canvas, ropes, turnbuckles, judges, referees, stools, spit buckets, all of it. Myria Gumm was slated for the final bout of the evening.

Myria's opponent was a stocky white girl with sandy blond hair, a mouthy, hot-headed, young firecracker from Texas. The two had exchanged words more than a few times over small things really, but the disdain was obvious. When it came time to match up the fighters, both knew they'd end up in the ring with each other.

"You got a nickname?" Sergeant Aponte inquired before the fight.

"Naw, I don't need a nickname," Myria replied.

Sergeant Aponte grinned, nodded, and filled out the bout sheet.

The two had become fast friends when Myria arrived in Iraq in November 2007. Upon meeting Myria for the first time, Sergeant Aponte instantly noticed her red-and-black Lo's Gym Boxing Club t-shirt.

"Tell me about Lo's Gym," Sergeant Aponte had asked, breaking the ice.

Myria, more so than any boxer my father ever trained, understood my father's vision. She understood that most of the kids in the gym weren't going to become champions, amateur or professional. She understood that boxing was an escape from all that was suffocating out on the streets of Cowen. She understood that most of the kids in the gym didn't have much to go home to. She'd lived their lives, cried their tears, felt their anger. During the two years Myria frequented the gym, she was a mentor, a counselor, an assistant trainer of sorts.

"Chris, why are you standing around? Don't just stand around and wait for Mike to work you out on the hand pads. Hit the bag."

"Hey, kids, stop spilling water everywhere. You're going to get Mike in trouble with the church."

"Hey, guys, you gotta stop cussing like that up here. You're gonna get Mike thrown out on the streets."

Myria can best be described as a *mother figure*, *best friend*, and *sparring partner*—a *cheerleader* for fighters at Lo's Gym. She'd mentor the younger girls on personal issues best suited for a woman-to-woman conversation. She'd show up at each and every community service activity (e.g., the winter coat drive) and would shame the fighters who didn't. She'd come to each and every Lo's Gym fight, even if she didn't have a fight, sometimes busing kids who didn't have a ride.

True to her National Guard background, Myria was also one hell of a recruiter. She talked her high school friends Jennifer Rhodes and Miranda Woods into joining the gym. Shortly thereafter, my father found himself with a steadily growing roster of female boxers. On any given night he'd have 30 or 40 kids in the gym, half of them young women. Some girls would lose their first fight and never come back. Others stuck with it for a while. Most just wanted a place to go, wanted to feel as if they belonged to something good. And that's exactly how Myria Gumm made people feel.

Myria Gumm's brief amateur boxing career at Lo's Gym is a different story altogether, however, a series of unfortunate mismatches—the story of Myria's life.

Myria's first time up was at the show in Ashland, Kentucky. She was matched against a girl from Nikki Eplion's gym in South Point, Ohio. Myria's opponent was a large African American girl—cornrows, tattoos, biceps, etc. She had a handful of fights and trained with the most accomplished female professional in the region. We knew it was a tough draw. It was.

Myria lost a unanimous decision, taking a beating but proving her grit.

"You got that first one out of the way. Now we have something to build off of," my father instructed.

Myria's second time up was at the West Virginia Golden Gloves in Charleston. There wasn't an active boxer in the state signed up for Myria's weight class, so they matched her up with an African American girl from Detroit—more cornrows, tattoos, biceps, etc. It was supposedly the girl's first fight, but you were never quite sure about that sort of thing.

Myria lost a tough one; the ref stopped it in the second round.

The following Monday, Myria was back at it. Losing those fights didn't temper her enthusiasm for boxing. And it was like that for a while. If Myria wasn't at Pizza Hut, she was down at Lo's Gym.

When Myria finally decided to go into active duty, they shipped her off to Hawaii. Myria kept up with the fighters at the gym, writing letters, sending pictures, and even sending part of her paycheck as a donation to the annual Lo's Gym coat drive.

At first, my father wasn't a big fan of Myria's decision. He'd watched his uncles return home from war. But Myria wasn't afraid of a mismatch and my father knew there was no talking her out of it. Sixteen months after arriving on the shores of Hawaii, Myria was deployed to Taji, Iraq.

"Fighting out of the red corner, representing Lo's Gym Boxing Club in Cowen, West Virginia . . . The Boxing Princess . . . Myria Gumm," the ring announcer's voice echoed through the speakers mounted on the steel ring posts.

Sergeant Aponte grinned from his ringside stool, well aware that he'd pulled a fast one over on Myria. She was anything but a pretty princess.

Myria's opponent was introduced second.

Whoops and hollers from the rowdy crowd.

The pressure was mounting; Myria's cohorts had gone 0–3 on the night. Her bout would be the last fight, the last chance to nab a win for Sergeant Aponte's company.

Myria was decked out in her red-and-black Lo's Gym uniform, the same one she'd worn in her two amateur bouts. Her white boxing gloves were a gift sent overseas.

"It was the only time I wasn't nervous before a fight," Myria told me.

"I was just thinking about the guys back at the gym. I was focusing on all those good memories. I was excited by the idea of phoning home, telling everyone I had won," she said.

The bell rang and the Texas firecracker jabbed and parried her way around the ring, begging Myria to chase. The ring generalship suggested that she'd boxed before.

When Sergeant Aponte first started training with Myria, he was impressed by her technique and her patience under fire. Myria held her position in the center of the ring, waiting for the Texas firecracker to engage. She followed Sergeant Aponte's game plan, as instructed.

Midway through the first round, Myria missed with the jab, landed a glancing right hand, and nailed her back-peddling opponent with a solid left hook that came all the way from downtown Cowen.

Whap!

The Texas firecracker was hurt by the punch, momentarily dazed, and Myria moved in for the kill.

One-two-one-two.

Elbows in.

Chin tucked.

Knees bent.

One-two-one-two.

For a second, Myria was back at Lo's Gym, working the mitts with my father.

One-two-one-two.

The ref jumped in and administered a standing eight count. There'd be more of those to come in the subsequent rounds, four in total.

The Texas firecracker was tough as nails, but clearly outmatched. Myria administered a three-round beating that silenced her Texas-sized mouth for the remainder of their time together in Iraq.

"The winner . . . by unanimous decision . . . from Lo's Gym Boxing Club in Cowen, West Virginia . . . the Boxing Princess . . . Myria Gumm."

"Ain't nothing tougher than a West Virginia *Mountain* Momma," a fellow soldier proclaimed as Myria exited the ring.

And, 1,000 miles away, across the oceans, far removed from the wartorn capital of Iraq, my father was likely down in a coal mine, or down at Lo's Gym Boxing Club, holding the hand pads for a coal miner's daughter.

Chapter 9

——

APPALACHIAN UNDERDOGS OF THE SQUARED CIRCLE

——

Talking Union was a risky move. You could be docked pay, fired, or branded a communist sympathizer. If the boss man pegged you a *Red*, that'd be the end of your coal mining career. *Talking Union* set off what most folks call the "Mine Wars." It started with the Cabin Creek and Paint Creek strike of 1912. Those old boys were looking for fair pay and safer working conditions; they were *Talking Union*. But King Coal wasn't a big fan of workers' rights back in those days. The mining companies refused the demands and hired Baldwin-Felts detective agents. Strikebreakers. Like most mismatches, the odds were apparent to all involved in the fisticuffs. Miners were evicted from their company-owned homes, forcing families into camps supported by the union. Things were rather testy from that point forward. Unionized miners armed themselves; the coal company boys did the same. The fight was bloody. It was part of the largest insurrection in the United States of America since the American Civil War, May 19, 1920, the Battle of Matewan, or as my father always called it, "The Matewan Massacre."[68] In the hurt business, even mismatches get a flashy nickname.

The shootout that occurred between the Baldwin-Felts agents and the local union miners is a key piece of West Virginia mythos. Back in junior high school, they'd show us John Sayles's 1987 film portrayal of the events and teach us about how the bloodshed ushered in a new era. It had all been worth it, they said. We'd listen to James Earl Jones's baritone voice and watch those good old West Virginia boys get shot and the teachers would talk about how the union pulled it off.[69] If I hadn't grown up a coal miner's boy, I might have fallen for the Hollywood ending.

To my knowledge, there is no film portrayal of the national coal strike in 1977, when 160,000 coal miners from West Virginia to southern Illinois waged a 111-day strike led by the United Mine Workers of America against the Bituminous Coal Operators Association,[70] but it was just as important as the Battle of Matewan. The 1970s were a hostile time in the coal business. The unions were successful in building membership and gaining a foothold in the industry, scoring safety regulations for workers. That much, I'll admit. But if you know anything about the hurt business, you know that rematches rarely go the other way. The fellow who wins the first one tends to do the same in the second refrain. In coal country, it's always two steps forward, two steps back. A tragedy has to occur before progress is made.

Still today, I can't help but view it all as one big *mismatch*. Since the formation of the state in 1861, all of West Virginia's economic eggs have been placed in the same metaphoric basket. My homeland's political voice has always been that of the coal industry, a ventriloquist act of sorts. At academic conferences I am sometimes politely accused of being stuck in the past, perhaps too focused on the days of coal camps and company scrip.

"Those days are long gone," folks say.

"Technology has advanced, workers have their rights, and a miner can purchase all kinds of nice things above ground as a result of coal mining."

To such a response, I often point to the most recent mining-related disaster in the region (e.g., the West Virginia water crisis of 2014) and the argument typically dissipates.[71]

"But how can you speak and write so critically of the industry when your own father is still a coal miner?" a professorly gent once asked. "How can you criticize an industry that provides for your own family?"

"I get it from my father, actually. I can't help but root for the underdog," I replied.

Down at Lo's Gym Boxing Club, my father and Jason Bragg inadvertently played good cop, bad cop with the boxers. My father liked the guy who could barely chew gum and walk. Those kinds of guys drove Jason crazy. If a guy couldn't fight, Jason would tell him. If a guy threw punches incorrectly, Jason wouldn't hold his tongue. My father, on the other hand, was attracted to the underdogs. That's how he saw himself. He liked the challenge of finding the one thing a guy could do correctly and using that one thing to get his ass out of trouble. I used to think it was ego, my father's unwavering belief in himself as a trainer.

"Dad, why aren't you giving Chris Short more attention in the ring?"

"Chris Ledsome has a fight coming up."

"Why are you wasting time holding the mitts for Bobby McCartney? He's never gonna fight," they'd say.

My father was born a coal miner, way in over his head. He found the one thing he could do and used that thing to get his ass out of trouble. Maybe that's how it is for most West Virginians. We can't help but root for the underdog.

***

Dustin Wood inadvertently played the role of coward—picture Ichabod Crane in boxing gloves. He'd make most fighters look like Brom Bones. Dustin wore his fear to the ring like a hooded boxing robe; it was a fear both honest and visible. He'd always been bullied and tormented, easy pickings out on the playground. Too skinny for football, too short for basketball, Dustin Wood was a perennial bench setter during his days at Richwood Junior High School. For those unfamiliar with bench setting, the bench is cold, the bench is lonely—Dustin's words, not mine.

The world had convinced Dustin that he was a failure. That he was a pussy. That he was less than human. Before fights Dustin would pester my father to no end.

"Hey Lo, do I have a fight?"

"Lo, I still have a fight, don't I?"

"That guy is still going to fight me, right?"

Dustin Wood wasn't afraid of being punched or knocked down. He was afraid that he wasn't going to get a chance to prove it all wrong. He was afraid of disappointing my father, afraid of disappointing himself, afraid that everyone had labeled him correctly. This fear made Dustin fight like a buzz saw.

On several occasions, I felt deep sympathy for the young men who were about to enter the right against Dustin Wood. He'd inadvertently hit after the bell, below the belt, behind the head, head butt, and elbow opponents in the face. Dustin had one talent—his ability to take punishment. He was a whirlwind of activity, a barrage of constant energy—a V8 engine fueled by fear. Dustin trained hard—very hard—could not follow my father's advice, and threw punches with his eyes closed. My father called him "buckshot." When you fought Dustin Wood, he was all over you.

Dustin Wood arrived at Lo's Gym Boxing Club when he was 15 years old. His mother, recently remarried, had noticed a change in Dustin. Her son had gradually become a withdrawn, sad-eyed shadow of himself. She'd read about our gym in the *Nicholas Chronicle* and figured it was time for Dustin to learn how to be a man.

Bullying culture is, in many ways, a typical by-product of socially and economically downtrodden communities, be it inner city poverty or rural economic strife. Long story short, folks feel dominated. They are always looking for some way to find agency within their socially and economically dominated lives. School-aged bullying is merely a symptom of a much larger sickness, one that West Virginia educators are well aware of.

In 2016, for example, West Virginia ranked seventh in the nation for its national suicide rate, first in the United States of America for its overdose rate, and took third prize in the bullying department.[72] Dustin Wood's mother wasn't going to wait around for antibullying legislation to pass. She drove her son from Richwood to Cowen. She drove her son to Lo's Gym Boxing Club.

When Dustin Wood climbed through the ropes for the first time, he looked like a stand-up comedian, Bob Hope perhaps. Dustin visibly personified the way most fighters really feel deep down within. Maybe that's why I took to Dustin Wood so quickly. After his first day in the gym, he turned to his mother and said, "Mom, I think I finally found something I'm good at." He was wrong, I thought, but the sentiment melted my heart anyway.

Those first couple of weeks, Dustin Wood pestered my father to no end.

"Hey, Lo . . . are you going to let me spar today?"

"You think I'm ready to spar, Lo?"

"Hey, can I get in there and spar a few rounds today?"

Finding a sparring partner for Dustin was not easy. After the Marvin Gothard Classic, our gym was flooded with football-player types. Those guys were too big for Dustin, who weighed 130 pounds at the time. Getting the football-player types to spar each other wasn't easy either. They'd puff their chests out and waltz into the gym ready to try boxing out, but they'd usually quit when they discovered they weren't any good at it.

"So, how did you like boxing?" my father would always ask after a fighter's first day in the gym.

They'd always answer with something stupid like, "I like boxing but I don't like getting hit."

The football-player types would come to the gym, train for a few weeks, get their asses kicked, and we'd never see them again. I figured we would never see Dustin Wood again after his first sparring session.

My father put Dustin in there with a 16-year-old kid named Wes Hice because, at the time, he was our only other fighter close to lightweight. Wes really beat the shit out of Dustin that day; my dad stopped the sparring session after the first round. I was embarrassed for Dustin and did my best to build him back up. When his mother dropped him off at the gym the next evening, I was shocked. After the second ass kicking from Wes Hice, I was certain we'd never see Dustin again, but at 6 p.m. the following evening, there he was, standing beside his mother's car, waiting for us to open the gym. The third time Dustin sparred with Wes Hice, it was a little closer; Dustin actually made it to round three. Hice carried the rounds, but Dustin landed a few wild shots. Wes Hice kicked Dustin's ass around Lo's Gym the entire month of July that summer. Then, one midsummer day, Dustin really gave it to Wes. If I had to guess, I'd say Wes Hice had probably been out drinking the night before and Dustin caught him with a mean hangover. Either way, Dustin really gave it to him.

Away from the rest of the fighters, when nobody was looking, while I was removing Dustin's gloves, I gave Dustin the biggest hug I could sneak in without showing my favoritism.

"Great fight, Wood . . . you kicked his ass," I said as Dustin nervously smiled through a bloody mouthpiece.

Wes Hice never boxed again.

Dustin Wood did.

***

The 2004 West Virginia Silver Gloves Tournament, ironically hosted in Ashland, Kentucky, was something of a coming-out party for Lo's Gym Boxing Club. Our club was relatively unknown in the Tri-State Boxing Association at the time. That first year, we were the underdogs.

Calvin White[73] hit Dustin with the first three jabs of the fight; each punch snapped Dustin's head backward. Dustin fought like his head weighed 150 pounds. He went into battle headfirst and sometimes head down. Sophisticated boxers would hit him with everything they had and would look damn good doing it.

Calvin White won the first minute of the round easily; he tripled up his jab, landed one-twos, one-two-threes, uppercuts, a few overhand rights—everything. For that first minute of the fight, it was the kind of round boxers dream up while they are whaling away on the heavy bag. Calvin White was a good young fighter, a South Charleston kid who came from a boxing family. He was the defending junior lightweight West Virginia Silver Gloves State champion and he knew his way around the ring. But what Calvin didn't understand was how a Venus flytrap does its business. The Venus flytrap needs you to get close; it relies on the overconfidence of its prey.

The final minute of a round was Dustin's favorite. It is the part of the round in which everyone is tired, ready for things to be over and done with. There is some semblance of equality in the final minute of a boxing round. It is a discomforting space to exist within. Dustin understood this. At the end of the first round, the referee had to peel Dustin Wood off of Calvin White's black skin.

Dustin Wood fights often took place within a phone booth. They were close and personal, an ugly three rounds of action. When Dustin was hurt, he fought harder. When he was reminded of the painful realities he was trying to escape through boxing, he became a frightened cat backed into a corner. Dustin didn't have an overly powerful jab, or an overly powerful uppercut, or an overly powerful left hook, or the kind of overhand right that would chop off an opponent's head—he was no Sir Gawain. If Dustin Wood was going to get you out of there, it'd be execution by 10,000 buckshots. He would not stop throwing punches. He'd eat as many punches as you could throw. He'd swarm you. You'd be winning the fight, but he'd keep swarming. You'd better be in shape. You'd better be willing to dig deep.

When I worked the corner with my father during Dustin Wood fights, I sometimes found myself holding my breath. He was never knocked down, that I remember, but referees would sometimes stop fights on Dustin—they didn't know they were refereeing Jason Voorhees. They'd give up on Dustin before they could see what made him special. This happened more than a few times over the years. My father and I were always one step away from throwing in the towel as well, although I don't think we ever did. During the second round of Dustin Wood's championship bout with Calvin White, I caught myself holding my breath and my father holding the towel.

Calvin White won the first minute of the second stanza. It was as if Calvin suddenly remembered that he was the better fighter and decided to get back to proving it. Fighting Dustin Wood, however, was not a sprint; it was a marathon. A sweeping overhand right finally broke through Calvin's tight defense and wobbled Calvin's knees. Showing pain or weakness against Dustin Wood was a bad idea—he was a shark, he could smell blood, he understood fear; he'd been baptized in it. Dustin swarmed a tired and overwhelmed Calvin White from one corner to the next. Calvin was taking punches that hurt his pride just as much as they did his face.

After the bell rang, closing the second round, Dustin collapsed on the red corner stool. As I placed the spit bucket between Dustin's long skinny legs, I caught an image of an exhausted Calvin White in the opposite corner.

"Am I winning?" was always the first thing that came out of Dustin's blistered lips when he returned to the corner.

"Goddamn Buckshot, I'd hate to have to fight you," my father joked, water bottle in hand.

When asked the difference between a hero and a coward, famed boxing trainer Cus D'Amato once said, "Nothing. They're both afraid of getting hurt, but it's what the hero does that makes him a hero, and what the coward doesn't do that makes him a coward."[74]

More so than any boxer my father and I ever worked with, Dustin Wood personified Cus D'Amato's idea of a hero. Dustin Wood always won the third round, even in the fights he lost. I don't know this for a fact. Dustin never said this to me, but I always imagined him exorcizing demons in the third round. I always suspected that he was fighting more than the opponent.

The referee gave the chief seconds the signal to exit the ring. My father returned Dustin's mouthpiece to its rightful place.

"This round, remember all of those bullies who picked on you," my father instructed.

Dustin nodded his headgear dutifully.

"Chief seconds out," the referee repeated.

"Remember those guys and all the shit they said to you and how they made you feel."

"Red corner . . . chief seconds out."

"Now go do something about it," my father called, finally exiting the ring.

My father brought six fighters to the West Virginia Silver Gloves tournament that night, but Dustin was the only one of our fighters who'd yet to compete as an amateur boxer. Two hellacious minutes later, the ding of the final bell saved Calvin White from someone else's beating. Dustin Wood really gave it to Calvin White in that final round, just as he did to Wes Hice down at Lo's Gym a few months prior.

When the ring announcer called Dustin's name, he leapt into the air, about five inches off the canvas, with hands raised in victory—think Ali vs. Liston.

Dustin "Buckshot" Wood was the unlikeliest West Virginia Silver Gloves lightweight champion in the history of USA Amateur Boxing, I'd argue.

"You will always be the 2004 state champion . . . this is forever . . . nobody can ever take that away from you," my father told Dustin after the fight.

It was the happiest any of us had ever seen Dustin. It was the happiest I'd ever seen my father.

Less than a year after The Edge opened its doors to the public, Lo's Gym Boxing Club gave birth to five West Virginia Silver Gloves state champions (Dustin Wood, Chris Short, Chris Ledsome, Jennings Barger, and Craig Wright). The following year, Lo's Gym would rack up five more state championships (Dustin Wood, Chris Ledsome, Chris Short, Max Anderson, and Lane Gillespie). Jimmy Utt's *Webster Echo* news articles consistently reminded everyone around town that my father's boxing gym was doing something special in the community. My father had championship jackets made up for the kids, and paid for the jackets out of his own pocket. He wanted the kids to walk around town with a sense of pride. Those first two years, everything fell into place. The gym was packed every night, fighters were winning fights, fighters were becoming a visible presence within the community, and Jimmy Utt kept the town in tune with all the comings and goings of the gym. But it was Dustin Wood who most eloquently personified Lo's Gym's success, at least in my father's imagination. Dustin was an underdog. He was my father's kind of guy—undersized with a big heart.

"That skinny kid from Richwood has more heart than any boxer I've ever seen in person or on television," my father would say.

"Dustin would fight the devil," he'd add.

Dustin Wood boxed at Lo's Gym in all four of his high school years. His winning percentage wasn't much over 500, but he was probably my father's favorite fighter. My father was proud of the way Dustin fought.

"Buckshot's DuPont fight. That's my favorite Dustin Wood fight and he didn't even win it," my father would always say.

In the DuPont fight, Dustin had taken on a slick southpaw from Ironton, Ohio, who had more wins than Dustin had fights.

"That kid dominated Buckshot for all of rounds one and two."

"Hell, the ref gave Buckshot two standing eight counts in the second round, I think."

"But that last round. Oh boy."

"Buckshot was on his ass."

"Ol' boy thought he had it over and done with."

"Didn't realize that West Virginia boys fight till the damn bell."

"You might whip Buckshot's ass, but you'd better pack a lunch."

My father would beam with pride, recounting Dustin Wood's lopsided loss in DuPont, West Virginia—my father's gold-capped teeth would always show when he smiled. When things went Dustin Wood's way, my father became an arbiter of fairness in an otherwise unfair Appalachian backdrop. And, West Virginia, as far as my father was concerned, became a somewhat better place than before.

***

Tunney Hunsaker was born in Princeton, Kentucky, but most folks know him as a West Virginia boy. At the age of 27, Hunsaker became the youngest police chief in the history of West Virginia. But that's not why most folks know Tunney Hunsaker. Three years after Hunsaker took office in Fayetteville, West Virginia, he traveled to Louisville, Kentucky, to box an 18-year-old heavyweight named Cassius Marcellus Clay. It was Clay's professional debut. Most folks know Cassius Marcellus Clay as Muhammad Ali, *the greatest of all time.*

The Clay vs. Hunsaker bout took place at Louisville's Freedom Hall on October 29, 1960. I've watched a few fights at Freedom Hall. Back in 2004, I watched Danny Williams knock out an aging Mike Tyson. At the prefight weigh-in, I asked Williams for a photograph, mostly because Tyson didn't appear to be in the photo-taking mood.

"Mr. Williams, can I get a picture?"

"No," Williams sternly replied, his eyes unchanging.

"Oh, I'm sorry."

"Just kidding, get over here," Williams said in his thick British accent, breaking into laughter, wrapping his tree-trunk forearm around my neck in a playful gesture.

The following night, Williams scored a sizable upset of the man who was once heralded as the "*baddest* on the planet." Freedom Hall, one hell of a place to catch a fight. But I digress.

Hunsaker knew that he was a sizable underdog that night in Freedom Hall, but didn't know much about his hometown opponent.

"I'd never heard of Cassius Clay. It was just another fight. When they told me he'd won the gold medal, it didn't mean a thing to me," Hunsaker once recounted in an interview with journalist Bud Poliquin.[75]

Hunsaker learned to box during his days in the Air Force. He'd been stationed at Lackland Air Force Base in San Antonio, Texas. The day he climbed in the ring with Cassius Clay, Hunsaker was hardly a spring chicken. He'd been in there with a few top professionals, such as Ernie Terrell and Tom McNeeley, fought on an undercard in Madison Square Garden, and had 27 pro fights under his belt. The Fayetteville police chief took the Clay fight without batting an eye.

"I gave him a hard time. Later, he said he almost lost the hamburger he'd eaten for dinner when I gave him some good chops to the stomach in the second and third rounds," Hunsaker recalled.[76]

The teenager who later became Muhammad Ali won a spirited, but relatively easy, six-round unanimous decision.

Tunney Hunsaker and Ali wouldn't meet again until the 1980s, when Hunsaker and Ali both signed autographs for fans at the West Virginia Golden Gloves in Charleston.

The two fighters would meet up on several occasions over the years. I grew up on those stories—tall tales of Ali wandering the streets of Fayetteville, stories of Tunney and Ali walking the New River Gorge Bridge, stories of Ali crashing backyard cookouts. Ali even made a surprise visit to Hunsaker's retirement party in 1992.

My father and I never had the pleasure of meeting Tunney Hunsaker, but we did get to know his wife, Patricia. When Tunney passed away in 2005, my father wrote Patricia to express his condolences; she responded to my father's letter and was kind enough to donate some of Tunney's photographs and newspaper clippings to Lo's Gym. The photographs and newspaper clippings of Hunsaker that hung in the corner of my father's gym demonstrated our vicarious connection to the West Virginia boy who'd gone the distance with *The Greatest*.

Back in 1999, my father and I met Muhammad Ali's third daughter, Laila, at Mountaineer Casino in Chester, West Virginia, after her fourth round TKO of Shadina Pennybaker. We posed for a quick picture, shook hands, and offered our congratulations. We'd meet Laila again in Louisville a few years later, at the weigh-in for the Tyson-Williams fight.

"Your dad was my hero," my father said.

Laila flashed that beautiful Ali smile. "Mine too."

Ali was my father's boyhood hero, but Hunsaker was his muse. Fighters from West Virginia don't have many hometown heroes. West Virginia's contributions to the history of boxing are scattered at best. West Virginia fight towns have never been fortunate enough to have a working-class champion, at least not in the same way Youngstown, Ohio, celebrates Ray "Boom Boom" Mancini. Our boys were always in the tune-up fights, the crossroads bouts, were always the last-minute replacements, the underdogs.

Most West Virginia folks are surprised when they discover the parents of legendary heavyweight champion Jack Dempsey were natives of Holden, West Virginia, and that despite being born in Boulder, Colorado, Dempsey spent much of his boyhood years in Logan County: one of Jack Dempsey's first jobs was working for the mines of the Gay Coal and Coke Company, a few miles west of Logan.

But that's not how most folks know Jack Dempsey, "The Manassa (Colorado) Mauler." Despite Dempsey's familial pedigree and coal mining background, he is rarely celebrated as a son of West Virginia. The history books will have you read him as a Colorado boy. Ours, as West Virginia's, is a history of being on the wrong end of a mismatch.

My father was friendly with a few ol' boys from the Mountain State who had the opportunity to get in the ring with boxing's elite— Appalachian underdogs of the squared circle. Tommy Franco Thomas (Clarksburg, West Virginia) went 10 rounds with Leon Spinks, took on Michael Dokes and Jimmy Young too. Tommy Small (Beckley, West Virginia) fought the great Julio Cesar Chavez in Chavez's hometown of Culiacan, Mexico, and had the balls to get in there with Meldrick Taylor, Keith Holmes, Raul Marquez, and Hector "Macho" Camacho. Perry Ballard (Madison, West Virginia) compiled a pro record of 26–2–1, took on the "Macho Man" as well. As for my generation, Mike Sheppard (Palestine, West Virginia) got in there with Antonio Tarver, Ruslan Chagaev, Clifford Etienne, and James Toney. Jeremy "The Beast" Bates (Charleston, West Virginia) mixed it up with Evander Holyfield, Andrew Golota, and Kirk Johnson. Eric Watkins (Morgantown, West Virginia) took a few lead left hooks from the great Roy Jones. Our boys always came out on the wrong end of it. They'd give it hell, but they'd always lose. My father admired those guys. He viewed their bouts as a pugilistic metaphor for both the beauty and horror of our struggle.

"The sun rarely shines in the state of West Virginia," President John F. Kennedy famously stated.

"But its people always do," he added.

"I'll take the guy who has the balls to climb through the ropes and give it hell knowing the odds are against him," my father always said.

"That's the kind of guy I want in the foxhole with me," he'd add.

* * *

And, there was Lane Gillespie, 11 years old. Lane looked like Tiny Tim when he walked through the door that first time; all of the girls in the gym wanted to pinch his rosy cheeks and pat his Eddie Munster haircut.

"Hey, buddy, I like those boots," my father said.

Lane showed up to box in a worn-out pair of cowboy boots.

"He's crazy about John Wayne," Eric, Lane's father, said.

Lane flashed a bashful smile, and mostly looked down at the hardwood floor.

"I'm going to start calling you . . . The Duke," my father replied.

That first day, Lane really took to it.

Favoritism was always a dirty word in my house. My father hated small-town politics, and couldn't quite accept the fact that some folks have it easier than others. But I played favorites in the gym, I'll admit. Long before I became a college professor, Lane "The Duke" Gillespie was my teacher's pet. Lane was a Willoughby Trailer Park kid, a back-lot kid, just as I had been. I'd always make sure Lane received extra rounds on the mitts whenever he wanted to get in the ring. His being from Willoughby Trailer Park garnered a little favoritism, I figured. My father played favorites with Lane as well, although he'd never admit to it.

The Gillespies didn't have much. Lane's father was drawing workers' compensation or welfare or both. His mother didn't work either, from what I remember. You couldn't help but feel sorry for them. But Lane had one thing on his side—time. He was starting the game at the right age; many of our other fighters were playing catch-up to kids who'd been boxing since they were ten years old. But that was the only thing going for Lane. We didn't find out about his medical condition, Type 1 diabetes, for some time. Eric was keeping it from us, I think.

I always hated taking fighters to amateur shows at Van High School in Boone County, West Virginia. The shows were always crooked and disorganized. You'd fight a kid, only to find out that his trainer was refereeing the fight, his uncle was a judge, and his grandmother was working the concession stand. We always caught a bad break at Van High School. Lane's first amateur bout was against Kevin Thurman[77] from the Van Boxing Club, an 11-year-old kid who already had a handful of bouts under his belt. Despite the experience difference, it wasn't much of a risk. At 11 years old, the gloves are too big for most kids to throw or land a meaningful punch. More often than not, it would be three rounds of pitty-patter. Sometimes a kid would get hit with a good one, cry, and the ref would stop the fight. We took the fight, despite the fact that everything was working against us.

It was three rounds of pitty-patter. Lane got the best of it, but you never quite knew how the judges would score it.

"Judge Ernie Roth has it 18–14."

"Judge Tommy Flanker has it 15–12."

"And Judge Michael Thomas scores it 14–12," the ring announcer called over the loudspeakers, his thick southern accent echoing the walls of the gymnasium.

"For the winner by close, but unanimous decision, from the blue corner, Lane 'The Duke' Gillespie."

My father and I escorted Lane over to the bleachers, where his mother, father, and little sister, Harley, were seated.

Lane's pudgy cheeks were flushed with exhaustion; the trophy, clutched in his chubby fingers, shimmered like something great.

"Mom, can I get a picture with the champ?" my father asked, kneeling down on one knee, wrapping his tattooed arm around Lane's neck as Candy Gillespie removed the Kodak from her purse.

Lane flashed a million-dollar smile, held up the trophy with his right hand, and formed a *number one pose* with his tiny left hand. He'd studied the victory poses of the champion fighters who decorated the walls of Lo's Gym. I jumped in for a pic as well.

And then the ring announcer's slick southern drawl returned to the speakers.

"Ladies and gentlemen, we have a correction for that last bout."

"Ladies and gentlemen, may I have your attention . . . we have a correction for that last bout."

My father gave me the look.

"The scores for that last bout were 18–14, 15–12, and 14–12 for Kevin Thurman of Van Boxing Club."

"We apologize for the mistake. I repeat, the scores for that last bout were 18–14, 15–12, and 14–12 for Kevin Thurman of Van Boxing Club."

"The fuck," my father smirked.

"Did I lose the fight?" Tiny Tim whimpered.

"Don't you pay any goddamn attention to that, Lane," my father instructed.

About ten minutes later, a goosey-looking fellow in a white USA Boxing polo came over to our side of the bleachers.

"I'm sorry for the mistake, fellas. Chad read the cards the wrong way," he said, extending his hand for a shake that never happened.

"Yeah," my father quickly replied, barely opening his lips.

Lane sat on the first bleacher, sandwiched between his mother and father, flashing the look kids flash when they're in trouble. We all just stood there for a second or two, our hands in our pockets.

"I'm going to need to switch those trophies. I need to give that one to Kevin, I'm afraid," the fellow in the white polo finally said. It took him a good 60 seconds to work up the courage.

"Give it back, Lane," Eric instructed.

Tears started to form in Lane's tiny green eyes.

"You'd really do that?" my father said, calmly at first.

Lane handed the trophy back to the goosey fellow.

"I'm sorry, Lane, you fought a real good fight," the goosey fellow said, removing the trophy from Lane's chubby fingers.

"You'd really do that? You'd take a trophy from an 11-year-old boy?" my father interjected, this time with more gusto.

"Lo, I'm sorry. Chad read the cards wrong."

The goosey fellow started to make his exit.

"Give that goddamn thing back to Lane. I don't give two shits what you write down in his passbook, but you give that goddamn thing back to him," my father said, his face becoming more irate by the minute.

"I'm going to get Kevin's trophy and give it to Lane," the goosey fellow promised, sensing things were getting heated.

"Give the goddamn thing back to Lane and go ask Chad, whoever the fuck that is, if all of this is worth getting his ass kicked over," my father threatened, placing his index finger squarely in the middle of the goosey fellow's chest.

The goosey fellow gave the trophy back to Lane, who at this point, was sobbing like the child he was.

Lane lost in the next two fights by decisions; the judges, a West Virginia good old boys club of sorts, had it out for him, I think. You don't see many kids go 0–3 to start their amateur careers and continue to stick with it. Hell, a good portion of the kids in our gym went 0–1 and never fought again.

"You really think Oscar De La Hoya is the best welterweight in the world?" my father asked Lane in the gym one evening.

"I don't know," Lane replied.

"He is the best welterweight in the world who didn't quit. He's the best welterweight in the world who didn't give up when things didn't go his way, when other guys would have packed it in," my father instructed.

Lane kept at it, won his next five fights in a row, and eventually became Willoughby Trailer Park's first and only two-time West Virginia Silver Gloves state champion.

***

Boxing showed Lane Gillespie the world beyond Willoughby Trailer Park, just as college had done for me. Lane saw his first shopping mall, his first set of escalator stairs, before an amateur bout in Charleston. Lane ate his first chain restaurant meal at the Wheeling Island Casino, didn't know what to do with the cloth napkin, before a fight card back in 2008. But no matter how many fights Lane won, how many state titles he collected, my father never stopped viewing him as the 11-year-old trailer park kid in the cowboy boots. I'm sure of it.

"When Eric would give him those insulin shots in the side, it'd break my heart," my father once reflected.

"Eric and Lane . . . those are my kind of people," he added.

Lane Gillespie boxed at Lo's Gym from age 11 to age 16. During his time at the gym, Lane was our most active amateur boxer. He'd win fights easily—pop shotting opponents and showboating his way to lopsided victories. He'd throw bolo punches like Sugar Ray. He'd pull those sneaky little veteran moves like James Toney. He'd grab the top rope with his right hand and jab opponents with his left, an illegal showboat tactic from the 1980s. During our hometown shows, he'd enter the ring to the sounds of Hank Williams Jr.'s "Country Boy Can Survive." Lane quickly became Cowen's hometown favorite. Lane "The Duke" Gillespie was, in many ways, emblematic of my father's genius as a boxing trainer. He grew into a lanky teenager with thin ropey muscles, stubble on his chin, and dynamite in his fists. Lane Gillespie represented both the possibility and the limitations of boxing as a way out for poor West Virginia kids.

"Got a boy whose gonna kick your ass," Bullet Bill Hopkins would always say to Lane after one of his lopsided showboating victories.

Bill was always judging or refereeing amateur bouts. He was at damn near every event. In fact, Bill once called our house on Christmas day to ask my father if he had a 140-pounder for his show in early January. Boxing was Bullet Bill's life.

"Got a boy in my gym, Buzz."

"He's coming for you, young man."

"Buzz is gonna humble you," Bill would tease.

It went on like that for about a year. Bill really did have a kid named Buzz in his gym, a stocky 14-year-old red-headed kid from Fairmont. We'd seen him win a few fights, but he really wasn't all that impressive. Bill was either bullshitting Lane or needed a new pair of glasses.

Finally, Buzz and Lane squared off at the third installment of the Marvin Gothard Classic. Lane stopped Buzz in the second round. It wasn't pretty.

"I'm'a find a boy to whip your ass," Bill threatened Lane after the fight, when my father wasn't around.

"I'll see that you're humbled," Bill added, basking in the convenience of my father's absence.

My father wasn't all that crazy about Lane's showboating either, but Lane had every right to taunt and tease his opponents, we figured. The world had dumped enough shit on Lane's life to justify a bolo punch or two. As a kid, I never fully grasped my father's affinity for the underdog. I never understood how much his underdog ethos was a product of the life he'd been forced to live as a teenage coal miner, following the family trade. Maybe that's why my father distrusted those from wealth and privilege, those with authority. We'd been cast into a rigged system, metaphorically up against more powerful opponents who held all of the physical advantages dictated by the tale of the tape. When we do catch a lucky break, some fella comes along and wants the trophy back—Lane's story is *our story*.

The lasting image from my five years working with Lane Gillespie is that of a weather-torn punching bag, hung from a poplar tree in Lane's front yard. When my father would give Lane a ride home from the gym, I couldn't help but smile at the decoration.

"Lane'll come home from the gym and go four or five rounds on that thing every evening . . . the kid's crazy about boxing," Eric once told us.

Lane is still in Willoughby Trailer Park, I hear. After his folks split up, Lane became a teenage father and dropped out of high school—all of this a year or so after the gym closed its doors for good.

He's humbled, Bill.

We're West Virginians, Appalachian underdogs of the squared circle, all of us.

We get humbled in the end.

I want to write Lane differently, I'll admit.

I want to tell you that my father turned him pro. I want to tell you that Lane got a shot at the title. I want to tell you that Lane is rich and famous. I want to tell you he was the kid from Lo's Gym who got the shot at the big dance in Atlantic City.

I want to write an Appalachian tall tale about ol' Tunney Hunsaker whopping the greatest fighter to ever walk the planet. But this is our story; this is who we are. Our guys take the fight on short notice, climb through the ropes, and slug it out with bigger and more athletic opponents. Most of us are Dustin Wood. Most of us are Lane Gillespie.

Stereotyped and stigmatized, Appalachian folks are easy prey, socioeconomically bullied by privileged society. We're the underdogs. We gather our strength from histories of exploitation and cultural degradation. Our stories are tragic and beautiful. In these parables of Lo's Gym's underdog champions, I write the story of Appalachia. This is who we are—fighters. We fight like hell, knowing the other fellow has the advantage.

PART III

SPLIT DECISIONS

Stories from the Championship Rounds

Chapter 10

PRIZEFIGHTERS

Jason Bragg didn't wake up one morning and decide to become a professional boxer. He didn't have an epiphany, didn't talk things over with his wife and come to the conclusion that professional boxing was something he had to do. Jason Bragg's prizefighting ambitions were a festering sore buried somewhere deep underneath the surface; the blister that finally popped and oozed was decades in the making.

It started with Steve Tincher and Matt McClung, two high school gym teachers/football coaches who'd met my father at the Lewisburg Fairgrounds the year Curtis "The Ice Man" Wright won his second straight Toughman Contest. Steve was a light heavyweight, had dark black hair, and looked half-Indian. Matt was a heavyweight, had bleached blond hair, and a thin goatee mustache. They were handsome, athletic guys who looked and fought like they belonged in the Gene Tunney era. When Steve and Matt heard my father was back in business, they phoned Jerry Thomas for the street address.

Steve and Matt carpooled all the way from Lewisburg two or three days a week to train with my father. That's a good 72-mile drive both ways. My father had the magic touch, they figured. I liked Steve and Matt right from the start. They worked well with the kids in the gym, and treated my father like he was Angelo Dundee. And, as an added bonus, Steve and Matt were great sparring partners for our amateurs. They were player-coaches; they'd even pick up the hand pads and help out. I was, however, somewhat leery of Steve and Matt taking my father's attention away from our crop of promising young amateurs. Steve and Matt were 20-something Toughman brawlers, epilogue characters with no long-term future in the sport.

Yet my father couldn't stay away from Jerry Thomas's Toughman circus. Jerry had him working corners, wrapping hands, judging fights. Jerry even talked my father into refereeing on a few occasions. When Steve and Matt came along, building a West Virginia Toughman champion had become something of a formula for my father. He was more than confident he could turn both guys into champions.

And he did.

Steve Tincher won the light heavyweight division of the tournament in October 2004 and Matt McClung won the heavyweight division the following year. That's when Jason Bragg started picking at the sore. That's when the pus began to slowly discharge.

At this point, Jason Bragg's place within the Lo's Gym hierarchy was tenuous at best. It was Lo's Gym; my father was the trainer and Jason was merely one of the helping hands. Jason had never boxed, won a fight, or been in a real street fight in all of his 31 years on planet Earth.

Sure, Jason had taken up weight lifting after high school, bought tons of weight-gaining supplements at GNC, added a few inches to his biceps, got a few tattoos, and grew some facial hair, but he still mostly walked around feeling like the kid who was too little for the Webster County High School basketball team. The boxers in the gym listened to Jason's advice, but not in the same way they listened to my father.

But "it's never too late," my father is prone to saying.

"It's never too late until it's too late."

When Jason Bragg accompanied my father to the 2004 Lewisburg Toughman Contest to help with Steve and Matt's fights, Jason found his second chance. Jerry Thomas had introduced a middleweight division to the mix, a space for boxers weighing 160 pounds or less.

In between rounds, my father glanced over at Jason, and caught the unmistakable look in his eyes. Jason was a 31-year-old boxing virgin, lusting.

"You'd like to fight in one of these, wouldn't you?" my father smirked, amid the cheers from the crowd. Jason didn't answer, but flashed what my father often refers to as a "shit-eating grin."

But it didn't happen all at once, as is usually the case with festering sores. Jason's prizefighting ambitions took their good old time before finally reaching the surface and revealing themselves to the world. It was a few months later, after the holidays, when Jason Bragg finally came to my father wearing the same sheepish look Curtis Wright once had. It was a look that roughly translates to "Make me young again."

Pop!

Ooze!

***

November 1999. Beckley, West Virginia.

Just over a year after watching Tommy Small fight Aaron "Superman" Davis on ESPN2 *Friday Night Fights*, we made a pilgrimage to Tommy's dilapidated boxing gym on the outskirts of Beckley. Tommy's gym was housed in a hollowed-out brick building at the end of a graffiti-adorned street located in the kind of neighborhood you don't want to pass through after dark. When my father parked his silver Ford F-150 alongside Tommy's gym, he flashed me a momentary look of indecision, as if to say, "We shouldn't be here."

Training with Tommy Small was a big deal to the 17-year-old version of myself. He was one of a handful of professional boxers from the state of West Virginia who had actually *made it* in the sport. Tommy's story was the Appalachian version of the typical professional boxer chronology: he started boxing at the age of six when his father built a makeshift boxing ring in the basement of their home. When he turned 18 years old, he entered and won a few local Toughman Contests and dreamed of becoming a world champion. He moved to a big city to follow his professional aspirations, made a decent living as a professional journeyman, fought a little bit too long, retired, moved back to West Virginia, opened up a gym, and started training local fighters. When Tommy greeted us at the curb with a firm handshake, it was the first time I'd ever met a boxer from my television screen. Looking back on that day, I imagine that it was hard for my father to shake the hand of someone who had lived his dream, someone who had taken the chances he didn't.

Tommy's gym was disgusting; it made Simon's Gym look like the Taj Mahal. There were plastic gray buckets placed around the gym to catch the water dripping from the leaky ceiling. Tommy had two heavy bags, two speed bags, and a makeshift boxing ring with droopy ropes. His gym smelled like fight.

Tommy's gym was full of black guys. He was the only white person in the gym that day. It was the first time in my young life I'd ever experienced being the racial minority.

"Lord Jesus, you got the *white man syndrome*—no rhythm, son," Tommy said after watching about two minutes of my shadowboxing routine.

Before I could respond, Tommy yanked me by the arm and all but stuffed me into the ring with Golden Gloves welterweight champion Kendall Rife.[78]

"Kendall, show this kid the ring run . . . he could use it . . . and turn on some of that rap shit, we need to shake the whiteness off this kid."

Tommy was as white as they come, looked like the bad guy in a 1950s movie, but had perfected his trade in the predominantly black gyms of Washington, D.C. He was a firm believer that great champions need rhythm and that most white guys didn't have it. From what I can remember, he was the only trainer we ever worked with who asked his fighters to play rap music in the gym.

"He's fucking wit you, don't let him bother you," Kendall muttered under his breath when Tommy was out of earshot.

In the middle of the boxing ring was a thick black circle of duct tape that gave way to an oval shape.

"Tommy calls this the *ring run*," Kendall explained as he glided his Everlast boxing shoes along the perimeter of the oval.

"When the bell rings, Tommy asks us to circle the ring twice before throwing a punch . . . it calms you down, helps you focus, keeps you from getting tagged early in the fight . . . if you are in there with a guy that doesn't know what he's doing, he'll chase you around the ring and walk into a punch," Kendall explained, shifting his direction from one foot to the other, gliding counterclockwise around the ring. My father, observing patiently in the distance, was taking it all in.

Tommy worked me on the hand pads for three rounds. He showed me a few defensive drills, watched me hit the heavy bag, watched me hit the uppercut bag, showed me how to work the double-end bag, and lectured to me while Kendall Rife sparred.

"Your boy has got some tools. He can hit. That left jab ain't bad. He ain't got rhythm, but he's got some tools," Tommy said to my father.

That was supposed to be a compliment.

"Loosen up, Todd. You're stiffer than a wedding dick," my father added between rounds, half joking.

"You bring him back and I'll get him looking like a fighter," Tommy boasted after the workout.

"I'll get him looking like this," Tommy said, removing his shirt.

It was a strange gesture.

"I've been taking Todd up to Simon's Gym in Morgantown. We've got a lot to learn, but we're going to put the work in," my father replied.

Tommy was still shirtless.

"I wouldn't waste my time," Tommy smirked.

That's how boxing gyms are in West Virginia. They always tell you the other guy doesn't know what he's doing. Tommy finally put his shirt back on.

On our way home from Beckley, we stopped at a Wendy's. I'd earned that spicy chicken sandwich. My father didn't know what to think of Tommy Small or his gym, but he liked the ring run and he liked the rap music. Years later, both would be a staple of Lo's Gym Boxing Club.

"Dad, I want to be a great fighter like Tommy."

"It's never too late."

"It's never too late until it's too late."

Be careful standing too close to dreamers; that kind of thing is contagious.

***

Starting a boxing career at the age of 31 is hardly a smart move. My father decided to play it safe with Jason Bragg, or as safe as one could play it at this point. He didn't want to see Jason get knocked out, become discouraged with boxing, and disappear from Lo's Gym altogether. Other than Jeff Dean, who worked mostly with the smaller children in the gym, Jason was my father's only full-time assistant trainer. I was off being a graduate student.

Because fighters with more than five amateur bouts are barred from Toughman competition, my father thought it best for Jason to fight in a few amateur bouts before jumping into the deep waters. When the second annual Marvin Gothard Classic rolled around in July 2005, Jason Bragg signed his name on the bout sheet.

Jason's opponent was a 26-year-old Mexican American fighter from Beckley, West Virginia. Decked out in satin boxing trunks in the colors of the Mexican flag, the kid was Julio Cesar Chavez, as far as the hometown crowd was concerned. Jason was going to get his ass kicked, they figured. Every Smooth coal miner not working evening shift was in the bleachers that night. If Jason had gotten his ass kicked, he would have had to transfer to another coal mine to escape the teasing he would have had to endure on a daily basis. But that isn't how it played out, not completely.

For the first minute or so, Jason stayed in a defensive posture, jabbing and moving, largely avoiding contact—winning the fight at a distance. Chavez landed a thundering left hook to the body, Jason dropped his guard out of instinct, and Chavez attacked upstairs with a one-two combination that instantly broke Jason's pointy white nose. A steady flow of blood stained Jason's boxing uniform and soiled Chavez's garb as well.

I worked the corner with my father that night, so I'm fairly certain the first words out of Jason's mouth, when he collapsed on the stool, were "He broke my goddamn nose, Lo."

It was one hell of a tussle. Both Jason and Chavez abandoned their pugilistic discipline and slugged it out. Chavez ripped Jason to the body with looping hooks and Jason returned fire with solid uppercuts that snapped Chavez's head backward in a whiplash motion. Every coal miner in the stands was on his feet. All of those ass kickings from Curtis "The Ice Man" Wright had paid off, apparently. The broken nose had only made Jason fight harder, with more gusto than we'd ever witnessed in the gym. The final two stanzas of the fight were as good as it gets in West Virginia amateur boxing—an all-out war.

I wasn't sure if Jason had won the fight, but it was close. Both combatants were beaten and bloodied, Jason's nose swollen three times its normal size.

The judges handed down a split-decision victory in Jason's favor. It was a nice *Cinderella Man* moment, a nice ending to Jason's James Braddock story. I hastily assumed Beckley Chavez had diverted Jason's ambitions. But that wasn't how it played out, not exactly.

Two months later, Jason signed the bout sheet for an amateur event in Belle, West Virginia. He wanted one more tune-up bout before fighting in the Lewisburg Toughman Contest in November. This time around, they matched Jason up with a 29-year-old lanky whiteboy-coal miner who, like Jason, had his eye on Jerry Thomas's newly created middleweight division. It was about the fairest fight we'd ever drawn, I think. Both guys had one amateur bout under their belts and were almost the same exact age and weight.

Jason fought a smart fight, using his jab, circling the ring, largely staying out of harm's way. In the second round, Jason landed a few straight right hands, scored a standing eight count, and controlled the overall pace of the fight. Jason's opponent, clearly not in fighting shape, quit on the stool after the second round.

And, just like that, Jason Bragg, a few months shy of his thirty-second birthday, was an undefeated amateur boxer. There was no talking him out of the Lewisburg Toughman Contest.

Jason's Friday night Toughman opponent, Jamal Turner,[79] was Lewisburg's first and only defending middleweight champion. Cinderella Man's luck had run out, I figured.

"Hell, might as well fight the toughest guy on the first night," my father joked upon viewing the bout sheet.

"Might as well fight the toughest guy in the tournament while you're fresh," my father added, placing the bout sheet back onto the table without even glancing over to gauge Jason's reaction.

My fears were largely confirmed in the opening round. Jason fought overly defensively and was knocked off his feet by a lead right hand. He wasn't hurt; the knockdown was largely the result of Jason's poor balance, but he was certainly down on the scorecards after the opening refrain.

"Okay, Lo. I'm ready to do what you tell me," Jason said the instant my father removed the mouthpiece.

A few weeks later Jason would admit to my father that he'd been talked into *brawling* by a few of his buddies down at the Smooth Coal Company.

"Jason, Lo's got you doing that boxing shit too much. This is a Toughman . . . we want to see you go in there and knock 'em out," they goaded.

After the first-round knockdown, Jason was ready to listen.

In the second round, Jason tightened his defense, moved his head laterally, and scored a lightning-quick one-two combination that planted

Jamal Turner on his ass. Coming back to the corner for the final round, the fight was likely even.

"You are gonna hate yourself in the morning if you don't go out there and give this everything you have, Jason," my father said calmly but sternly.

"Everything you've always wanted is right there waiting on you."

Jason fought like hell, scored two standing eight counts, and the ref stopped it on Jamal Turner before the end of the final round.

And there I stood at ringside, dumbfounded once more, fully convinced that my father could "teach a rock to box," as he often bragged.

As my father predicted, Jason's next three fights were far easier than his Friday night bout with Jamal Turner. In total, Jason Bragg went 4–0 (with three knockouts) in capturing the 2005 Lewisburg middleweight Toughman Championship. When Jason Bragg returned to Lo's Gym the following week, the kids saw him differently—wanted to work with him on the mitts just as much as they did my father. All of this was going to do wonders for Jason's career as an amateur boxing trainer, I figured. But that wasn't how it played out, not exactly.

A few months later, Jason Bragg found himself right back in there, fighting for the Beckley Toughman Championship. It's like art or fashion—proving one's Appalachian manliness is an ongoing process, never quite complete. Jason won the whole damn thing in Beckley, going 4–0 (with two knockouts).

Less than one year into it, Jason was 10–0 (with six knockouts). This was one hell of a pugilistic ethos boost, especially for an undersized 30-something coal miner.

My father had done some of his best work as a trainer, turning Jason into an undefeated boxer. Winning back-to-back Toughman Championships was a nice ending to Jason Bragg's *Cinderella Man* story, I figured. But that wasn't how it played out, not exactly.

***

December 1999. Clarksburg, West Virginia.

"Welcome, Mr. Snyder. This must be your son, Todd. Welcome."

Jerry Thomas was putting it on real thick. He was a dresser and a talker.

"Mike, Todd, let me introduce you to my brother."

"Tommy, this is Mike Snyder and his son, Todd. They drove up here all the way from Webster County."

"Pleased to meet you fellas."

We shook hands.

Tommy was big and intimidating, but it was hard to believe he fought Jimmy Young and Leon Spinks. He seemed too nice, too civilized. Tommy had his police uniform on that day. It was impossible to believe he'd fought those guys.

"Now let me introduce you to the rest of our staff."

Jerry paraded us around his Clarksburg boxing gym, introducing us to anyone who mattered.

"Tim, this is Mike Snyder and his son, Todd."

"Tim Wheeler, nice to meet you fellas."

We shook hands.

"Nice to meet you, Tim."

Tim Wheeler, probably in his late forties, was a local Clarksburg boxer who'd won a few of Jerry's Toughman Contests back in the day and had since gone on to become one of the top boxing referees in the state—I recognized him from Beckley. Tim was a funny, energetic, handsome guy who favored Billy Ray Cyrus; he seemed too nice to be a boxing trainer.

"And this is Dennis Quinn. He's our other head trainer."

"Dennis Quinn. Nice to meet you fellas."

We shook hands.

"Nice to meet you, Dennis."

Dennis Quinn, probably in his early sixties, was a grizzled fight veteran who had come up in one of the toughest fight towns in America— Philadelphia, Pennsylvania. And let me tell you, from the accent to his demeanor, Dennis Quinn was all Philadelphia. He was the Diet Coke version of Burgess Meredith's Mickey Goldmill character. He looked the part more than the rest of them.

"I heard you used to train with Smokin' Joe Frazier," I once naively said.

"That man is a goddamn drunk and a bully," Dennis swiftly replied.

I never asked Dennis about Frazier again.

Because Tommy Thomas was often busy with his duties as a police officer and Jerry Thomas was preoccupied with the business side of the

Toughman Contest enterprise, Tim Wheeler and Dennis Quinn typically opened and ran the Tommy Thomas Boxing Club. Tim and Dennis were probably my two favorite characters I met during our bimonthly boxing pilgrimages around the state. Both guys would always keep me laughing, often for different reasons. These guys were full of Jesus-like parables on the sweet science. They had a story to explain every facet of the fight game. If you could get them talking, you'd end up doing more talking than training.

"Now, let me introduce you gentlemen to some of our most accomplished fighters," Jerry said, whisking us around the gym. Jerry was like a politician—he knew how to socialize in a crowded room.

"This is Darren 'Bam Bam' Abraham. He fights professionally at the 175 pound division. Thus far, Darren is 5–0 with two wins coming by KO."

Jerry would slip back into his announcer voice every now and then.

"Nice to meet you, Darren."

We shook hands.

"The pleasure is all mine."

Darren "Bam Bam" Abraham looked like an insurance salesman. He was clean-shaven, wore khakis and polo shirts to the gym, and sported a slicked-back Wall Street haircut. He spoke like a city boy and wasn't the least bit intimidating. But he was tall and slender and didn't have an ounce of fat on his body. When he boxed, it looked like ballet. His movements seemed choreographed and precise. Darren took to me right away; he'd always buddy up with me and tell me that I was doing well. He was like a schoolteacher who makes each of his students believe they are his favorite. I trusted Darren. I'd brag to my high school friends about knowing a real-life professional boxer. I'd reference him to boost my own ego.

I hadn't planned to spar that day.

Darren "Bam Bam" Abraham was supposed to go six rounds with Billy Fox. My father had driven me to Clarksburg that Friday just to see Darren and Billy spar. This was going to be some kind of lesson, I figured.

But after all of us had sat around waiting for almost an hour, Billy Fox called Tommy and said he wasn't going to be able to make it down from Pittsburgh. Everyone else had gone home.

"Looks like it's you and me," Darren said.

"Me?"

"Yeah, I've got a fight next weekend. I need to get six rounds in or it's going to throw everything off."

"But I'm no good. I can't go six rounds with you."

My father didn't like me talking like that in front of everyone.

"Todd, get in there and learn from him. Darren isn't going to tee off on you," he said, trying to save face.

I climbed in the ring with Darren "Bam Bam" Abraham.

Pop. Pop. Pop.

His punches stung like Cowboy Jack's tattoo needle.

Darren wasn't trying to get me out of there, but there was *mustard* on those punches. After the fifth round, I was completely exhausted. In the corner, I tried to quit.

"Dad, I can't go anymore," I said through my slobber-filled mouthpiece.

"Son, you're going the six rounds."

"I can't."

Ding!

"Get back out there."

So I did.

My gloves felt like cinderblocks. My legs were shot. Darren started landing his perfectly choreographed punches again.

Pop. Pop. Pop.

Pop. Pop. Pop.

Pop. Pop. Pop.

Darren shouldn't have been hitting me that hard, I thought. It pissed me off. My father pissed me off. Billy Fox pissed me off too. This should have been his beating. Pissed off but mostly tired, I ducked a straight right jab and countered. The punch landed squarely on Darren's chin. I doubt it shook him up much, but it made a CRACK and I heard Dennis and Tim whoop it up for a second.

Pop. Pop. Pop.

Darren started throwing back with a little more gusto. I was exhausted, but I fought back. It was a nice little tussle there for a second.

Ding!

I made it.

Out in the parking lot, my father gave me a big kiss on the cheek. He never did that.

"You made me very proud in there. Son, you just went six rounds with an undefeated professional boxer."

That's how I remember my first day in the Tommy Thomas Boxing Club. I'd found something deep within myself that I didn't know was there.

And that's precisely how Jason Bragg felt after winning those Toughman Contests. He'd found something.

***

Jerry Thomas had been around the professional game most of his adult life; he'd been ringside for all of his brother's big fights, had promoted shows alongside Don King, promoted fights across the U.S. and abroad— Mexico, Switzerland, Italy, South Africa, France, England, and Canada. If there was a professional boxing match going down in his home state of West Virginia, Jerry was likely in on it. Wheeling Island Casino in Wheeling, West Virginia, and Mountaineer Racetrack and Casino in Chester, West Virginia, were his playgrounds. My father would often tag along, working as judge, inspector, and referee—whatever Jerry needed. Every now and then he'd find himself in the corner, working as a stand-in chief second for local professionals such as Kenny George (Elkins, West Virginia). When Jason Bragg decided to turn professional, Jerry Thomas was the best and most obvious choice to serve as his promoter/manager.

"Jerry, I'm gonna be honest with you."

"Jason's 32 years old, I know he ain't got no long-term future in the sport."

"We just want to win a pro fight, no gimmies, but we want to win one."

"Maybe a few local fights, then a casino fight, but that's it," my father cautioned over the phone.

Jason Bragg had a fan-friendly disposition in the ring, and had been impressive enough in his two Toughman victories. Jerry was quick to take him on. The third annual Marvin Gothard Classic, only a few months away, was the logical venue for Jason Bragg's professional debut—Jason had fought *the* fight of the night against Beckley Chavez at the previous year's event. Adding a professional boxing match to the already popular lineup of local amateurs was a smart move for the third installment of the Marvin Gothard show, Jerry felt. He was right—there wasn't an empty bleacher seat in the house.

Ken Kellum[80] was a light-skinned 23-year-old kid out of Warren, Ohio. He had a clean-shaven, pretty-boy face. My father and I had seen Ken fight as an amateur. My father was a little concerned with his stick-and-move style, but it was the fairest fight Jerry could cook up on short notice; my father wasn't about to let Jason step in the ring with an experienced pro. Jerry faxed the contract to my father's office at the coal mines and Jason signed on the dotted line. And just like that, little Jason Bragg was a prizefighter.

Jason Bragg whipped himself into tremendous shape that summer; he'd run the steps down at the Smooth Coal Company treatment plant each morning, and fixed himself up a chin-up bar as well.

"I was always training . . . even when I was at the coal mine," Jason once reflected.

Each evening, Jason and my father dedicated extra hours to preparing for Lo's Gym's first crack at professional boxing. Jason's wife, Tiffany, a registered nurse, made sure he was eating the right foods, and tended to his bumps and bruises. It was one hell of a training camp and the results showed. Six-pack abdominals. Ripped biceps. The scrawny kid who was too little for the Webster County High School basketball team found himself in the body of a professional boxer. All of the coal mining and boxing was beginning to take a toll on my father's aging body. He had a torn bicep, nerve damage in his lower back that caused his left leg to feel numb, a bleeding ulcer that kept him up at night, and the sore wrists and elbows that go with holding the mitts for power punchers. Every month or so my father would drive to Webster Springs Hospital to have fluid drained from his right elbow. The sand was draining out of the hourglass.

Leading up to the fight, none of us really knew what was going through Jason Bragg's mind. Jason had something of a class clown attitude and none of us could tell if he was keeping it all inside or wasn't taking the risk seriously. He was keeping it all inside.

"The night before the fight, I just 'fessed up and told Tiffany the truth," Jason said to me years later.

"What's bothering you?" Tiffany asked.

"I'm scared," Jason replied.

"Scared of getting hurt?" Tiffany questioned.

"Hell no . . . scared of losing . . . scared of feeling that way again."

Ken won the first round, sticking and moving his way around the ring. Jason was the aggressor, but Ken blocked most of the power shots. The second round went to Jason—an all-out assault of left and right hooks to the head and body. The third round was too close to call. I change my mind every time I watch the tape. If you scored it for Ken, I wouldn't call you crazy. The final round of the bout belonged to Jason Bragg, as was always the case. Our Lo's Gym amateurs, led by an impressive KO performance by Lane Gillespie, had gone 4–1 in their undercard bouts. If Jason had won the decision, it would have been our boxing club's best hometown showing. He didn't. The judges handed down a majority decision for Ken Kellum.

The first professional boxing match in Webster County history was all folks around Cowen were talking about for a week or so. You couldn't go into Foodland or down to the post office without hearing somebody gossip about the fight.

"Lo, ol' Jason Bragg got robbed."

"Them judges were blind."

"That wasn't the way I scored it," the guys down at the Smooth Coal Company declared.

And, for a short while, things got back to normal at Lo's Gym. My father had other fighters to train, Toughman fights to referee, and amateur events to attend. Jason again picked up his former role as Lo's Gym's helping hand.

Jason tried to hide it, and made an honest effort.

But the festering sore remained.

"Lo," Jason called out to my father on Main Street one night.

"Tell Jerry Thomas I want a rematch."

***

The Ken Kellum–Jason Bragg rematch was set for October 5, 2007, at Elkins High School gymnasium. The event was an all-pro card featuring local talent such as Kenny "Mr. Opportunity" George, Justin "The Lumberjack" Howes, John "The Jaw Breaker" Boggs, and Tanya "Redneck Momma" Colvin. The rumor was that William Joppy, the former WBA middleweight champion of the world, was scheduled for the main event, and credible boxing websites even suggested as much. Joppy never made it to Elkins, West Virginia, that night.

My father put everything he had left into Jason Bragg's second training camp as a professional boxer. He even coaxed Curtis "The Ice Man" Wright out of retirement, talking him back into boxing to assist with Jason's training. Winning a real professional boxing match was a bucket-list item for both Jason and my father, two coal miners who'd cooked up new identities late in life. It was now or never, they figured.

When the bell rang, Jason shot out of the corner, reckless and angry. He fought the first two minutes of the fight as if a million dollars were on the line. Ken smacked Jason with a few countershots, but spent most of the round backpedaling.

Pop! Pop!

Pop! Pop!

Pop! Pop!

Jason landed one-two combinations with power and accuracy, slipping countershots and bulldogging his opponent to the ropes. During the final 30 seconds of the round, Ken was trapped in the blue corner. Jason quickly transformed a left hook to the body into a left uppercut, snapping Ken's head backward, a combination that was quickly rewarded by the applause of the Webster County faithful who'd made the drive to Elkins.

Ding!

The bell sounded an end to the round. Jason returned to the corner, my father entered the ring, and I slid the stool underneath the bottom rope.

"Okay, take a deep breath," my father instructed, removing Jason's mouthpiece.

"You feeling, okay?"

"Yeah, I won that one," Jason announced, in-between gasps for air.

"Okay, Jason. Stay calm. Take another deep breath," my father instructed, providing Jason with a sip of water from the bottle.

"Keep your chin tucked, elbows in, everything straight and down the middle."

"Pace yourself."

"Don't case this guy," my father instructed, placing the mouthpiece back in Jason's mouth.

That's when referee Tim Wheeler tapped my father on the shoulder.
"That's it, Lo," Tim instructed.

Ken's chief second had called a halt to the bout. His boxer was either unable or unwilling to continue.

Jason Bragg's fight was over.

Chapter 11

HILLBILLY JEFFERSON

Zack Kuhn was the most decorated amateur boxer in the state of West Virginia. Zack fought out of the Van Boxing Club in Boone County. Long ropey arms, shaggy hair, the kid didn't look like a champion, but he was. Zack won multiple state championships and had success at the national level. He'd fought in well over 100 amateur bouts by the time he was a high school sophomore. Zack was a high school sophomore when he lost his mother.

My father met Zack Kuhn at the first Marvin Gothard Classic and instantly took a liking to his family. Zack's father, Scott, trained fighters, Zack and his older brother were fighters, and Zack's mother judged fights. Our boxing clubs were in-state rivals, but my father maintained a healthy respect for the opposition.

"Promise that when you hit it big, you'll score me some free tickets to your first championship fight at Madison Square Garden," my father would joke with Zack after bouts.

When my father heard that Zack's mother had been killed in a car accident in June 2005, he took to the phone, got the necessary town permits, and organized a road stop on Main Street in Cowen. The Kuhn family was having trouble coming up with money for the funeral expenses, we'd heard from Bullet Bill Hopkins.

Lo's Gym fighters toed the yellow line and collected money in rubber buckets. My father pitched in his donation at the end.

"No, Zack doesn't box out of Lo's Gym," my father repeated throughout the day, explaining the purpose of the collection to motorists.

***

Marine Corp. Bryan J. Richardson, of Summersville, West Virginia, died in Al Anbar Province, Iraq, on March 25, 2005. He was 23 years old.

Patrick W. Richardson, of Hominy Falls, West Virginia, died in an automobile accident on February 1, 2006. Patrick was 27 years old.

Patrick was Bryan's older brother.

When news broke of the Richardson family's second tragedy in less than a year, my father decided Lo's Gym should do something to help honor the legacy of the two Nicholas County boys. The Bryan and Pat Richardson Memorial Boxing Event was his brainchild. Hosted at the newly opened Summersville Armory on April 1, 2006, the event featured over 25 amateur bouts, pulling together clubs from Ohio, Kentucky, Pennsylvania, and West Virginia (six or seven of our Lo's Gym guys fought on the card as well). The $5,000 in proceeds went to a scholarship to honor the legacy of Bryan and Pat Richardson, two West Virginia boys my father had never even met.

"Bryan and Pat are all of our brothers," my father said to the local news reporter before the first bout.

***

Three years into it, Lo's Gym had donated over 500 new coats to the four local schools that made up the Webster County District. Donations came from the Smooth Coal Company, other town businesses, and from my father's own paycheck. During the winter months, you couldn't drive down Main Street in Cowen without catching a glimpse of one of those coats.

Three years into it, Lo's Gym had established an annual Easter Sunday field trip to Sunny Grove Nursing Home in Cowen. Fighters delivered Easter baskets to the residents, and stayed to talk, laugh, and share stories.

"There is a lot we can learn from these folks, let's treat them like we'd like to be treated," he'd instruct the fighters before entering Sunny Grove.

It was an ego check for some guys, rough-around-the-edges man-boys who'd almost rather die than be caught holding an Easter basket.

Three years into it, my father had become pen pals with more than a few local kids locked away in the Central Regional Jail, kids doing time in juvie. Some were violent, some were rapists, others were in for drugs or larceny or both.

"Mike, I don't like you sending letters with our home address to those boys," my mother finally said at the dinner table one night.

"I was in prison and you didn't come to see me," my father responded, without looking up from his spoonful of mashed potatoes.

Cowen, West Virginia's, Street Preacher was destined for politics. When a spot opened on the Webster County Board of Education, folks around town talked my father into running for the position.

"I'm just an old coal miner," my father would say, trying to downplay his significance in the community.

It took some nudging before my father agreed to run for the position. He didn't hang a single campaign sign or knock on a single door. He agreed to place his name on the ballot, but did absolutely no campaigning whatsoever. My father won his spot on the Webster County Board of Education by a landslide.

Mike "Lo" Snyder, the warehouse manager at the Smooth Coal Company and head trainer at Lo's Gym Boxing Club, served on the Webster County Board of Education for the next six years. He was an advocate for the kid who was falling through the cracks. He was the unofficial affiliate of the alternative school boys.

"Mike, you can't help some kids," a fellow board member once warned.

"I'm not worried about what I can't do. I'm interested in seeing what I can do," he replied.

Three years into it, Mike "Lo" Snyder was living a life of service. Cowen had fallen on difficult times; folks were out of work, as the mines were gradually shutting down one by one. There was more than enough poverty to go around.

Three years into it, my father had developed an Ahab-like obsession with living Jesus's Sermon on the Mount.

And folks around town began to take notice.

***

Sue Anderson was the principal at Glade Elementary in Cowen, West Virginia. She was the only principal I'd ever known during my nine years at Glade. Sue was stylish, outgoing, and classy—the smartest woman in all of Webster County, for all I knew. She was the boss lady of Glade Elementary, a woman of power in our small West Virginia mountain town. Sue Anderson first became involved with Lo's Gym when my father introduced the coat drive into the mix, a few years before he joined the Board of Education. She was all for giving new coats to poor kids, but wasn't enthusiastic about the sport of boxing. Sue Anderson didn't become connected with Lo's Gym until Alec and Max caught the bug.

Sue Anderson had two boys. Alec was five years younger than me, Max a good nine years or so. I'd see them around school when they were little, but didn't know either boy that well. When they walked through the doors that first day, I figured they'd be boxing tourists. Alec, 17 years old when he first arrived at Lo's Gym, didn't look the part. He was a good-looking, clean-shaven kid with nice clothes. He was tall, athletic, and outgoing, but I didn't take him seriously. Alec looked more like a lover than a fighter.

Max, 13 years old at the time, was a stocky all-American-looking kid with curly hair and straight teeth. He didn't look the part any more than his older brother. Max and Alec had a college-educated daddy and a principal for a mommy. Boxing wasn't for those kinds of folks, I figured.

"You can go down to Mike's gym and work out . . . but I don't want you fighting," Principal Sue Anderson likely instructed her two boys.

Sue had it all wrong.

I did too.

The Anderson boys were naturals. They took to it quickly.

Alec and Max both won their amateur debut bouts in dominating fashion. If they hadn't won so easily, I doubt their mother would have tolerated much more of it. She was, without question, the loudest screamer in the crowd that night.

By the end of their first year at Lo's Gym, the Brothers Anderson had been transformed into small-town boxing royalty. Alec won the West Virginia Middleweight State Championship four fights into his amateur career and Max won the Super Middleweight Silver Glove title a month later. Alec was the technician; he wasn't great at anything, but he was good at everything. He was a counterpuncher, a slickster on defense, a textbook fundamentals kind of guy. Max was more of a front-foot attacking fighter—good defense and fundamentals, but always looking to turn the fight into a scrap. Alec and Max were model pupils for my father. They would've jumped off the New River Gorge Bridge if he had asked them to do so. When the Anderson boys fought on the same fight card, they never lost—perhaps gaining strength from the brotherly rivalry. The only problem they ever caused my father was when they sparred each other. My father had to keep an eye on the Anderson boys when they got in the ring as those sparring sessions would always turn into Gatti-Ward-style brawls.

The Anderson boys quickly lost interest in high school sports, becoming mainstays at Lo's Gym. Max even jumped in Cowboy Jack's tattoo chair and pledged his allegiance to my father with a Lo's Gym tattoo along the lower right side of his abdomen; my Lo's Gym tattoo would come a few years later. If my father worked an amateur boxing match, you would likely see Alec or Max (or both) by his side. After turning 18, Alec voided his amateur status by fighting in and winning the Beckley Toughman Contest; Max eventually did the same by winning the Summersville portion of the Rough-N-Rowdy. By the time Alec and Max showed up on the scene, my father had already established a core group of talented boxers. Chris Short was the recipient of West Virginia's most prestigious boxing award, the Governor's Cup. Chris Ledsome was the most feared heavyweight under the age of 16. Claudia Cline was making her name as one of the best female boxers in the state. The Edge was packed full of hungry young fighters. Alec and Max simply added to my father's already impressive tally of accomplishments as a local boxing trainer. When Jason Bragg decided to turn professional, Alec Anderson did the same.

Sue Anderson became a fixture at Lo's Gym boxing events as well. She wasn't there just to cheer on her boys. She was there to cheer on the kids she'd watched grow up under her supervision as principal of Glade Elementary. She, like a lot of folks in the community, was inspired by the community service—inspired by the kids who'd found discipline and self-respect via humankind's most primal activity, fighting. And, in the privacy of her home office, Sue Anderson made the decision that changed everything.

"Your father was giving so much back to the community. I wanted to ensure that he received recognition for his service," Sue once told me.

Although we didn't know it for some time, it was Sue Anderson, the mother of Lo's Gym's boxing Anderson brothers, who wrote the recommendation letter that would validate all that my father had given back to his hometown.

***

The Jefferson Award was the brainchild of Jacqueline Kennedy Onassis, U.S. Sen. Robert Taft Jr., and Samuel Beard. Their charge was to establish a Nobel Prize for Community Service. Named after the third president of the United States, the Jefferson Awards Foundation was created in 1972 by the American Institute of Public Service.[81] The goal was to highlight the accomplishments of ordinary folks who did exceptional things in their communities without expectation of recognition. Recipients are recognized at the state level and then proceed to a national recognition ceremony in Washington, D.C.

None of us had ever heard of the Jefferson Award. When my father received the call, he was stocking warehouse shelves down at the Smooth Coal Company.

"If they hadn't asked for Mike Snyder of Lo's Gym . . . I'd have figured they were looking for another Mike Snyder," my father once reflected.

Winning the West Virginia Jefferson Award was one of the proudest moments in my father's life, but he'd never admit it. My father was a giver, and givers like to revel in the joy of others, never wanting to be praised for their selflessness.

"This lady called me at work. She said I have to give a speech at the capital in Charleston . . . at a dinner with Gov. Joe Manchin," my father said over the phone, trying his best to fight the urge to be excited.

"And then they're gonna fly me to D.C. for the National Jefferson Awards Ceremony," he added.

My father had never been to our nation's capital. I'm not sure if he had ever been to West Virginia's state capital. He hadn't been much of anywhere outside of the Tri-State Boxing Association.

"My God, I never dreamed this boxing stuff would take me all the way to Washington, D.C. . . . I never once dreamed I'd get to see the capital," he gushed over the phone.

My father's enthusiasm shed light on a side of my father that was, in many ways, unfamiliar to me. His joy had always come from the triumphs of others. This was his prize.

"Who'd have ever thought when we built that little boxing ring in the back of your mom's beauty shop that all of this boxing stuff would lead us down this path," my father reflected.

He was right. It was that makeshift boxing ring that had set us both adrift. What we didn't know at the time, however, was just how far away from Cowen, West Virginia, our ships would sail.

***

I hid the three-ring binder underneath my bed, not unlike a teenage boy with a dirty magazine. Roxanne Aftanas had given it to me after class; she was Dr. Kirkwood to me back then. I nodded at all the things she told me, pretended to understand, pretended to be brave, and carried the three-ring binder across Huntington, West Virginia's, snow-covered Fifth Avenue and back to my apartment. But I didn't even take a little peek. The three-ring binder stayed underneath my bed for just over seven days.

At first, I didn't tell my father about the three-ring binder underneath my bed. I didn't even tell Stephanie. They'd think I was crazy, I figured. The plan was to hide the three-ring binder underneath my bed without anybody knowing that it was in my possession. I'd wait a week or so and then give it back to Dr. Kirkwood. If I gave it back to her in less than a week, she'd know that I hadn't read it. I didn't want to hurt Dr. Kirkwood's feelings, seeing that she had been so nice to me over the past few months. That's why I kept the three-ring binder underneath my bed for that first week. Back then I was an over-thinker, a planner/schemer, not unlike Shakespeare's Hamlet.

I had it all figured out. I'd eventually give the three-ring binder back to Dr. Kirkwood and say something like, "Thanks for going to all that trouble, Dr. Kirkwood. I photocopied the pages I needed. You should keep the binder in your office for the next student who needs it."

She'd say something like, "Great, Todd. I'm happy to help."

Or, "Are you sure? I made it for you to keep."

And then I'd say something like, "No. I insist. I copied everything I need. You should keep it here for the next student."

I'd give the three-ring binder back to Dr. Kirkwood, never mention it again, she'd eventually get the hint, and my parents and Stephanie would be none the wiser. That was the plan.

Dr. Kirkwood asked me about the three-ring binder the following Thursday. I knew that she was going to do that. I was ready for it.

I said something like, "There is a lot of information in there. I'm still looking through it."

I hadn't.

"Make sure you check out Ohio University. It's only about 70 miles from here," she added.

That was just the push I needed. If she hadn't said that, you certainly would not be reading these words.

When I made it back to my apartment after class, I removed the three-ring binder from underneath my bed, and carefully flipped through the pages.

Florida State University.

I didn't know a thing about Florida outside of oranges and NCAA Championship football teams.

The University of Louisville.

Muhammad Ali was from Louisville. They made quality baseball bats there. This was the extent of my knowledge about Louisville.

The University of Texas at Austin.

I'd never heard of Austin, Texas. All I knew of Texas was cowboy movies, and Dallas Cowboys, and cowboy hats, and delicious toast. At this point in my life, I wasn't exactly well traveled. I was a kid from coal country. Like my father, I hadn't been much of anywhere.

And then I flipped the page and there it was.

Ohio University.

Athens, Ohio.

"Seventy miles from Huntington, West Virginia," I remembered.

I looked it up on MapQuest just to make sure Dr. Kirkwood wasn't mistaken.

She wasn't—72 miles exactly.

I wasn't looking for prestige. I wasn't looking for famous professors.

I didn't know anything about teaching assistantships or research stipends or WPA administrative opportunities. I was a first-generation college student who had fallen in love with the dream of becoming a college professor, a writer/scholar.

"You can't get a tenure-track job without a PhD," somebody told me along the way.

Tenure-track job means that you are actually treated like a human being by your employer, I learned.

The dreamer inside of me was brave enough to pursue the magical PhD that would allow me to stay in the ivory tower for good. The hillbilly inside of me figured PhDs were for city boys or rich folks or geniuses. The dreamer inside of me didn't want to go back to the realities of life in Cowen. The hillbilly inside me was more than ready to do so.

"What makes you think you're smart enough to get a PhD?"

"Boy, you getting too big for your britches."

"They goin' laugh at you, boy, . . . when you apply to them fancy schools and don't get in . . . they goin' laugh at you," the hillbilly said to me.

But I found what I was looking for on the fourth or fifth page of that three-ring binder—a PhD program in rhetoric and composition that was close to *home*.

***

Midway through my first semester as a graduate student, Dr. Kirkwood asked if I had time to speak with her after class, in her office. I thought that I might be in some kind of serious trouble.

"I've committed accidental plagiarism," I figured.

Dr. Kirkwood didn't pass my essay back when she distributed the rest of the grades to my peers. When your paper doesn't get passed back with the others, that's never a good sign.

"I'm an accidental plagiarizer and now they are going to kick me out of graduate school," I imagined.

Back in Dr. Kirkwood's office, on her desk, sat my essay on the role of parental involvement in the college-going decisions of first-generation college students from rural Appalachia. Our class had gone through the IRB process and conducted our own little makeshift ethnographic studies. Mine was a 35-pager that blended scholarly writing with personal writing. At this point in my life, writing was the only subject in which I had any confidence whatsoever. I went into adolescence thinking that I was a good writer, a clever writer, but along the way there were plenty of people who told me that writing was not a realistic profession. When I glanced down at my ethnographic essay on Dr. Kirkwood's desk, I figured she was about to say something worse than that.

But she didn't.

Dr. Kirkwood told me that my little makeshift study was the best graduate student paper she had ever read and that she was going to help me get it published. She started talking about Victor Villanueva's *Bootstraps*, Katherine Kelleher Sohn's *Whistlin' and Crowin' Women of Appalachia*, and some guy named Mike Rose. She started talking to me about academic conferences and Doctor School. She said we should meet again and come up with a *graduate school game plan*. At the time, I didn't believe any of it.

But I enjoyed the fantasy.

I likened our after-class meetings, our conversations, to the discourse my father and grandfather would indulge in about winning the lottery. She was bluffing, I figured.

She wasn't.

The following class session, Dr. Kirkwood showed up with a three-ring binder that contained the admission requirements for every single PhD rhetoric and composition program in the United States of America, as far as I knew.

During my second year of graduate school, my life changed quickly and drastically. All of Dr. Kirkwood's fantastic predictions came true—all of them. My little makeshift ethnographic study was accepted for publication in *The Community Literacy Journal*. It was also accepted as a conference paper for The Thomas R. Watson Conference on Rhetoric and Composition. Just like that, I had a scholarly article and a conference presentation on my CV. Just like that I had a CV.

Success was a new and contagious feeling for me. I wanted to attend Doctor School more than anything I had ever wanted in my entire life. The problem was that Dr. Kirkwood didn't exactly understand the world I was from. She didn't quite understand my insecurities or the limitations people from my neck of the woods often place on themselves. Half of the universities in that three-ring binder were out on the West Coast.

Telling my fiancée or my parents that I wanted to go to Doctor School out on the West Coast would have been like telling them I wanted to move, become an astronaut, and go to Mars. Rural Appalachian kids often come from socioeconomically disadvantaged communities that give way to defeatist world views. These kids come from isolated mountain communities that maintain cultural frameworks that, in many ways, discourage nomadic lifestyles. But Doctor School sounded like a dream to me—all of it but the moving-away-from-*home* part.

"It's just a few years of your life," Dr. Kirkwood said.

"Go hang out on the beach for five years and then come back to Appalachia," she added.

In my mind, Ohio University was the only realistic option. Ohio was as far away from *home* as I was willing to move. But I'd give it a shot. I'd give it my best. If I didn't get into Ohio University, I was going back *home*, back to Lo's Gym. That was the deal I made with myself.

The following day I unveiled my Doctor School ambitions to Stephanie and my parents. I'd be a liar if I wrote that they were receptive to the idea. However, all parties eventually agreed to my Ohio-or-bust game plan. That is, all parties except Dr. Kirkwood.

"You need to apply to at least three or four schools," Dr. Kirkwood said.

"These programs sometimes accept only two or three students per year and they can be very competitive. Let's research your top three or four schools and apply a little more broadly," she added.

"Okay, I'll pick a top four," I replied.

But I didn't, not really.

That winter I applied to Ohio University and West Virginia University. WVU didn't even have the program that I was looking for, but I applied anyway.

A few months later I gave Dr. Kirkwood and a few other recommendation letter writers the names and addresses of two additional schools that I had no intention of ever applying to. Some poor secretary at those schools started admission files for Todd Daniel Snyder that would never be completed. If Roxanne reads this piece, she'll know the truth for the first time.

For the hillbilly inside me, it was Ohio or West Virginia or bust. She didn't know who she was dealing with. Then again, maybe she did.

In March 2006, I received the rejection letter from West Virginia University that I likely deserved. The Ohio University envelope showed up in the little tin mailbox outside my apartment a few weeks later. I was so frightened by the contents of that letter that I made Stephanie open and read it. I was *wait listed* and consequently devastated. I'd been quasi-accepted to Ohio University's program, but my optimism vanished instantly. I went back to my apartment and wrote Dr. Kirkwood a sad little email thanking her for everything that she'd done for me.

"It appears that my vacation in the ivory tower was about to come to an end. I'll probably just move back to Cowen and help my dad with his boxing gym," I wrote.

She replied quickly, her email was of the keep-your-chin-up variety. "I can help you get an adjunct position here at Marshall. We'll apply to more schools next time. We'll get you in more conferences. We'll help you publish again," she wrote.

But I'd already given up.

The following week I started applying to public school teaching positions back *home*. There weren't any public school teaching positions back *home*, just coal to be mined. I cursed that three-ring binder. I hated myself for removing it from underneath my bed.

Two weeks later, a 704 area code came up on my caller ID. It was 3 p.m. on a Friday afternoon. It was Dr. Josie Bloomfield of Ohio University.

The hillbilly was going to Doctor School.

***

Three weeks into my career as a doctoral candidate at Ohio University, I mustered up the courage to ask Dr. Holt for permission to skip her graduate seminar on pragmatist rhetoric. My father was being honored as the state's Jefferson Awards recipient at the West Virginia state capital. My grandmother bought my father a JCPenney suit for the award ceremony. It was probably the first suit he'd ever owned in his life. I'd recently purchased my first professor blazer at the Grand Central Mall, and learned how to tie a tie by watching YouTube videos. We looked like a distinguished family that day, my mother, sister, and fiancée all looking more beautiful than ever before. The dining hall at the University of Charleston was too fancy for an old coal miner like my father. It was all cloth napkins and shiny silverware. The room was full of local politicians and news anchors.

"Look, there is my favorite weatherman," my mom whispered at dinner.

My father gave a brief but rhetorically powerful speech, his hand slightly shaking the cue cards. He began by telling the story of how the gym found its way from the back of the Classic Curl Beauty Shop and then moved to The Edge. He thanked the church, his family, Jeff Dean, and Jason Bragg. My father talked of Bobby McCartney, told a few stories of other Bobby McCartneys in our gym. He talked about the coats, and the nursing home visits, and the road stops, and the money we'd raised, and the people it had helped. If I remember correctly, he didn't mention any of the impressive accolades his boxers had accomplished in the ring.

"I do this," my father said toward the crescendo of the speech.

"I do this for *the least*. Jesus told us that what you've done unto the least, you've done unto me," he said, closing the show.

My father shed his tears openly. The crowd offered hearty applause. Gov. Joe Manchin stood up from his table and hugged my father on his way back to his seat. There for a second, West Virginia's governor and the old coal miner looked like two high school buddies reunited.

I wasn't used to seeing my father all dressed up. He probably wasn't used to seeing me that way either. We'd made a few good decisions along the way, it appeared.

"I guess this makes me Hillbilly Jefferson," my father joked, as we hugged and said our good-byes in Charleston.

"I'm pretty sure Ol' Thomas Jefferson and his family was from the other Virginia," he added.

"Yeah, I think you've got it right, Dad."

"You're Cowen's minister of fisticuffs," I said.

After the ceremony, my father, mother, and sister made their way back to Cowen, and Stephanie and I back to our new life in Athens, Ohio.

I didn't accompany my father, mother, and sister to Washington, D.C., for the national Jefferson Award Ceremony the following month. I had a heavy course load as a graduate assistant and Stephanie had just begun her new job at Health Recovery Services, a nonprofit chemical dependency center in Athens. We were big kids now, off on our own for the first time—our marriage sanctified at the First Baptist Church of

Cowen, Pastor Donne presiding over the ceremonies. Stephanie and I were the first in our families to move *away*.

My father made the usual touristy stops during his celebration weekend in Washington. He visited Honest Abe, the White House, the Washington Monument, and the Pentagon. They even snuck in a quick visit to Joe Louis's grave in Arlington Cemetery, my father jumping the rope to pose with the gravestone in a picture.

My father gave the same speech that night, my sister, Katie, tells me. He ended with the "remember the least" crescendo and shed a few tears.

"Joe Biden was there . . . I swear it," my father insisted.

But you can never quite be sure with a storyteller like him.

***

I've only one regret. I should have attended the parade. My father didn't get to puff out his chest and trot around the bases all that often. He was a man constantly in search of approval, never quite feeling loved or appreciated. His crazy childhood made him that way, I think. He needed to be thanked. He needed to know that you thought he was a *real swell guy*. Otherwise, he pretty much felt like something the cat dragged in. Perched on the back of that white 1964 Chevy convertible, with those red Everlast gloves proudly displayed on each side of his thighs, I imagine he felt validated, if only for a day. I should have been there.

But this isn't an apology, not really. I've exorcised no demons in making this confession. Rather, I'm simply at a place in my life where I am comfortable admitting the festering guilt that is a by-product of my willful absence. On that sunny July afternoon in 2008, I was a few hundred miles away in Athens, Ohio, writing seminar papers and conference proposals, I suppose. I don't particularly remember what I was doing that day.

With each passing year of my doctoral education, I gradually withdrew from it all. I missed Jason Bragg's professional bout with Jason Colvin at the Wheeling Island Casino. I missed Alec Anderson's pro bout with Jesse "The Rooster" McCutchen. I skipped out on Curtis Wright's comeback fight against Bobby Thomas Jr. at Beckley Armory. The visits to Lo's Gym became less frequent and I eventually stopped going to fights altogether.

I blame Stephanie Nicole's beautiful green eyes. They made the past seem small and not worth my time. We'd fallen in love and decided to start living in the future. Becoming professoriate is serious business, don't you know? Living in the past is a laborious existence.

The Cowen Railroad Festival was founded back in 1980 as a response to our neighboring town's annual shindig, The Webster Springs Wood Chopping Festival.

"Those old boys on that side of the county can have their annual shindig. By God we're gonna start one of our own," I imagine somebody from Cowen saying.

Every summer, during the final week of July, the Cowen Railroad Festival planning committee hangs a laminated banner over Main Street. They host beauty pageants in the Glade Elementary gymnasium. They host a pig roast on the Glade Elementary football field. They host fishing tournaments down at Big Ditch Lake. They host a car show in the Foodland parking lot. And they wrap it all up with a small-town parade. Fresh off his Washington, D.C., coronation, my father was the grand marshal of that parade back in 2008.

If I am ever bestowed such an honor—asked to be grand marshal of a parade—no matter how small or insignificant my accomplishments or how small and insignificant the parade, I hope my son would want to be there to cheer me on. I'd want him to say, "Dad, I'm proud of you," or "You've done good, old man." That much I'll admit.

My father wore that same oversized gray suit jacket that day. I know this because my sister took a photograph for me. I still have it. My father is smiling in that picture, showing his gold-capped teeth, dimples borne by a genuine smile. My father hated getting all gussied up. If he was getting all gussied up, it usually meant he was going to a funeral. But he wasn't going to a funeral, not really.

It would have been a perfect ending that day. I imagine my father riding off into the sunset in his oversized JCPenney's dress clothes.

If this were a piece of fiction, I might have closed the show that way, with Mike "Lo" Snyder, number 22 coming out of the backfield, perched on the back of a white 1964 Chevy convertible, two bright-red Everlast gloves displayed accordingly, the grand marshal of a victory parade lumbering its way down the freshly painted yellow lines of Main Street in Cowen, West Virginia.

Chapter 12

PREMATURE
STOPPAGE

Anthony Capone's[82] voicemail was the beginning of the end. Everything else is epilogue, the steady *pop* and *crack* of the mirror that doesn't yet realize it is broken.

Auditors were scheduled to arrive at the Smooth Coal Company that day and, as warehouse manager, auditors always put my father on edge. My father's cell phone was tucked away in his dinner bucket while the auditors were on the premises, so he missed the call. My father didn't notice the voicemail message until he arrived home from Lo's Gym later that night.

Hello. This is Anthony Capone of TKO Promotions. I'm looking to contact Mike Snyder. I have you listed as Alec Anderson's trainer and manager. Long story short, I'd like to offer Alec the opportunity to fight Daniel "The Golden Child" Jacobs in a scheduled four-round middleweight bout on Saturday, October 18. This bout will take place at Boardwalk Hall, Atlantic City, New Jersey, and will likely be featured as a televised undercard bout for an HBO Pay-Per-View event. I can offer Alec $1,200 for the fight. Your fee as a trainer will, of course, come out of that $1,200 purse. If this sounds like something that will work for both you and Alec, I can take care of travel accommodations and hotel rooms. Again, this is Anthony Capone calling for Mike Snyder concerning a potential fight between Daniel Jacobs and your fighter, Alec

Anderson. If you could give me a call back as soon as possible, that would be
fantastic. Thank you.

My father listened to the voicemail three or four times over, wagging
his head in disbelief each time. His was the look you wear when the doctor
says the tumor is malignant.

"I thought somebody had died, or something tore up at the mines and
he was getting called back to work or something," my mother said.

My father called me first, even before phoning Alec. I was at the
movies with my wife, Stephanie, so I missed the call. I didn't get the
voicemail until we arrived back at our apartment later that night.

"Todd, this is Dad [he'd always say that sort of thing on voicemail, as
if I wouldn't recognize my own father's raspy voice] . . . just got a call from
a matchmaker . . . they want to put Alec in there with Daniel Jacobs . . .
Atlantic City . . . on HBO Pay-Per-View . . . haven't talked to Alec yet . . .
give me a call . . . love ya."

I didn't believe him, figured somebody at the gym was pulling a prank.
Maybe Alec?

Or maybe my father was trying to pull a prank on me?

By the time I returned my father's call the following morning, he'd
already spoken with Anthony Capone. Their brief phone conversation
produced no new information. It was a take-it-or-leave-it offer. Capone
didn't pretend to think Alec stood a chance against Jacobs. World-class
prospects earn the luxury of padding the early portion of their records
against inferior opposition, scoring highlight-reel knockouts on nationally
televised undercard bouts.

At this point, Jacobs had a handful of professional wins. Alec was 0–2
as a pro (both losses coming by close but unanimous decisions). Capone
had been combing the internet boxing databases for opponents with
upside-down records to showcase his fighter's punching power in front
of the HBO Pay-Per-View audience. He didn't insult my father's boxing
intelligence by suggesting otherwise.

"Does Alec want to do it?"

"Haven't talked to him about it yet," my father said.

The lack of enthusiasm in my father's voice troubled me.

"Part of me thinks you ought to do it, Dad. This might be the only
time you get a chance like this."

"This ain't how I wanted to do it," he replied.

"You think Alec even knows who Daniel Jacobs is?"

"I know who Daniel Jacobs is," my father tersely responded.

Raised in the Brownsville section of Brooklyn, New York, Daniel Jacobs compiled a stellar amateur record of 173 wins to only seven losses, won four New York State Golden Gloves Championships, and two PAL National Championships on his way to becoming the 2006 United States national champion. My father and I had watched Jacobs make his pro debut on the undercard of the Floyd Mayweather Jr. vs. Ricky Hatton Pay-Per-View the previous year. You didn't need to be a boxing aficionado to know that Daniel "The Golden Child" Jacobs was going to eventually become the middleweight champion of the world.

"Alec is going to want to do this, Dad. Why aren't you excited?"

"Todd, he'll get hurt. I ain't in this to get people hurt."

"There is no way Alec turns this down. He'd fight anybody."

"That purse won't cover the hospital bill," my father said, half joking.

The conversation quickly turned into an argument.

"This is *your* shot, Dad. This is your chance to put a Lo's Gym fighter on HBO."

"This ain't how I wanted to do it," my father interrupted.

"Dad, if you don't want to take the fight . . . then what is the point of all this? Training these fighters day in and day out . . . Killing yourself at the mines all day and killing yourself down at the gym every evening and coming home at nine o'clock each night . . . All I ever hear you talk about is taking a local boy to the big dance . . . This looks like the big dance to me, Dad. It's everything you've always wanted."

My father remained silent.

"You're going to tell him, right? You have to tell Alec, Dad. You've got to give him the chance to decide. You can't keep this from him," I urged.

"This ain't how I wanted to do it," my father repeated for the final time.

We ended the conversation shortly thereafter. The graduate student was off to a doctoral seminar. The Smooth Coal Company warehouse manager had auditors to deal with.

Later that evening, my father pulled Alec to the side, away from the rest of the boxers, and informed him of the phone call he received from Anthony Capone.

"Your dad came over to me kinda nervous like. I could tell something was wrong by the way he was acting," Alec said.

Alec was no dummy. He understood the score. Alec and Max had watched Daniel "Child" Jacobs on the Mayweather vs. Hatton undercard as well. This was an opportunity to get knocked out on live television, the chance to play Tunney Hunsaker to a future world champion, the strangest of small-town bragging rights.

"Fuck it. We should do it," was Alec's gut reaction.

But the story of Lo's Gym doesn't end at Boardwalk Hall in Atlantic City, New Jersey, under the bright lights of an HBO Pay-Per-View telecast.

The younger version of my father would have said, "What if?"

Or something like, "One lucky punch can change all of our lives forever."

Or, "Fuck it. We should do it."

But this wasn't the younger version of Mike "Lo" Snyder.

My father had exhausted his own fantastic imagination. That voicemail from Anthony Capone was confirmation of what he already knew.

"Think I should do it?" Alec asked my father, out on Main Street, underneath the Cowen streetlights.

"I'll support you either way," my father reportedly said.

"It's a crooked deal, isn't it?" Alec both stated and asked.

"Yeah, it is, Alec. I'm in this game to help people. Not to get them hurt."

"So, it's just a set-up fight," Alec replied.

"We've had a good run, Alec. This little boxing gym has had a good run," my father said.

"Think I should do it?" Alec asked one final time, testing my father.

"This ain't how I wanted to do it," my father replied.

Tyrone Watson, a kid out of Pittsburgh, got the fight. We watched him get in there with Daniel Jacobs in the first televised bout of the Bernard Hopkins vs. Kelly Pavlik HBO Pay-Per-View on October 18, 2008. I was home from Ohio University for the weekend. My father and I watched from the comfort of the living room sofa.

Daniel Jacobs dropped Tyrone Watson with a thunderous right hand in the first round. Watson was a game fighter, but clearly outclassed. Jacobs finished him off in the second.

"Should have done it," I joked during slow-motion replays of the knockout, gruesome images indeed.

"Fighting out of Lo's Gym Boxing Club in Cowen, West Virginia . . ."
I added, mimicking Michael Buffer's trademark cadence.

"Alec . . . The Executioner . . . Anderson."

My father grinned, nodded, and made his way to the bathroom to
take a piss.

One year later, in October 2009, Daniel Jacobs defeated titleholder
Ishe Smith to become the WBO/NABO middleweight champion of the
world.

And Lo's Gym Boxing Club would be closed for good.

***

Gary Boone could have been a champion, my father says. But he wasn't.
Gary arrived at Lo's Gym in his mid-thirties, a fruit much too ripe to
take up a hobby like boxing. That's my opinion, not his.

Gary Boone was a tough man from Lewisburg; he'd fought in a
handful of Lewisburg Toughman Contests, winning a few fights here
and there, but never captured hometown glory. He'd watched my father
work the *champion's corner* for almost a decade. He'd watched local boys
Steve Tincher and Matt McClung win titles via their long-distance
commutes to Lo's Gym. Somewhere along the way, Gary scored my
father's phone number from Jerry Thomas and decided to give Lo's
Gym a try. He and my father became fast friends.

Gary had been a wild one back in the day; bar fights and street
fights, always looking for a fight. Gary was tall, muscular, with a Clint
Eastwood snarl. But married life had settled him down. And becoming
a father gave him some measure of perspective.

But, as is the case with most tough guys from around my way, Jerry
Thomas's traveling circus always brought it out of him. Gary's rage was
a jigsaw puzzle not easily put back together again. He couldn't fight the
urge to prove how tough a son-of-a-bitch he was. Gary Boone was going
to keep fighting until he won a Toughman Contest.

"Nobody was any tougher or worked any harder than Gary Boone.
I wanted to help him win a Toughman so bad," my father says.

He didn't. Gary Boone lost a unanimous decision in the semifinal
bout of the 2009 Lewisburg Toughman Contest, Gary's first and only
training camp under my father's tutelage. Later that night, Gary Boone
was medevac'd to Greenbrier County Hospital, was diagnosed with a

hematoma of the brain, and was rushed into emergency surgery. My father was on the road, making his way back to Cowen, when all of this occurred. He didn't find out about Gary's misfortune until he received a call from Jerry Thomas the following morning.

Gary Boone posted a picture of his scar to Facebook a few years ago. It wasn't pretty. The scar begins at the tip of Gary's left ear and snakes around his skull like a reversed C before ending its journey just above the left eyebrow. Doctors removed part of Gary Boone's skull to let the swelling in his brain go down, my sister tells me. She's the medical expert in the family.

But the story of Lo's Gym doesn't end with Gary Boone's reversed C scar tissue. If I were writing a screenplay, that would have been the way to go. Gary's injury was simply the second shard of glass to fall from the broken mirror. The *Big Guy Upstairs* had to get my father's attention in some serious kind of way. Otherwise, he'd have never even tapped the brakes. Gary Boone's injury did just that.

In March 2009, my father closed Lo's Gym for the summer, with plans to reopen in the fall. At least that's his version of the story. I'm not so sure he was actually planning on reopening the gym. My father was exhausted, both physically and mentally.

"If I close the gym for a week, I'll come back to find my shit piled in the corner, or worse," he'd always say.

He was right. That's why I figured he was finally waving the white towel. He knew the good Christian soldiers of the First Baptist Church of Cowen were dying for a chance to give him the old heave-ho.

"Why don't you take a few weeks off? You're working yourself ragged," the deacons would always say.

"If you don't want me down here doing this, please just let me know," my father would always reply.

"Oh no, it's not that," they'd always respond.

"They're dying for me to take a week off so they can pile my shit in the corner," my father would say.

He was right.

But like the maulers and sluggers who plead with the referee after the bout has already been stopped, my father dreamed of going out on his own terms. Four weeks after Gary Boone's surgery, my father received his eviction notice in the mail.

Cowen First Baptist Church
April 6, 2009

Dear Mike,

We at Cowen First Baptist Church would like to take time to thank you for the many years you put into taking care of the Youth in our Community. Last month me and Eugene Arnold stopped by your home and asked you if you were going to continue the Boxing Program at the Church and you stated it may be fall. We had also discussed about people picking up there boxing equipment. Up until now no one has responded. We at the Church feel that the upstairs at the Edge is valuable space that is needed and that can be use for the kids and most of all it can be sued to lift up the name of the Lord. We held our first Business Meeting in March and the Church has voted to stop the Boxing Program and move in a different direction. Even though it was a great program, we fill it only targeted some youth.

We at Cowen First Baptist want to be able to set up a program where we can reach all youth. It is very important that all youth have a place in the Church. Jesus said let them come for they are the Kingdom of God.

I am writing you to ask if you can make arrangements to remove all the boxing equipment out of the Edge upstairs. We would like to get started on our vision for the upstairs by 15 May 2009. This will give you plenty of time to move the equipment out. I will place my home number and work number at the bottom of this letter. Please give me a call when you want to get the equipment and I will make sure someone is there to let you in.

Mike, if you do not respond by 15 May 2009. We will be under the understanding at the Church that you don't want the Boxing Equipment. At that time we will get rid of it, so we can have the space for the Church. Again, I want to say if you want the equipment, please respond to this letter.

Mike, I want to personally thank you for the love you have for the Youth and we would love to have you and your family on our Team at the Church winning souls for the Lord. May God Bless You, but most of all Bless the Lord for He is worthy.

With Love,
Pastor Shawn Boggs[83]

Poor old Pastor Donne got the ax first. He didn't have anything to do with my father getting voted off the island, so to speak. It wasn't Eugene Arnold's fault either. When the church sent Pastor Donne packing, Eugene Arnold and his family jumped ship to the Baptist church on Erbacon Road. The new guy at Cowen First Baptist Church was of the fire-and-brimstone variety and didn't much like the idea of a boxing ministry. That's how churches operate in my neck of the woods, or maybe in every neck of the woods. They'll shuffle the deck every now and then just to keep things interesting.

Getting the old heave-ho from the good Christian soldiers of the First Baptist Church of Cowen rejuvenated my father at first. He'd show them, he figured. In the summer of 2009, my father purchased a 24-by-24-square-foot tin building and planted the makeshift boxing gym in our backyard. That purchase nearly drove my mother crazy.

"It was supposed to be Lo's Gym: Round Three," my father joked in hindsight.

"You couldn't beat the location," he added.

The 24-by-24-square-foot tin building in our backyard was just big enough to house the remains of my father's makeshift boxing gym, a heavy bag, an uppercut bag, and a double-end bag. It wasn't pretty. The plan was to train fighters out of that little tin building until a better location revealed itself. Chris Short, fresh off his high school graduation, won a pair of Rough-N-Rowdy competitions training out of that little tin building in our backyard. Claudia Cline, training on weekends home from college, did the same. If I remember correctly, Max Anderson trained in that building as well. My father could have gone on like that, running private training camps out of the tin building in our backyard. He'd have been content, I suppose. Then came the storm.

Tornados are pretty damn rare in West Virginia, but every now and then, a good one will blow past. In the summer of 2010 a tornado ripped through Cowen and wrecked the hell out of everything. A branch from the large oak tree in our backyard landed on the roof of Lo's Gym. My father didn't even bother fixing the roof.

I've lost track of most of our Lo's Gym fighters. After the storm, they scattered about. Curtis Wright fought one professional fight and hung 'em up. Curtis remarried, had another child, and now he's a Little League football coach in Webster Springs. Jason Bragg hung 'em up as well. He was at peace with all he'd achieved in the ring. Jason, like each of Lo's

Gym's auspicious locations, had squeezed every little bit of potential out of his small frame. Craig Wright, Chris Short, and Chris Ledsome took to the coal mines. After a few years in the mines, Chris Short said to hell with it and went back to school. He's now the toughest X-ray technician in the state of West Virginia, I'd wager. I couldn't tell you what became of Jeremiah and the other two Ledsome Bears. I couldn't tell you what became of Wes Hice or Bobby "Wild Boy" McCartney. Myria Gumm served her time in the military, moved back to West Virginia, and has a little boy of her own. Lane Gillespie is still in Willoughby Trailer Park, I hear. A few Lo's Gym fighters shipped off to college, just as I had done back in the fall of 2000. Dustin Wood graduated from Glenville State College, became a cross-country star, and now he's a physical education teacher in Richwood, West Virginia. Claudia graduated from Furman University, married a boy from New Zealand, and is now a physical therapist in San Diego, California. Alec Anderson shipped off to college, but he kept at it for a while, training with Bullet Bill Hopkins in Fairmont while attending school.

In October 2010, Alec scored a pro bout with Mike Robinson, a local boy who'd beaten him as an amateur a few years back. The Summersville Armory is no Boardwalk Hall, Mike Robinson no Daniel Jacobs, but it was decent money and a winnable fight. Alec immediately called my father after receiving the offer, his voice full of excitement.

"Lo, I want you to work my corner. It won't be the same without you in my corner," Alec pleaded.

"Alec, it just don't seem right to work somebody's corner if I didn't train them," my father replied.

"Bill has a previous commitment with amateur boxers in Pittsburgh that weekend. C'mon, Lo, I need you," Alec urged.

"I guess I'm retired," my father said, stating the obvious.

Jason Bragg agreed to serve as Alec's chief second that night in Summersville. It didn't matter. Alec never made it back to the corner. Minutes into the fight, Alec landed a hard overhand right that TKO'd Mike Robinson in the first round. Mike made it back to his feet, but the ref called it. It would be Alec Anderson's first and only professional boxing victory and my father didn't even get to see it. He was back in Cowen, working an extra shift at the Smooth Coal Company.

Today, Alec is a police officer in Summersville, West Virginia. He's married and has a son. His younger brother Max graduated from Fairmont University in 2012 and subsequently joined the United States

Army. Max is now a football coach in Lewis County. Boxing gradually slipped away from the Anderson boys just as it did my father.

"Every single time I hear something about Daniel Jacobs on television, I think about Lo's Gym. Don't get me wrong. Jacobs would have killed me. But I could have always said I got in there with a world champion," Alec confided to me, years after his decision to turn down the fight.

My father blinked and Lo's Gym Boxing Club disappeared.

And then came the storm.

***

As part of my responsibilities as the assistant director of composition at Ohio University, I helped organize and host fall orientation for the new teaching assistants in the English Department. It was a Friday, the final day of orientation, and I was nervous as hell. I probably checked my cell phone 200 times that day. If I remember correctly, the event ran late and we didn't finish up until around five-thirty that evening.

I drove slowly the entire way back to my apartment because I had a feeling that when I opened my apartment door, Stephanie would be waiting for me with bad news.

She was.

I burst into the room and said something stupid like, "Have you heard anything about Mom's biopsy?"

I should have known better. The Snyders aren't a no-news-is-good-news kind of family. We're all paranoid and neurotic.

Stephanie had bloodshot eyes and streaming tears—that much I remember.

"It's not good, Todd."

I don't remember much after that. I'm not being overly dramatic or romanticizing. I'm being honest with you. I can't recall a single thing about the rest of that evening. I don't even remember talking with my mother on the phone. Maybe I didn't.

"I think Lo's Gym was supposed to end like it did," my father said years later.

"I think the Good Lord took the gym away from me because he knew that I needed to be in your mother's corner to help her fight breast cancer," he added.

Nobody can spin a boxing metaphor like my father.

"God's always trying to show me what to do . . . But I'm always too stupid to read the signs."

My mother made it through the radiation, and the surgeries, and the pills, and all the other bullshit cancer puts a person through. She didn't complain or question the fairness of life. She kept right at it, living more boldly than ever before, perhaps. Appalachian women are as tough as they come, especially McCoy girls.

And, to my father's credit, he really did go cold turkey on boxing when my mother was diagnosed with breast cancer. He even went cold turkey on refereeing and judging fights. In fact, my father stopped watching boxing altogether. For some reason, that bothered me the most.

My father blinked and the love of his life was a cancer patient at the Ronald McDonald house in Morgantown, his son a college professor in Albany, New York, his only daughter a college student at Marshall University. It had all slipped away from him.

And then came the storm.

***

I was writing in a Starbucks coffee shop in Rensselaer, New York, just across the Hudson River from Albany, when I got the call. A publisher had expressed interest in turning my graduate school dissertation into a book and I was doing my best not to screw it up. I spent my first full summer in New York editing and reshaping the hell out of that dissertation.

My father never called during the day, so when his number came up on my cell phone I knew something was wrong.

"They finally shut the fucking thing down," my father said before I could say "hello."

He was in a bad way.

"They finally shut it the fuck down," he repeated when I didn't say anything.

The Smooth Coal Company had been purchased by a few big shots from St. Louis, who, if you believe my father's version of the story, had no intentions of keeping the mine open—Smooth was apparently a small piece in a much larger business deal.

Earlier that morning, mining officials gathered all 170 Smooth employees to make the announcement. A Smooth Coal Company bigwig informed the men "they were selling the coal at $56 a ton, but it was costing $70 a ton to operate with all of the equipment they used."[84] Everyone at the mine would be laid off. The company offered the men two months' severance pay and health care benefits up till Thanksgiving.

The following month, Alpha Coal slashed 508 positions in Naoma, West Virginia, and Whitesville, West Virginia; Blackhawk Mining let go of 146 men in Eskdale, West Virginia, Gilbert, West Virginia, and Lyburn, West Virginia; Walter Energy cut 120 jobs in Powellton, West Virginia, and Summersville, West Virginia; Alpha slashed another 527 jobs in November and closed things down in Clintwood, Virginia, and Nora, Virginia.[85]

"What happened to the coal industry?"

"Why hasn't West Virginia's economy expanded past the extractive industries?"

"Do West Virginian's think coal mining will make a comeback?" my colleagues sometimes ask.

King Coal is a shot fighter, I say. China doesn't want Appalachian coal anymore. They've pledged to reduce their carbon emissions and exports are down.

But things aren't so bad out west, I hear.

Those old boys are mining coal used to make steel. Coal production in Wyoming and Montana has remained steady. "Appalachian thermal coal is dying," analyst James Stevenson argues.[86]

If folks hadn't held on to romanticized notions of the good old days so fervently, they may have seen it coming. King Coal hit the canvas face-first, no need for a ten count.

***

When the Smooth Coal Company shut down, just about every *working man* in Webster County lost his job, my father and Jason Bragg included.

The guys who really gave a damn transferred to other coal mines, if they were lucky enough to do so. The rest took low-paying jobs elsewhere or stopped working altogether.

My father was one of the guys who gave a damn; he was paranoid about losing his health insurance while my mother was due for more cancer treatments.

The new regime eventually transferred my father to a coal mine in Grafton, West Virginia, about two hours north of Cowen. My father moved into a little two-bedroom apartment a few miles down the road from the coal mine in Grafton. The apartment used to be Johnson's Funeral Home but the funeral home went belly up during the economic downturn and somebody converted the building into a rental. My father's bedroom in that apartment used to be an infirmary, he says. The coal miner sleeps in the infirmary.

According to Griffin Moores, "from 2007 to 2012, West Virginia's annual coal production dropped by 31.7 million tons annually, falling over 20 percent."[87] The Smooth Coal Company's demise was symbolic of a larger national trend. According to data published by the Bureau of Labor Statistics, "The United States has lost approximately 191,000 jobs in the mining industry since September 2014."[88] Appalachia was hit the hardest.

"This new mine in Grafton should provide a good ten years of coal mining," my father's new bosses proudly declared.

"I'd say we've got a good ten years."

A puncher's chance?

**

My father packed on the pounds after moving to Grafton. Training fighters and working the mitts had always kept him in shape. After his first Christmas in Grafton, my father signed up for a gym membership at the Tygar Gym, the only public gym in town. His doctor said he needed to lower his blood pressure. My father was on the exercise bike when Derek Roth approached him for the first time. Derek had heard about my father's boxing glory days from his mother, a beautician at the shop where my mother worked in Grafton.

Derek was one of those mixed martial arts guys; my father hates MMA, but likes Derek Roth.

"Are you Mike Snyder, the boxing trainer?" Derek asked.

"Yes, sir," my father replied, a little surprised he'd been recognized as such in Grafton, West Virginia.

They shot the bull for a few minutes and Derek finally got to it.

"You think you could help me work on my stand-up game? I fight MMA and want some help on my combinations," Derek asked.

Derek and my father worked the mitts in the spare room in the back of the gym for a few weeks before Cody Goff came into the picture.

Cody Goff was Derek Roth's friend from Grafton High School. He was a good-looking kid with sandy blond hair and one of those chiseled jawlines movie stars try to achieve through surgery. Cody was only 18 years old at the time; Derek was a few years older.

"Hey, Mike, this is my buddy, Cody. He's planning on fighting in that Clarksburg Toughman Contest next month. You mind working with him too?" Derek asked my father one evening—he was back on the exercise bike.

"He's not one of those MMA underwear wrestling guys, is he?" my father asked, breaking the ice and getting a chuckle out of both young men.

Cody Goff wasn't into MMA, but he was a wrestler. He had been the West Virginia state wrestling champion in the 154 pound division during his junior year at Grafton High School. Cody was built like a skinned squirrel, my father said.

"I've never boxed," Cody warned, trying to temper my father's expectations after Derek went on about that state wrestling title.

"Good, you won't have no bad habits," my father replied.

Just like that, Lo was back at it.

The following evening my father measured it out and placed four orange cones in the spare room at the back of the Tygar Gym. This would be his last makeshift boxing ring.

Cody and my father trained in the spare room for just under four weeks. They mostly worked the mitts, but my father put him through a host of other drills as well. They didn't have any sparring partners or even a heavy bag.

"Cody Goff was a hard worker and an even better listener," my father said.

For a guy who'd never boxed, Cody Goff took to it quick. He went 5-0 with four knockouts that weekend and won the whole damn thing.

"He threw everything right down the middle."

"Hell, he even ducked and slipped better than you'd expect," my father said.

"He's bit by the bug, you can tell."

My father was right. A few weeks later, he and Cody were right back at it—training in the back of the Tygar Gym in preparation for the Elkins Toughman Contest, the last event of the season.

"You think he'll win?" I asked my father over the phone the night before the tournament.

"That kid is a winner. I'd bet on him in a chess tournament," he joked.

Cody Goff did win the whole damn thing: he went 5–0 (with three knockouts). But that's not the part of the story that makes me smile. Before the event, Cody's folks took his boxing trunks to a local seamstress to have "Lo's Gym" sewn on the back. The seamstress accidentally printed "Lowes Gym" on the trunks, so Cody had to buy another pair and have the seamstress do it correctly the second time around. It was a big surprise; my father didn't have a clue.

I've never had the pleasure of meeting Cody Goff, but I love him for going to all that trouble to help preserve my father's small-town ethos. I was happy to see my father get one last ride on the carousel.

"Like my new trunks?" Cody asked my father back in the locker room, a rhetorical question.

"Lo's Gym ain't dead."

Shiny satin trunks with "Lo's Gym" printed on the back.

My father deserved that moment after all he'd been through. They hadn't stolen it from him after all.

Cody Goff had it right. Maybe Lo's Gym was never really a physical space.

Maybe it wasn't a spare room in the back of a women's beauty shop. Maybe it wasn't a boxing club located in a Baptist Youth Center. Maybe Lo's Gym wasn't a tin building in the backyard of my home on Mason Street. It sure as hell wasn't four orange cones placed in the back of a knockoff YMCA in Grafton, West Virginia. Maybe Lo's Gym was nothing more than an Appalachian boy's daydream.

***

I made the call at about six-thirty in the evening in February 2013. My father had just made it home from the coal mine in Grafton. I sent him a "Facetime request" and he quickly accepted the iPhone video call. My father looked tired that day, frustrated. I'd caught him at a bad time. I was happy to have caught him at a bad time.

"What do you need, Professor?" my father answered.

Who was this old man, balancing microwavable dinner on his lap, setting on the edge of the couch in nothing but a white tank top and nylon workout shorts? Certainly not the Beowulf I'd grown up with in Willoughby Trailer Park. Certainly not Mike "Lo" Snyder, number 22 coming out of the backfield. Didn't look a thing like "Smokin' Lo."

Didn't look a thing like Bobby McCartney's Street Preacher. My mother's bout with cancer drained my father of his invincibility. After the biopsy, both my mother and father became human to me for the first time. There are some things an old West Virginia coal miner just can't mend.

"I don't need a thing, Dad. Just calling to check in," I said.

"Can I call you back? I'm eating my gourmet Smart Ones dinner," my father joked.

After I moved to New York, my father and I didn't talk on the phone all that much. He was getting adjusted to his new life in Grafton and I was doing the same 600 miles away in New York's capital city. Life ebbs and flows, not unlike a good boxing match. Ask any good boxing trainer and he will lay it out for you. Proximity and distance dictate relationships.

"Hey, Mike," Stephanie called, leaning into the iPhone camera shot, pretending to be casual.

"Hey, Steph."

"How's New York?" he asked, setting the microwavable dinner to the side.

"New York is great," she quickly answered, wearing her best poker face.

"I'm proud of you guys. Brag on both of you all the time," my father said.

I was a big-shot college professor in the Big Apple, with scholarly conferences, and scholarly publications, and plenty of educated folks patting me on the back and telling me how far I'd come. I was some kind of big shot, a first-generation college student turned big-shot writer. And there was my father, eating his microwavable dinner in his two-bedroom apartment in Grafton, lonely and aging. The old West Virginia coal miner sleeps in the Grafton infirmary and the war stories are now left for me to tell. Who was this old man? He couldn't be my father. I wanted to blame King Coal. Forty years in the coal mines was enough. He shouldn't have to work so long, shouldn't have to get so old. King Coal had always provided for my family. He kept a roof over our heads. He kept clothes on our backs and food on the table. King Coal helped pay for my fancy college education, helped turn a coal miner's son into a big shot, helped pay for my sister's fancy college education as well. Imagine this small-town Appalachian scenario—a coal miner and a hairdresser raise a *college professor* and a *dentist*.

Todd Daniel Snyder, PhD.

Katie Nicole Snyder, DDS.

"You look good today, old man," I finally said, advancing the conversation.

"What the hell are you talking about?" my father replied, showing those shiny gold teeth as he smiled.

"Hell, you look good is all," I repeated.

"You do look good, Mike," Stephanie added.

"What are you guys getting at?"

"Can I not tell my own father he looks good?"

"Yeah, I suppose. But what the hell are you up to?"

I let a few moments of silence build the suspense.

"I'd say you look like someone who is about to become a grandfather."

And I've been finding pieces of my father in the mirror each day since.

***

It's been a good seven years since I set foot in a boxing ring. Lo's Gym isn't around anymore, and all of our fighters have moved on to new phases in their lives. Yet the story begged to be written. I began work on this book of scattered memories shortly after discovering Stephanie was pregnant. More specifically, the day I found out I was going to have a son. I conjure these scattered memories onto the page for him.

This book is for you, Huntington Jay Snyder. You've given me the courage to get back into the ring with Noah Milton.

My first memory of my son will always be the quivering of his mother's bottom lip as she slowly opened the bathroom door, spilling light into our darkened bedroom. Tears welled up in both eyes, she didn't say a word, just nodded her head up and down. It wasn't until my wife opened the bathroom door that I truly understood how fathers dream up their sons. With my arms around my teary wife, I conjured up a poet, a critically acclaimed author, a film director, a cosmopolitan thinker, an intellectual, a world traveler, an Ivy League graduate, the idea of someone better than myself—lofty expectations for two thick red lines in a plastic tube.

Little boys mythologize their fathers. Fathers dream up their sons. Both see each other through romanticized eyes. Both struggle to look beyond their predetermined expectations and fantastic imaginations.

This book is for you, Huntington Jay Snyder. These are stories of manly men conditioned to repeat mistakes of the past.

The woman in the cat's-eye glasses placed the cold ultrasound jelly on Stephanie's skin and Stephanie jerked at first contact. The monitor lit up and there he was.

"Do you want to know the sex of the child?"

"Yes, of course, we want to know."

"Momma, what is your guess?"

"I think it's a boy."

"Papa, what is your guess?"

"I think it's a girl."

I wanted a boy, but was afraid I'd jinx it. I'm superstitious.

"Well, Momma got it right. Congratulations! It's a boy."

We cried tears of joy in front of the lady in the cat's-eye glasses and her computer screen and her ultrasound jelly.

"Do you have a name picked out yet?"

We did.

Huntington Jay Snyder was named after the small college town where my wife and I fell in love—Huntington, West Virginia—the place where our lives truly began.

Huntington Jay Snyder was born in Schenectady, New York, on August 31, 2013. I have no male siblings, only a younger sister, Katie, who is now married, so my son is the last name-bearing Snyder of the bunch, the only Snyder boy not born and raised in West Virginia. The Appalachian namesake was the least I could do for the little upstate New Yorker, the son of a college professor.

Growing up with a symbolic namesake is messy business, I'll admit. But maybe that's how it has to be with fathers and sons. I assigned symbolic meaning to my big-man feeling and gave it to him, just as my father had done for me. My son's name is a reflection of loving and subconsciously selfish notions of his father's success. My college degrees, my publications, and the nameplate on my office door—they'll all be a part of the mythology that hangs over Huntington's head. He will never be the Huntington of my dreams; he'll be something better. And it'll bother him much more than it does me.

This book of scattered memories is for you, Huntington Jay Snyder. You've given me the courage to look back, the courage to risk becoming a pillar of salt.

The story begins with Noah Milton's sneaky right uppercut and ends with the truth you have shown to me, my beautiful boy.

These old Appalachian yarns don't ever have to end.

They get better each time you tell them.

And it turns out that my father and I aren't that different after all. We're dreamers and storytellers. That's who we really are.

And in our stories we've done something great.

DEDICATION

Fighting Naton Leslie

Naton Leslie lived my life and he wrote it all down and the stories were sad and funny and beautiful. He was a working-class Appalachian kid who wrote his way out of the sticks and into the pages of literary journals. He was Todd Snyder before I ever had a chance to be. The first 35 years of my life read like the pages of a Nate Leslie biography.

Small-town Appalachian poverty. Check!

Working-class family history. Check!

Working-class pipe dream of becoming a writer. Check!

The identity struggles associated with being a first-generation college student. Check! Graduate school at Ohio University. Check!

The winds of the academic job market blew us out of Appalachia and north to Siena College in New York's Capital District. Nate arrived at Siena in 1990; I'd show up some 21 years later. Nate and I were destined to meet and collaborate.

On December 27, 2013, Naton Leslie passed away after a long and courageous battle with cancer. He was a Kennedy Award–winning scholar. He was the author of seven books of poetry. He was the author of a nonfiction work about secondhand culture in America, *That Might Be Useful*,[89] and a collection of short stories, *Marconi's Dream*,[90] which won the George Garrett Fiction Prize. He was a prolific poet and essayist. He was a working-class hero. He was my colleague. He was my friend.

During my early days at Siena College, Nate and his wife Susan were incredibly kind to Stephanie and me. They took us to our first horse race in Saratoga Springs, made us home-cooked meals, made two kids from Webster County, West Virginia, feel at home in upstate New York. Nate also played a key role in helping me finish and eventually shop my first book *The Rhetoric of Appalachian Identity*.[91] When I completed my final revision of the manuscript, I asked Nate to take a look at it. He read my 300-page book in one day and returned it to me with extensive comments—that is the kind of friend Nate was. If he had told me my book was rubbish and that I should throw it in the Hudson River, I would have. That is how much I respected his opinion. Our relationship defied the typical professor-colleague boundaries. Nate wasn't my department chair or my tenure-track supervisor or even in charge of my productivity as a scholar, but he most certainly took up those unofficial duties. Nate would blow into my office, barging through the door, full of big ideas. He'd damn near assign me writing homework.

"Have you ever written anything about boxing?"

"No."

"Why not? You love it."

"Well, maybe because I'm a professor of rhetoric and composition. I'm not a creative writer like you," I said.

"Can you show me a style of writing that isn't creative?" Nate swiftly answered.

"If you're a real writer, you can write in more than one genre," he added.

"Well, back in graduate school . . . I wrote this short story about my father's boxing gym . . . but I've never done anything with it," I replied, after giving Nate's rhetorical question some thought.

"Okay. We'll start there."

"Huh?"

"Send it to me tonight and I'll give you some feedback," Nate responded before leaving my office just as quickly as he'd arrived.

Nate was rail thin and his skin somewhat discolored from the chemotherapy by the time I met him. He looked sickly, a good ten years older than he really was. But Nate's energy, work rate, and discipline as a writer, teacher, and scholar were unmatched. He'd get up each and every morning and punch the clock, so to speak.

"If you're a real writer . . . you write every day. It ought to hurt you not to write," he'd say.

After reading my Lo's Gym story, Nate pressured me into joining the Siena College writing group he spearheaded in his free time.

"This stuff is dynamite. This is the kind of stuff you should be writing. I'll add you to my writing group and we can get to work on this project. Also, is that Flex character for real or did you make him up?"

The final lines of a 1:00 a.m. Naton Leslie email.

Nate cared about me, for whatever reason. Maybe Nate saw a younger version of himself in my working-class ignorance. Maybe he was just like my father, always trying to convince some underdog that he had *the stuff*. After my first year at Siena College, Nate and Sue drove all the way to West Virginia to visit my hometown of Cowen. Nate was enamored with the idea of Lo's Gym. Nate wanted to see Willoughby Trailer Park, wanted to see the coal town he'd read about, wanted to meet the man with the tattooed arms and the raspy voice who served as my lead character. Nate wanted me to get it right.

Well, here we are, Nate.

Do I have *the stuff*?

Did I get it *right*?

There is an old coal mining helmet that sits on the corner of my desk at Siena College. My grandfather Lowell gave that helmet to Nate when he and Susan visited Cowen back in 2012. To be completely honest, I don't know why Lowell gave the helmet to Nate. Maybe my father told Lowell that Nate was a "picker," loved rummaging through old antique stores and attending auctions. Maybe Lowell pegged Nate as some big-time New York professor and this was his idea of a Cowen, West Virginia, souvenir. Nate dressed more like a handyman than a poet, so that last one probably wasn't the case.

"This is who you are, Todd," Nate said as he held the old relic in his hands, our eyes meeting briefly.

"All of it."

"This town."

"These curvy roads."

"All of it. This is who you are," Nate said, playing front-porch philosopher.

At Nate's funeral, Susan pulled me to the side.

"I have something to give you. Come out to my car."

We made our way through the crowd and outside to the snow-covered gravel parking lot. Susan popped the trunk of her car and there it was—the old coal mining helmet my grandfather had given Nate, refurbished with a lantern.

"This was going to be Nate's gift to you when you earned tenure."

"He was going to tell you to put it on your desk as a reminder of where you are from . . . a reminder to work hard," Susan said, fighting back tears.

Beginning that first semester without Nate didn't feel right. I longed for our impromptu hallway conversations on writing, philosophy, and life in Appalachia. I still do. The old coal mining helmet that rests at the corner of my office desk reminds me of Naton Leslie, perhaps more than the fate I escaped by shipping off to college back in August 2000. During the course of writing this book, I'd often think of Nate as I walked the hallways of Kiernan Hall, trying to avoid writer's block. I wanted him to sort it all out for me. What does the future hold for Appalachian boys in post-coal West Virginia, Nate? Do the mining towns become fracking towns? What happens to the *shot fighter* after the ref calls it?

Writing this book would have been a lot easier if Naton Leslie were still around. But rather than feel sorry for myself, I did what that old *Appalachian-crow-turned-college professor* would have wanted me to do. I got back to writing. Sometimes the questions are more important than the answers.

Rest in peace, Nate.

NOTES

Prelude

1. Jane Eggleston, "History of West Virginia Mineral Industries—Coal," West Virginia Geological and Economic Survey, http://www.wvgs.wvnet.edu/www/geology/geoldvco.htm.

2. The *continuous miner* is a piece of machinery equipped with a drive mechanism, a cutting head, and a conveying system. The *dragline* is a type of excavator used in surface mining. *Longwall* coal mining is a form of mining where a wall of coal is sliced into single units by machinery.

3. This information was obtained from the official website of the "Biographical Directory of the United States Congress," http://bioguide.congress.gov/scripts/biodisplay.pl?index=c000822.

4. This information was obtained from the official website of the 'Biographical Directory of the United States Congress," http://bioguide.congress.gov/scripts/biodisplay.pl?index=c000822.

5. John F. Stover, *History of the Baltimore and Ohio Railroad* (West Lafayette, IN: Purdue University Press, 1987), 163.

6. In R. L. Thompson, *Webster County History-Folklore* (Webster Springs, WV: Star Printers, 1942), Thompson states the following: "The municipality was named for John F. Cowen, a director and one of the larger stockholders in the West Virginia Railway Company" (99). However, it was John Kissig Cowen, of Millersburg, Ohio, who served as president of the B&O Railroad from 1896 to 1901. When the town of Cowen was incorporated in 1899, it was John K. Cowen who was president of the B&O Railroad, which eventually absorbed the West Virginia Railway Company.

7. "Town of Cowen, West Virginia," official West Virginia Government website, http://www.local.wv.gov/Cowen/Pages/about.aspx.

Chapter 1: Fighting Noah Milton

8. Alex Haley, *The Autobiography of Malcolm X* (New York: Ballantine Books, 1989).

9. Ibid.

10. Kurt Vonnegut, *Mother Night* (New York: Delta Trade Paperbacks, 1999).

11. Haley, *The Autobiography of Malcolm X*.

12. This is a reference to my first book: Todd Snyder, *The Rhetoric of Appalachian Identity* (Jefferson, NC: McFarland, 2014).

13. When I was a child, local graffiti artists spray-painted "I-66" along buildings and bus stops throughout the county. The graffiti campaign was an attempt to protest the expansion of Interstate 66, which was scheduled to pass through Webster County.

14. The Smooth Coal Company is a pseudonym for the company my father and grandfather worked for in Webster County.

15. Thompson, *Webster County History-Folklore*.

16. Dinty Moore, *Between Panic and Desire* (Lincoln, NE: The University of Nebraska Press, 2008).

17. Dinty, *Between Panic and Desire*.

Chapter 2: Tough Men

18. "History—It's Got Violence, Sex, and It's Not Fattening," official Toughman website, https://wvtoughman.com/history.aspx.

19. Ibid.

20. All boxing records for professional boxers (e.g., Tommy "Franco" Thomas) have been verified by the "BoxRec" database, http://boxrec.com/.

21. Mitch Cooner is a pseudonym.

22. This Rocky Marciano quote can be found in the following documentary: *Boxing's Best: Rocky Marciano*, HBO Home Video, 1995.

Chapter 3: Lo's Gym

23. Devin Dwyer, "Craving Coal Dust 'Like Nicotine': Why Miners Love the Work," *ABC News*, April 7, 2010, http://abcnews.go.com/US/Mine/west-virginia-coal-miners-allure-dangerous-profession/story?id=10305839.

24. Ibid.

25. Ibid.

26. Charles Bukowski, *Hollywood* (New York: Ecco, 1989).

27. Ibid.

28. Charlie Cummings is a pseudonym.

29. Tom Butcher is a pseudonym.

Chapter 4: Flex and the Rumble on the Hill

30. Eric Drath, *Assault in the Ring*, HBO Films, 2008.

31. Bill Summers is a pseudonym.

Chapter 5: Street Preacher

32. Eugene Arnold and Pastor Stanley Donne are both pseudonyms.

33. Harold Johnson and Chip Dawson are both pseudonyms.

34. Bill Hopkins is a pseudonym.

35. Drew "Bundini" Brown was an assistant trainer for Muhammad Ali. He was Ali's motivator and cheerleader.

36. Muhammad Ali with Richard Durham, *The Greatest* (New York: Random House, 1975).

37. In *I Know Why the Caged Bird Sings* (New York: Ballantine Books, 2009), Maya Angelou paints a vivid picture of what Joe Louis meant to the African American community during her childhood.

38. Deborah Brandt, "The Sponsors of Literacy," *College Composition and Communication* 49, no. 2 (1998): 165–89.

39. Bobby McCartney is a pseudonym.

40. Robert Higgs, *Appalachia Inside Out* (Knoxville: University of Tennessee Press, 1995), 365.

Chapter 6: The Unlikely Reincarnation Story of Rick Cogar

41. "Hominy Falls Mine Disaster," *West Virginia Archives and History*, http://www.wvculture.org/history/disasters/hominyfalls02.html.

42. "Monongah Mine Disaster," *West Virginia Archives and History*, http://www.wvculture.org/history/disasters/monongah03.html.

43. "Eccles Mine Explosion," *The West Virginia Encyclopedia*, http://www.wvencyclopedia.org/articles/1995.

44. "Benwood Mine Disaster," *West Virginia Archives and History*, http://www.wvculture.org/history/disasters/benwood03.html.

45. "Buffalo Creek Disaster," *West Virginia Archives and History*, http://www.wvculture.org/history/buffcreek/buff1.html.

46. Ibid.

47. Ibid.

48. Frank Langfitt, "A Bitter Saga: The Sago Mine Disaster," *NPR*, January 7, 2006, http://www.npr.org/templates/story/story.php?storyId=5134307.

49. Brooks Jaroz, "W.V. Mine Widows Bring Fight to Supreme Court," *WSAZ News*, October 2, 2012, http://www.wsaz.com/news/headlines/98286214.html.

50. "Timeline for Upper Big Branch Mining Disaster Events," *Charleston Gazette Mail*, November 13, 2014, http://www.wvgazettemail.com/article/20141113/gz01/141119618.

51 Pete Whomsley is a pseudonym.

52. Tony Clevenger is a pseudonym.

53. Billy Rogers (like the names of the before-mentioned Rick Cogar opponents) is a pseudonym.

54. Randy Prayter is a pseudonym.

55. Steve Walker is a pseudonym.

Chapter 7: Jeremiah and the Three Bears

56. Roger Hatfield is a pseudonym.

57. Brandon Holcomb is a pseudonym.

58. Shannon Elizabeth Bell and Richard York, "Community Economic Identity: The Coal Industry and Ideological Construction in West Virginia," *Rural Sociology* 75, no. 1 (2010): 119.

59. Ibid.

60. John Alexander Williams, *Appalachia: A History* (Chapel Hill, NC: University of North Carolina Press, 2002), 226.

61. Editorial Board, "Coal Companies Have a Filthy Dirty Trick for Miners," *St. Louis Post Dispatch*, October 7, 2015, http://www.stltoday.com/news/opinion/columns/the-platform/editorial-coal-companies-have-a-final-dirty-trick-for-miners/article_a20b1351–1ea4–5310–98e8–be7a038b1692.html.

62. Ibid.

63. Sarah Jones, "J. D. Vance, the False Profit of Blue America," *New Republic*, November 17, 2016, https://newrepublic.com/article/138717/jd-vance-false-prophet-blue-america.

Chapter 8: Ring Girls

64. Janet Greene, "Strategies for Survival: Women's Work in the Southern West Virginia Coal Camps," *West Virginia History* 49 (1990): 37.

65. Ibid.

66. I am referring to The Special Supplemental Nutrition Program for Women, Infants, and Children, which provides federal grants for states to supplement the food and health needs of poor families.

67. This is a phonetic spelling of the term "home." This is how folks in my neck of the woods pronounce it.

Chapter 9: Appalachian Underdogs of the Squared Circle

68. "Matewan Massacre," *West Virginia Archives and History*, http://www.wvculture.org/history/labor/matewan04.html.

69. I am referring to John Sayles's 1987 film *Matewan* (Cinecom Pictures). The film stars Chris Cooper and James Earl Jones.

70. Adam Turl, "The Miners' Strike of 1977–78," *International Socialist Review* 74 (2010), http://isreview.org/issue/74/miners-strike-1977–78.

71. For information on the West Virginia water crisis, see Krista Bryson's website, *West Virginia Water Crisis*, https://wvwatercrisis.com/.

72. The 2016 Wallethub poll alluded to in this sentence was conducted by using a national analysis of "17 metrics and data from the Center for Disease Control, ranking states on data such as the cost of truancy in schools, and instances of cyber-bullying and suicide attempts." The rankings discussed in this sentence were found in Bob Brenzing, "Michigan Ranks Worst for Bullying," *Fox 17 West Michigan*, August 16, 2016, http://fox17online.com/2016/08/16/report-michigan-ranks-worst-for-bullying/.

73. Calvin White is a pseudonym.

74. The quote by Cus D'Amato was cited from James Toback, *Tyson* (Wild Bunch Productions, 2008).

75. Bud Poliquin, "Muhammad Ali's First Opponent was Tunney Hunsaker, Who Never Did Forget The Greatest," Syracuse.com, October 13, 2013, http://www.syracuse.com/poliquin/index.ssf/2013/10/muhammad_alis_first_pro_oppone.html.

76. Ibid.

77. Kevin Thurman is a pseudonym.

Chapter 10: Prizefighters

78. Kendall Rife is a pseudonym.

79. Jamal Turner is a pseudonym.

80. Ken Kellum is a pseudonym.

Chapter 11: Hillbilly Jefferson

81. Information about the history and scope of the National Jefferson Award can be found on the organization's official website: http://www.jeffersonawards. org/.

Chapter 12: Premature Stoppage

82. Anthony Capone is a pseudonym. Alec's offer was, however, actually for a bout with Daniel Jacobs.

83. This is a word-for-word copy of the letter mailed to my father in 2009. Shawn Boggs is a pseudonym.

84. Guy Raz, "Miner's Weather the Slow Burn of Coal's Demise," *NPR*, July 14, 2012, http://www.npr.org/2012/07/14/156784701/miners-weather-the-slow-burn-of-coals-demise.

85. Nathan Bromey, "Coal's Demise Threatens Appalachian Miners, Firms as Production Moves West," *USA Today*, April 19, 2016, http://www.usatoday.com/story/money/2016/04/19/coal-industry-energy-fallout/82972958/.

86. James Stevenson is quoted in Bromey, "Coal's Demise."

87. Griffin Moores, "West Virginia Coalminers, Families, Struggle with Departing Industry," *Scripps Howard Foundation Wire*, April 14, 2014, http://www.shfwire.com/wva-coal-miners-struggle-1/.

88. These statistics were quoted in Moores, "West Virginia."

89. Naton Leslie, *That Might Be Useful: Exploring America's Secondhand Culture* (Guilford, CT: The Lyons Press, 2005).

90   Naton Leslie, *Marconi's Dream: And Other Stories* (Huntsville, TX: Texas Review Press, 2003).

91. Todd Snyder, *The Rhetoric of Appalachian Identity* (Jefferson, NC: McFarland, 2014).

INDEX

C S 0 0 0 0 4 5 2 6 J R N *